PENGUIN BUSINESS

FORKS IN THE ROAD:
MY DAYS AT RBI AND BEYOND

Forks in the Road

My Days at RBI and Beyond

C. Rangarajan

BUSINESS

An imprint of Penguin Random House

PENGUIN BUSINESS

USA | Canada | UK | Ireland | Australia
New Zealand | India | South Africa | China

Penguin Business is part of the Penguin Random House group of companies
whose addresses can be found at global.penguinrandomhouse.com

Published by Penguin Random House India Pvt. Ltd
4th Floor, Capital Tower 1, MG Road,
Gurugram 122 002, Haryana, India

First published in Penguin Business by Penguin Random House India 2022

Copyright © C. Rangarajan 2022

ISBN 9780670096992

Typeset in Adobe Caslon Pro by MAP Systems, Bengaluru, India
Printed at Thomson Press India Ltd, New Delhi

www.penguin.co.in

To Dr Manmohan Singh, whose vision and courage opened up new vistas and opportunities for India

'Two roads diverged in a yellow wood,
And sorry I could not travel both.'

—'The Road Not Taken',
Robert Frost

Contents

Introduction   xi

PART I: At RBI between 1982 and 1991   1

  1. Tryst with IMF: 1981   3

  2. BOP in the 1980s: A Crisis in Making   7

  3. Monetary Policy in the 1980s   20

  4. The Crisis Years: 1990–92   45

  5. At the Planning Commission   58

PART II: At RBI between 1992 and 1997   71

  6. The Beginnings of Autonomy   73

  7. External Sector Management 1992–97   118

  8. Strengthening the Banking Sector   156

  9. Social Responsibility of Banks   177

10. Widening the Knowledge Base   188

11. Emerging Contours of Monetary Policy   195

12. Men (and Women) and Matters   217

PART III: Beyond RBI   231

13. The Days at Raj Bhavan   233

14. Fiscal Federalism: At the Finance Commission   247

15. Interacting with the Political System   262

16. Advice to Government   268

17. Some Ruminations   310

Acknowledgements   337

Notes   339

References   345

Introduction

Should one write about one's own story? Who benefits from this? In fact, after I left the Reserve Bank of India (RBI) in 1997, I did not think of writing about the fifteen years I was part of it. I thought the *History of the Reserve Bank of India*, when it was written covering this period, would take care of it. During these fifteen years, I was at a level where I could influence the policy decisions of RBI. The history of this period (Volume IV) has done its job. It is very detailed, but it lists all the events with the same emphasis. Also, while the events of the 1980s are described in detail, the description of the early nineties misses out the dramatic character of changes. Perhaps something more will come out in the next volume. Even then I was not keen to write about the events. Also, I was pulled into public policymaking for another two decades. It was only in the last few years that I felt I should write about all the events since 1982 in which I had a role to play. I have tried my best not to project myself as the centrepiece. It is more a chronicle of events, explaining not only what happened but also the motivations and processes behind such events or policies. Publishers have one angle. They want the personal element and anecdotes to be highlighted. In their opinion, that is what makes the narrative appealing. I have tried to underplay that angle.

The narration begins in 1982. I had spent nearly three decades prior to this in academia both as a student and a teacher in India and abroad. Perhaps this period as well as my childhood need to be written about.

But I do not know whether I will get the time to do it. I am already 90. Perhaps that will never get written about. Each individual's life has its own ups and downs. Perhaps there is something to learn from the story of each life. Writing an autobiography may have some use and some meaning.

One doesn't plan one's life fully. Some of it is planned, but some of it is purely accidental. As someone said, much of life is a matter of circumstance. Perhaps in my life, the first part of my adult life, which was spent in academia, was a matter of gradual planning. But moving to RBI in 1982 was purely an accident. I did not plan it. I made no effort towards it. Again in 1991, when I had left RBI, I thought I was doing so for good. But going back to it as governor was again an accident or an unplanned event.

When I first came to RBI, the frequently-asked question was whether the transition from academia was difficult. As I have explained in one of the chapters, it was not so. Prior to it, I had been basically a monetary economist. My thesis at the University of Pennsylvania was on some aspect of the monetary transmission mechanism in the US. My writings were mostly about financial systems. I could claim at that point that I must have read most of the significant literature on monetary economics. There is some advantage in looking at practical problems from a theoretical perspective. As Martin Bronfenbrenner once wrote, policy recommendations and decisions are the result of a confluence of analytics flowing from theory, data and judgement[1]. Those who despise theory need to remember what Keynes said. 'The ideas of economists and political philosophers, both when they are right and when they are wrong, are more powerful than is commonly understood. Indeed the world is ruled by little else. Practical men, who believe themselves to be quite exempt from any intellectual influences, are usually the slaves of some defunct economist.' Steven Levitt in *Freakonomics* and Tim Harford in *The Undercover Economist* show how economic tools and analysis can be applied to understand problems that are not traditionally considered as part of economics. 'It is detective work all the way,' says Harford. Economists do differ. That is how that profession thrives. But that is because of differing assumptions and value judgements.

The 1980s, when I was deputy governor, RBI, was a period marked by a pickup in growth rate but was also a period of rising fiscal deficit and a difficult balance of payments (BOP) situation. However, the period was also characterized by marked changes in the monetary policy environment. The Chakravarty Committee Report was a landmark development followed by changes in the short-term money market, both in terms of instruments and institutions. In fact, the transition to the post-1991 liberalization regime was smooth because of these changes. How the crisis of 1991 was handled is spelt out in detail in various chapters in this book. The reforms of 1991, as far as RBI was concerned, related to three important areas—monetary policy tools and environment, banking systems and exchange rate management, and foreign exchange controls. These again are delineated in detail in various chapters. Taken together, the reforms completely modified the role and structure of RBI. RBI acquired new tools such as open market operations (OMOs), which were not possible as long as interest rates were not market-determined. With a new agreement between RBI and the government, the earlier system of automatic monetization of the fiscal deficit through the issue of ad hoc treasury bills came to an end. The liberal trade policy ushered in would not have been complete without changes in the exchange rate system and the opening up of the sources of financing the deficit. Without doubt, the external sector management was a success story of the liberalization regime. The rules governing the safety and soundness of the banking system underwent significant changes. The first five years were packed with changes such that they truly constituted a paradigm shift. Reforms have continued since then. In the final chapter titled 'Some Ruminations', I discuss what the impact of reforms has been on India's growth and efficiency as well as poverty reduction.

From the governorship of RBI, I moved to become governor of Andhra Pradesh. During this period, I held additional responsibility as the governor of Odisha for nearly two years and that of Tamil Nadu for six months. While the position of governor of a state is largely ceremonial, one also has to be a keen 'night watchman'. Perhaps there have been only two governors of RBI who went on to become governors of states!

The chairmanship of the Twelfth Finance Commission which followed gave an opportunity to strengthen fiscal federalism. Apart from the recommendations on the correction of vertical and horizontal imbalances, the commission recommended a route through which states could move to a situation where they did not require the permission of the Centre to float loans. Many have missed this.

My nomination to the Rajya Sabha provided interesting insights into the functioning of the parliamentary system. I, however, had my own doubts about the utility of a second chamber.

The reconstitution of the Economic Advisory Council to the prime minister and my appointment as its chairman took me back to economic administration even though in an advisory capacity. It lasted almost eight years. What made the long stay worthwhile was the trust Prime Minister Manmohan Singh had in me and my colleagues in the Council.

In the long stretch of three decades and more since 1982, half the time was spent in RBI. The governorship of RBI came at a time when far-reaching reforms were being introduced to transform the economy under the leadership of Narasimha Rao and Manmohan Singh. I was happy to have been part of the team that ushered in the reforms. Many people ask me, 'Did you enjoy being governor of RBI?' My answer is, 'I am enjoying it in retrospect.' At that time, when we were dealing with the crisis and later with the reforms, it was not smooth sailing. There were moments of acute anxiety and concern.

I have written this book to share with you my thinking and my actions on the various issues that came up for consideration before me between 1982 and 2014.

PART I

At RBI between 1982 and 1991

1

Tryst with IMF: 1981

It was in February 1982 that I joined the Reserve Bank of India (RBI) as deputy governor. I was in academia for the previous three decades either at home or abroad. The entry into the realm of policymaking was both a challenge and an opportunity. It was a rare appointment and I was almost the first one to be appointed directly from academia as deputy governor.

Almost the very first task that I had to deal with after joining RBI was the management of the International Monetary Fund (IMF) Programme. I was part of the group that met every week to analyse the data and take action so that the conditionalities associated with the programme were met.

Since Independence, the external sector had been a continuous source of concern. This was particularly so in the first three decades. India embraced an import-substitution policy that had an adverse effect on exports and impacted the overall BOP severely. To overcome the BOP problem, India had to approach IMF four times between 1955–56 and 1980–81. The decision to approach IMF in 1966 and also to devalue the rupee became a contentious issue. Devaluation of the rupee in 1966 had almost become inevitable. But we did not reap the full results of devaluation for a variety of reasons. First, there was the drought of 1966. Second, the expected and promised aid was

3

not forthcoming. All this left a bitter taste. However, the approach to IMF in 1981 was different. We had no acute problem on hand. It was anticipatory in character and that made a big difference.

An Extended Fund Facility (EFF) was approved by IMF in November 1981, which allowed India to draw Special Drawing Rights (SDR) 5 billion. This was to be availed of in three instalments, namely, SDR 900 million in June 1982, SDR 1800 million in June 1983 and the balance by November 1984. The performance criteria included limits on overall expansion of credit with a sub-ceiling on the credit to the government. Besides, there was a broad statement regarding the economic policies to be pursued.

Anticipating approval from IMF, RBI had put in place a tight monetary policy from the middle of 1981. The Cash Reserve Ratio (CRR) was raised from 6 per cent to 7 per cent in May 1981. The Statutory Liquidity Ratio (SLR) was also raised from 34 per cent to 35 per cent. To send out a strong signal, the Bank Rate was raised from 9 per cent to 10 per cent in July 1981 after a lapse of nearly seven years. This also resulted in an upward rise in refinance rates for food and export credit. After the approval of the programme, the anxiety to keep the credit expansion within the limits led to further tightening of monetary policy. As the negotiations were reaching a close, the CRR was raised to 8 per cent, to be achieved in four equal phases. The net result was a sharp decline in bank credit in the second half and even more importantly, this led to widespread defaults in the maintenance of CRR and SLR by banks. Obviously the limits set in the IMF Programme on the expansion of credit for the period were met. Perhaps this was a case of overkill! Money Supply (M_3) expansion was brought down to 12.5 per cent in 1981–82 from 18.5 per cent in 1980–81. This money supply growth was perhaps one of the lowest recorded in the history[1] of RBI. The inflation rate in 1981–82 came down dramatically to 2.1 per cent from 16.7 per cent in the previous year. The banking system was caught in such a liquidity bind that the RBI had to loosen monetary policy. CRR was brought down to 7 per cent in April 1982. The vigilance over credit expansion continued through 1982–83 and 1983–84 though in a somewhat relaxed atmosphere. The money supply expansion in 1982–83 was 16.6 per cent, but it rose to 18.2 per cent in 1983–84.

India approached IMF for assistance in 1981, primarily to take care of the impact caused by the oil shock. Oil prices went up from $18 per barrel in 1978 to $35 in 1979. Indian authorities went for an extended facility arrangement rather than a standby arrangement because it was felt that a facility extended over several years would give an opportunity for the country to not only adjust to the immediate problem faced on the BOP account, but would also give time for undertaking structural changes in the economy. The programme was a success in the sense that the current account deficit came down from 1.7 per cent of gross domestic product (GDP) in 1981–82 to 1.5 per cent in 1983–84 and further down to 1.2 per cent in 1984–85. In fact, as is well known, India did not draw the last instalment because the situation did not warrant further withdrawal from IMF. The foreign exchange reserves rose. Indeed, the increase in reserves became somewhat of an embarrassment and had to be hidden in some way. India's foreign exchange reserves increased from $4390 million at the end of March 1982 to $6520 million at the end of March 1986. Looking at the trade account, India's exports did not show a great pickup during this period. Exports on an average grew at 4.5 per cent between 1980–81 and 1984–85. This rate of growth has to be seen in the context of a global situation that was not encouraging. The import growth was contained because of the bonanza accruing from the increased production of oil from Bombay High. India's oil import bill came down from $6.6 billion in 1980–81 to $4.5 billion in 1984–85. India's exports of oil products rose from $32 million to $1.5 billion in 1984–85. The much-talked-about structural changes were to come much later, even though some changes in industrial licensing policy and more particularly in trade policy were put in place. The Central government's fiscal deficit kept increasing from 4.9 per cent of GDP in 1981–82 to 6.8 per cent in 1984–85 partly contributing to a worsening of the current account deficit. In fact, India's BOP started deteriorating after 1983–84. The current account deficit touched 2.1 per cent of GDP in 1985–86.

India went to IMF in 1981 to tide over the BOP crisis. Similarly, a decade later in 1991, it went to IMF for the same reason. What are the differences? In 1981, thanks to the foresight of people like M. Narasimham, I.G. Patel and others, India approached IMF well ahead of time and much before the problem had become acute. It had its own advantages particularly at the time of negotiations. But in 1991, India went late, and by the time it approached IMF, the situation had deteriorated sharply. The 1981 programme was a success only to the extent that the current account deficit was brought under control. In the absence of deep structural reforms, the position deteriorated soon after the programme was concluded. But in 1991, far-reaching structural reforms followed the IMF arrangement. The external sector went through a metamorphosis. There was thus a paradigm shift and since then until the present, there has been no serious BOP problem except for a hiccup in 2013. The ten-year itch was overcome. Touch wood.

2

BOP in the 1980s: A Crisis in Making

The 1980s started and ended with a BOP crisis. It was not a steady deterioration. There was some improvement in between. But towards the end of the decade, the crisis was worse than what it was at the beginning. The immediate trigger on both occasions was the sharp rise in oil prices. Resorting to IMF became imperative on both occasions.

Trends in Balance of Payments

As mentioned earlier, the BOP situation was comfortable in 1978–79. The current account deficit was negligible. Then came the sharp increase in oil prices. The current account deficit deteriorated to 1.7 per cent of GDP in 1980–81. The assistance from IMF came in handy to finance the deficit and also to add to the reserves. We have explained in the earlier chapter the developments during the period when the programme under IMF was in force. The termination of the performance ahead of schedule was largely made possible because of the improved production of domestic crude and the consequent decline in the import bill on oil account. We patted ourselves on our backs. IMF was also pleased and congratulated us for not drawing the full amount.

During the three-year period beginning 1982–83, the current account deficit remained stable. This was the result of subdued growth in exports and imports. The average annual export growth rate during these three years was only 4.3 per cent. Imports growth also remained modest, once again helped by the increase in domestic oil production. In fact, in 1984–85, overall imports in dollar terms fell. Invisibles showed some decline. These three years saw an increase in foreign exchange reserves because of the financial support provided by the IMF programme. Foreign exchange reserves increased from $4890 million in 1981–82 to $5952 million in 1984–85. Thus, the situation as of end-March 1985 seemed satisfactory.

The situation started deteriorating beginning 1985–86 as exports fell by 9.9 per cent and imports rose by 10 per cent during that year. Services fell. All of these led to a sharp increase in the current account deficit, which touched 2.1 per cent of GDP. Since the normal sources of financing the current account deficit were not adequate, there was a drawdown of reserves of $707 million. In 1986–87 and 1987–88, the current account deficit moderated a bit but still remained high. Export growth was strong, particularly in 1987–88 when exports rose by 21 per cent. Imports also rose by 12 per cent but invisibles declined. Non-resident Indian (NRI) deposits, however, remained robust. Once again there was a drawdown of reserves in both 1986–87 and 1987–88.

1988–89 turned out to be another bad year with the current account deficit rising to 2.7 per cent of GDP. While exports rose by 13 per cent, imports jumped by 18 per cent. There was a sharp rise in imports on government account. Trade deficit amounted to 2.2 per cent of GDP. Invisibles receipts and payments taken together provided much less support. The surplus on this account was only 0.5 per cent of GDP. Payments rose because of the additional interest payments, including those on IMF facilities. Also on the receipts side, there was a one-time accrual because of compensation for the Bhopal gas victims of the order of $443 million. On the financing side, NRI deposits rose strongly. The normal sources were again inadequate and there was a drawdown of reserves of the order of $1001 million. The crisis was already on us. Foreign exchange reserves which stood at $4802 million were equal to two and a half months of imports. Thus, in a short period of four years, complacency turned into concern. But policymakers hoped for the best.

Before making an assessment of the developments relating to BOP in the 1980s, two aspects, one relating to the exchange rate and the other relating to financing the current account deficit, need to be noted.

Exchange Rate Movements

In September 1975, the rupee was delinked from the pound sterling and the exchange rate was determined with reference to the daily exchange rate movements of a selected number of currencies of the countries that were India's major trading partners. The shift to a basket of currencies was done to reduce the volatility of the rupee. The RBI was required to maintain the exchange rate within a band of +/-2.25 per cent—widened to +/-5 per cent in January 1979—on either side of a base 'basket' value. This was the exchange rate arrangement that prevailed in the beginning of the 1980s and it continued through the decade.

The exchange rate of the rupee was fixed by RBI every morning. At that rate, RBI was obliged to buy and sell the intervention currency. Even though the exchange rate was fixed in relation to a basket, the intervention currency was pound sterling.

Initially, when the basket arrangement was in force, the number of changes made was very few. However, as volatility in currency rates increased the world over, the number of changes started increasing. At one point, RBI was making a change almost every day. For example, in 1987–88, the number of adjustments in the rupee–sterling rate was 150 and in 1988–89, it increased to 229. In the 1980s and particularly towards the end of the decade, there were a number of international conferences to bring some stability in the foreign exchange market, even though the system of fixed exchange rate was gone forever. Given India's serious BOP situation, the exchange rate arrangement was operated in a way that it would provide a stimulus to exports and dampen imports. In 1980, one dollar was equal to Rs 8.69. It became Rs 12.36 in 1985, Rs 13.91 in 1988 and Rs 16.22 in 1989. The pound sterling, which fetched Rs 12.54 in 1981, could get Rs 26.55 in 1989. These are in nominal terms. In the mid-1980s we began constructing the nominal and real effective exchange rate to guide policy decisions on exchange rate adjustment. However, it is clear that the rupee did depreciate sharply over the decade. We shall discuss the relevance of this policy in relation to the requirements later.

Financing the Deficit

In the 1980s, the BOP capital account remained restricted. There were no equity flows. Portfolio investment by foreigners in Indian stock markets was prohibited, except for some opening for NRIs. Foreign Direct Investment (FDI) was restricted because of the various limits imposed on inflow of direct investment. Majority ownership of Indian companies by foreigners was virtually prohibited. Thus, the three types of inflows that financed the current account deficit were external assistance, commercial borrowings and NRI deposits. For example, in 1987–88, the current account deficit was $4852 million. This was met by external assistance of $2271 million, commercial borrowings of $976 million and NRI deposits of $1419 million. As India was running current account deficit year after year and since all the financing was done only through borrowing, the stock of external debt started rising. As a ratio of GDP, external debt rose from 12.5 per cent in 1980 to 16.6 per cent at the end of March 1988. The debt service ratio rose from 9 per cent in 1981–82 to 29.8 per cent in 1988–89. To some extent, the sharp rise in the ratio in 1988–89 was due to a big jump in repayments to IMF.

An important source of financing the current account deficit was NRI deposits, that is, deposits placed in Indian commercial banks by NRIs. This was an innovation introduced in the late seventies and it gathered momentum in the 1980s. There were two types of accounts, one in which the exchange rate risk was borne by banks and the other in which the risk was taken by the depositors. In fact, the adjustment in 'interest' rate was done in such a way as to make them attractive, sometimes too attractive, for the depositors. The flow of NRI deposits during 1982–83 was $398 million. These flows rose to $1419 million in 1987–88 and to $2550 million in 1988–89.

Global and Domestic Developments

Before assessing the performance of the external sector of the Indian economy in the 1980s, we need to take into account two developments— one global and the other domestic.

The global situation at the beginning of the 1980s was dismal. The ultra-tight monetary policy of the Federal Reserve System (Fed) in the US led to a steep rise in interest rates, and this put an end to the hopes of strong growth in many developing economies, more particularly in South America. Many strongly growing countries like Brazil wrote off the 1980s as the 'lost decade'. Growth came to a sudden halt and the debt crisis loomed large. The world growth rate came down to 1.08 per cent in 1981–82 and continued to remain low for several years. World trade slumped. Exports of goods and services kept falling from 1980 to 1985. Coupled with this was the volatile situation that prevailed in the foreign exchange markets. The abandonment of the fixed exchange rate system resulted in a 'non-system' with currencies fluctuating widely. There had been a number of meetings of developed countries to come to some understanding and each meeting was followed by some stability only for a short period. The Louvre Accord of February 1987, the G7 meeting in Washington in April 1988 and in Toronto in June 1988 are some examples of such collaboration. Nevertheless, volatility in exchange markets was a persistent problem in the 1980s. Developing countries had to cope with this situation. India opted out to maintain stability with a basket of currencies. In actual practice, it turned out to be something different.

The domestic development that was crucial was the move towards a more liberalized regime, particularly with respect to foreign trade. India had long adopted a strong import substitution policy. This had its impact on the efficiency of domestic production and on exports. Consequent upon accepting the recommendations of the Alexander Committee, a more liberalized foreign trade policy was put in place primarily to facilitate exports. Apart from the traditional incentives, such as duty drawback, cash compensation, etc., the import policy was liberalized to enable exporters to import raw materials and capital goods necessary to produce goods meant for export at internationally competitive prices. This led to a higher imports bill, but it was recouped by the proceeds of exports. This also required analysts to look not at gross export earnings but at net export earnings. Domestic producers continued to be protected by high tariff walls. While industrial licencing policy underwent some change, it was limited in scope. But the beginnings of a liberalized regime were visible.

Policy Options

By 1988–89, India's BOP had almost crossed the danger mark. How well were the policymakers aware of this? What did they do to forestall further deterioration? Did they act in time? Two things the policymakers did were in the right direction. The first was with respect to the exchange rate and the second, the liberalization of the trade regime to facilitate export growth. As mentioned earlier, the exchange rate of the rupee was being adjusted in relation to a basket of currencies. The weights of the different currencies in the basket were never revealed. In any case, such a basket with a margin of + or −5 per cent could achieve at best nominal stability. However, this did not make it a policy instrument. The exchange rate arrangement needed to be supplemented by an exchange rate policy.

Exchange Rate Policy

When I joined RBI, I had my ideas on what could be done on the exchange rate. However, I was told at that time that matters relating to the exchange rate were not to be put on paper and that they must only be discussed. When Manmohan Singh took over as governor, he had a clear view on the exchange rate. He did not want an overvalued rupee. Sometime in 1984, Montek Singh Ahluwalia came to spend a week at RBI. At that time, he prepared a note on exchange rate management which, in substance, advocated devaluation in real terms. Governor Manmohan Singh and I discussed it later and took the view that, given the situation with respect to BOP, the exchange rate of the rupee would need constant readjustment partly because India's inflation was well above inflation in the rest of the world. When Vijay Joshi was with RBI as special adviser, he took the initiative to construct a series on Nominal Effective Exchange Rate (NEER) and Real Effective Exchange Rate (REER). Governor Malhotra also stood solidly behind a policy of depreciation. During these years, I had the responsibility to fix the exchange rate every morning. We took on an aggressive posture after 1985. In fact between 1988 and 1989, the rupee value of the dollar rose from Rs 13.9 in 1988 to Rs 16.2 in 1989. The export weighted 36-country NEER with a base 1985 equal to 100 came down from 105.5 in 1982 to 68.59 in 1989. (Of course, these were calculated much later.) The REER came down from 109.5 in 1981 to 74.4 in 1989. The extent of depreciation achieved could not have been done with any basket arrangement with fixed weights for various currencies. Thus, it remained a basket arrangement only in name. In fact, IMF classified

India as coming under the category of managed exchange rate. This exchange rate regime can be best described as an adjustable NEER peg with a band and it helped to achieve the medium-term REER objective through changes in the NEER.

Growing Debt

On the financing of the current account deficit, a comment is appropriate. Almost all sources of financing as mentioned earlier led to the creation of debt. The equity investment was confined to retained earnings of multinationals and direct investment by NRIs. The opportunities for NRIs were widened during this period. The source unique to all developing economies was non-resident deposits. This was true of India. But the question that arose from time to time related to interest rates. In early 1982, the government wanted the rate of interest on NRE accounts to be raised to a level equal to 2 per cent over domestic deposits of similar maturities. This was illogical. Domestic interest rates were related to domestic factors, such as inflation. Too high a rate could only lead to arbitrage. *History of RBI* records, 'Before the introduction of this measure, the Reserve Bank had opposed this move on technical and prudential grounds, but the Government held to its views.'

Since commercial borrowings were on the rise, it also became necessary to talk to rating agencies because the rating given by these institutions had an impact on the rate of interest charged. State Bank of India chief D.N. Ghosh, Dr Y.V. Reddy from the finance ministry and I met with these agencies. We had to be careful not to overstate our case. But at the same time, we had to impress on them that we were doing our best. We didn't make much headway. But the rating agencies and foreign banks at least understood that India had a core of good professionals.

Another aspect of the growing foreign debt was the increasing share of short-term debt. A good part of oil imports was financed through acceptance credit, which was short term. This was going to haunt us very severely when we faced a crisis of confidence.

Rising Government Imports

The question is why, with a substantial reduction in the value of the rupee and the efforts made to liberalize the foreign trade regime, the current account deficit continued to remain high. Part of the answer is that exchange rate depreciation had no effect on imports. A devaluation is normally expected to stimulate exports and reduce the demand for imports. But in the situation that prevailed in the 1980s in India, imports were strictly controlled. Exchange rate elasticity had very little role to play. In fact, oil prices, which had risen sharply to $37.89 per barrel in 1980, came down to $14.4 per barrel in 1986. Despite this, overall imports continued to increase. The impact of Bombay High wore off as consumption of petroleum, oil and lubricants (POL) continued to rise. Could liberalization of imports have caused a sudden surge? Certainly some part of the increase in imports could have been due to this. But it has to be noted that there was no 'general' liberalization. Only import of goods and services needed for the purpose of exports was relaxed. In the absence of such liberalization, exports could not have picked up the way they did. The net earnings were certainly positive. There is another aspect of imports that needed to be taken into account. That is the difference between imports as reported by the Directorate General of Commercial Intelligence and Statistics (DGCIS) and imports as reported in the BOP statements. The difference is accounted for by the imports that do not pass through customs. These normally include defence imports, purchase of aircrafts and ships, and a few other items. The difference also came because of the timing of the recording of imports and exports. In the case of customs, imports were recorded at the time of the arrival and in BOP statistics at the time of payment. However, the major contributor to the difference is government imports of certain types. The difference between the two estimates that stood at $1.68 billion in 1982–83 rose to $4.1 billion in 1988–89. This period saw a substantial increase in defence expenditures. They rose from an average of 2.7 per cent of GDP during 1980–81 and 1984–85 to 3.8 per cent in 1988–89. Some of this must have spilled over to imports. In fact, the crux of the problem was excessive increase in government expenditure in relation to revenue.

Bulging Government Expenditure

There is a link between aggregate demand and BOP. If the aggregate demand exceeds availability, it spills over into current account deficit. The fiscal performance during this period deteriorated sharply. Up to

1979–80, the Central government had a revenue surplus. By 1988–89, it had turned out to be a deficit of 2.45 per cent of GDP. The net fiscal deficit of the Centre was 4.89 per cent of GDP. The fiscal deficit of the Centre and states taken together rose to 9.06 per cent of GDP. This was at a time when the total savings of the household sector in financial assets was low. It was but inevitable that excess expenditure was getting reflected in growing current account deficit. As mentioned earlier, concerns relating to BOP were never out of the radar of the policymakers. The tone of the economic survey was no different from the annual reports of RBI. The danger of rising aggregate demand was also known. On speaking about BOP, I had said in March 1987: 'Above all, the domestic resources constraint should not be allowed to spill over to the external sector by using imports funded by borrowing as a soft alternative for domestic resources mobilization.' The Economic Survey 1988–89 said,

'A compression of the present scale of fiscal imbalance is also essential for bringing about an improvement in our balance of payments. Though it is not often appreciated, it must be recognized that high levels of fiscal deficits tend to spill over and contribute to high current account deficits in the balance of payments. An improvement in the current account in the balance of payments requires a commensurate reduction in the overall savings-investment gap of the economy.'[1]

The steady rise in the fiscal deficit was also happening at a time when the Government of India had put out a long-term fiscal policy aimed at improving the tax structure and administration and setting long-term goals to ensure the stability of tax rates. It was the drive to grow fast at any cost that bore the seeds of a crisis that finally bust a few years later.

Table 2.1 CAD/GDP and Debt-Service Ratio

(per cent)

Year	CAD/GDP	Debt-Service Ratio
1981–82	–1.7	9.3
1982–83	–1.7	11.4
1983–84	–1.5	14.0
1984–85	–1.2	15.3
1985–86	–2.1	22.6
1986–87	-1.9	29.6
1987–88	-1.8	29.8
1988–89	-2.7	29.8
1989–90	-2.3	27.7

Source: History of RBI, Vol. 4.

Table 2.2 India's Overall Balance of Payments

(US$ million)

Item	1981–82	1982–83	1983–84	1984–85	1985–86	1986–87	1987–88	1988–89	1989–90
I. **Merchandise**									
A) Exports, f.o.b.	8697	9490	9861	10061	9461	10413	12644	14257	16955
B) Imports, c.i.f.	15970	16468	16575	15715	17294	17729	19812	23618	24411
Trade balance (A–B)	**–7273**	**–6979**	**–6715**	**–5654**	**–7834**	**–7316**	**–7168**	**–9361**	**–7456**
II. **Invisibles, net**	**4094**	**3572**	**3499**	**3238**	**2967**	**2756**	**2316**	**1364**	**615**
III. **Current account (I+II)**	**–3179**	**–3407**	**–3216**	**–2417**	**–4867**	**–4560**	**–4852**	**–7997**	**–6841**
IV. **Capital account (A to F)**	**657**	**2087**	**2655**	**3147**	**4506**	**4512**	**5047**	**8064**	**6977**
A) Foreign investment						195	434	357	410
B) External assistance, net	835	1168	1148	1184	1370	1414	2271	2216	1856
C) Commercial borrowings, net	164	761	761	934	954	1966	976	1894	1777
D) Rupee debt service									
E) NRI deposits, net	231	398	688	740	1444	1290	1419	2510	2403
F) Other capital	–573	–240	58	289	738	–353	–53	1087	531
V. **Overall balance (III+IV)**	**–2523**	**–1319**	**–561**	**730**	**–361**	**–47**	**195**	**68**	**136**
VII. Reserves (Increase – / Decrease +)	1812	–649	–750	–779	577	573	737	1001	740

Source: Handbook of Statistics on Indian Economy, RBI.

Table 2.3 Forex Reserves and Import Cover

(US$ million)

Year	Forex Reserves	Imports during the Year	No. of Months' Imports
1981–82	4390	15173	3.3
1982–83	4896	14786	3.6
1983–84	5649	15311	4.1
1984–85	5952	14412	4.5
1985–86	6520	16067	4.5
1986–87	6574	15726	4.4
1987–88	6223	17156	3.8
1988–89	4802	19497	2.5

Table 2.4 Exchange Rate of the Rupee

(Calendar Year—annual average)

Year	SDR	Rupee as Per Unit of Foreign currency			
		Dollar	Pound Sterling	Deutsche Mark	Japanese Yen
1981	10.2418	8.6926	17.5423	3.8512	3.9600
1982	10.4766	9.4924	16.5954	3.9129	3.8200
1983	10.8310	10.1379	15.3653	3.9760	4.2600
1984	11.6482	11.3683	15.1469	3.9979	4.7900
1985	12.5625	12.3640	15.9904	4.2282	5.2200
1986	14.8083	12.6053	18.4924	5.8414	7.5400
1987	16.7617	12.9552	21.2366	7.2207	8.9800
1988	18.6994	13.9147	24.7729	7.9297	10.8700
1989	20.7906	16.2238	26.5515	8.6438	11.7600

Table 2.5 India's Exports and Imports

Period	Exports and Imports (on BOP basis) (US$ million)		Exports and Imports (based on Customs data from DGCI & S) (US$ million)	
	Exports	Imports	Exports	Imports
1982–83	9490	16468	9107.6	14786.6
1983–84	9861	16575	9449.4	15310.9
1984–85	10061	15715	9878.1	14412.3
1985–86	9461	17294	8904.5	16066.9
1986–87	10413	17729	9744.7	15726.7
1987–88	12644	19812	12088.5	17155.7
1988–89	14257	23618	13970.4	19497.2
1989–90	16955	24411	16612.5	21219.2

Source: India's Balance of Payments Statistics, Handbook of Statistics on Indian Economy, RBI.

3

Monetary Policy in the 1980s

The 1980s saw a continuous 'battle' between RBI and the Ministry of Finance on the control of inflation and the need to contain the fiscal deficit and more particularly its monetization. Though this period recorded an average annual growth rate of a little over 5 per cent, the growth path was uneven. There were five years when the growth rate was well below 5 per cent. The average inflation rate was 6.4 per cent. But if we exclude the inflation rate of 2.6 per cent in 1981–82 when the programme with IMF was launched, the average inflation rate was close to 7 per cent (Table 3.1). As mentioned elsewhere, the gross fiscal deficit of the Central government rose from 5.4 per cent of GDP in 1981–82 to 8.9 per cent in 1989–90 (Table 3.2). The average annual M_3 growth rate between 1981–82 and 1989–90 was 17.1 per cent. CRR, which stood at 6 per cent in 1980, ended at 15 per cent. SLR rose from 34 per cent in 1981 to 38 per cent in 1989. The task of the RBI was reduced to one of offsetting the impact of the expansionary fiscal policy by raising the CRR and SLR to extraordinarily high levels. While the RBI was continuously urging the government to limit its borrowing, the government, while seemingly agreeing with RBI, acted differently. Non-inflationary deficit financing seemed to have an elastic limit for the government! Leaving aside this issue, monetary policy achieved clarity on three fronts. First, in deciding on the desirable or acceptable

Table 3.1 Growth in M₃, GDP and WPI

(per cent)

Year	M$_3$	GDP at Factor Cost at Constant Prices*	WPI end-March
1981–82	12.5	5.6	2.6
1982–83	16.6	2.9	7.1
1983–84	18.2	7.9	7.2
1984–85	19.0	4.0	5.6
1985–86	16.0	4.2	5.1
1986–87	18.6	4.3	5.3
1987–88	16.0	3.5	10.7
1988–89	17.8	10.2	5.5
1989–90	19.4	6.1	8.6

Source: Handbook of Statistics on Indian Economy and Office of the Economic Adviser, Ministry of Commerce and Industry, Government of India.
* GDP at Factor Cost at Constant Prices—Base Year 2004–05.

Table 3.2 Gross Fiscal Deficit and Revenue Deficit of the Central Government as Percentage of GDP at Market Prices

Year	Gross Fiscal Deficit	Revenue Deficit
1980–81	6.10	1.50
1981–82	5.42	0.25
1982–83	5.97	0.73
1983–84	6.28	1.22
1984–85	7.53	1.83
1985–86	8.34	2.25
1986–87	9.02	2.66
1987–88	8.13	2.75
1988–89	7.83	2.66
1989–90	8.05	2.69

rate of growth of the money supply, a new analytical framework was put in place from the mid-1980s. This followed the Chakravarty Committee Report. Second, an attempt was made to move away from the straitjacket system of controls and move in the direction of greater freedom for banks and market participants, though it was not successful at times. Third, the short end of the financial market, that is the money market, saw many changes with the introduction of new products and new institutions. Thus, some signs of reforms were already visible.

Salient Events of the 1980s

Before examining the issues that arose during the 1980s, a brief narration of important events associated with monetary policy may be appropriate.

1981–82 was the year in which India entered into an agreement with IMF to tide over a difficult BOP situation caused by the steep rise in oil prices. RBI put in place a very tight monetary policy that resulted in a substantial reduction in the growth of the money supply. As already pointed out, M_3 growth in the year was 12.5 per cent, the lowest recorded over several decades. In March 1982, the year-on-year inflation was 2.6 per cent. The banking system went through a very painful period.

1982–83 was the only year in the decade of the 1980s when the CRR was lowered. It was brought down from 8 per cent to 7 per cent. Overall, there was an easing of monetary policy. M_3 increased by 16.6 per cent. Inflation on a year-on-year basis was 7.1 per cent. Real growth was low because of the poor performance of agriculture.

Growth picked up in 1983–84. Both agriculture and industry performed well. But inflationary pressures were strong. CRR was raised in stages from 7 to 9 per cent. An incremental CRR of 10 per cent was also imposed. That year ended with M_3 growth of 18.2 per cent and an inflation rate of 7.2 per cent.

In 1984–85, it was realized that CRR as an instrument of control had been used to the hilt. Besides an average CRR, there was an incremental CRR that was in operation. In fact, it was estimated that the effective CRR was close to 12.5 per cent, which was very close to the legal ceiling of 15 per cent. The government showed some inclination to limit the money growth to 15 per cent and tailor the government borrowing consistent with such a target. But that was a short-lived aspiration. The year ended with a money supply growth of 19 per cent. But inflation moderated to 5.6 per cent, partly benefitting from the good performance of the economy in the previous year.

1985–86 saw a moderation in inflation again. It stood at 5.1 per cent. Money supply growth slowed to 16 per cent. CRR remained untouched. However, SLR was increased by 1 per cent. Some efforts were made to lower the lending rates of banks. The tax on interest income imposed on banks was removed, which also helped to lower the lending rate. The only tightening that was made was through raising the base of refinance. An attempt was made to give more freedom to banks in fixing short-term interest rates. But the effort had to be abandoned in light of the manner in which banks chose to use that freedom.

1986–87 was again another year of low growth. GDP grew by 4.3 per cent. It was a bad agricultural year. An important event during the year was the submission of the report of the Chakravarty Committee on the reform of the monetary system. There was extended consultation between RBI and the government on how to implement the recommendations of the Chakravarty Committee. One of the committee's recommendations was to evolve a close coordination between RBI and the government to limit the extent of borrowing and its monetization consistent with the desired or acceptable level of growth in the money supply. In a year of poor growth, the reserve money rise was strong. So CRR was raised from 9 per cent to 9.5 per cent. The year closed with a money supply growth of 18.6 per cent. Inflation at the end of the year was 5.3 per cent.

1987–88 was another bad year. Real growth was 3.5 per cent. There was negative growth in agriculture. While innovations were being initiated in the operations of the money market after the recommendations of the Vaghul Committee, the need to contain the money supply growth was felt in view of the difficult economic situation. CRR was raised from 9.5 per cent to 10 per cent. SLR was hiked to 38 per cent. The effective CRR had almost reached the legal limit of 15 per cent. The pre-emptions in the form of CRR and SLR exceeded 50 per cent of demand and time liabilities. Inflation ended in double digits. It touched 10.7 per cent.

1988–89 was a good year for the economy. Real growth touched 10.2 per cent after four years of sub-5 per cent growth. Agriculture, industry and services rose substantially. CRR was raised to 11 per cent. Steps were being taken to raise the ceiling of CRR by making suitable amendments to the RBI Act. 1988–89 ended with a money supply growth of 17 per cent and an inflation rate of 5.5 per cent.

In 1989–90, real GDP grew at 6.1 per cent. But the money supply increase was extremely high at 19.4 per cent. Wholesale Price Index (WPI) inflation was 8.6 per cent. The fiscal deficit remained high and so was the current account deficit. CRR was made applicable at a uniform rate of 15 per cent for all deposit liabilities. Thus, the average CRR and incremental CRR prescriptions were merged. This was the statutory limit.

This narration of events also brings out the issues that engaged the attention of RBI and the government. I discuss in the paragraphs that follow three sets of issues: first, the engagement between RBI and the government on the course of monetary policy and the efforts of RBI to get away from 'fiscal dominance'; second, the policy framework adopted by RBI after the Chakravarty Committee report; and third, the reforms that were introduced by RBI in modifying the monetary system to respond to the needs of the economy more efficiently.

RBI–Government Dialogue

The institutional arrangements that prevailed in the 1980s established a close link between monetary policy and fiscal policy. To put it crudely, fiscal actions called the tune. The tangency point between monetary policy and fiscal policy was the market borrowing programme of the government. If the borrowing was fixed at a level that was well above what the market could absorb, the excess would have to be absorbed by the RBI, which in turn would lead to an expansion in the reserve money and money supply. If the expansion in the money supply turned out to be in 'excess' of what was desired or acceptable, it had an effect on price level and inflation. RBI, charged with the responsibility to maintain price stability, had genuine concerns when the market borrowing programme exceeded what it considered reasonable. In such an 'excess' situation, RBI could only manage the situation by raising the CRR to contain the secondary expansion. The increase in SLR was also an attempt to channel a larger part of the resources of banks for investment in government securities. It is not as if the government was unmindful of the consequences of inflation. But their concern for growth compelled them to take a less concerned view on inflation. A concept close to the heart of the government was non-inflationary deficit financing. From the time of the First Five-Year Plan, this doctrine was invoked. The First Plan said, 'Judicious credit creation somewhat in anticipation of the increase in production and availability of genuine savings has also a part to play[1].'

As an economy grows, a rise in the money supply is needed to facilitate growth and to take care of larger transactions. Therefore, the basic argument for expanding the money supply with real growth is valid. But the crux of the problem is the determination of what that growth in the money supply should be. In fact, this was the burden of the arguments between RBI and the government.

Somewhere in the middle of the 1980s, RBI started writing formally to the government sometime in December every year outlining its projections of money and deposits, and indicating what the borrowing programme of the government should be. After some negotiations, the borrowing programme would be fixed. If this was fixed at a level that was in excess of its view, RBI felt uncomfortable and kept writing to the government. However, there was a need for some prior understanding on the expansion of reserve money. The exchange of views between the government and RBI highlighted the difference in emphasis between the two.

Soon after taking over as governor, Manmohan Singh, in a speech in November 1982, emphasized that the fiscal system must be so operated as to avoid excessive recourse to RBI to finance public expenditure. He added, 'If we take seriously the objective of accelerated growth in a regime of reasonable price stability and viable balance of payments, we cannot assume that the resources which are not mobilized can somehow be made available through expansion of bank credit. Unless this is clearly understood, monetary policy cannot be expected to operate smoothly and effectively. Here lies both a challenge as well as an opportunity.'

The annual report of RBI for 1982–83 (in the writing of which I had a major role) said,

'Another concern that may be of relevance not only for the immediate future but also over the next several years, related to inflation and its control. It is now well recognized that inflation is a phenomenon that is hardly conducive to economic growth. The option of "living with" inflation is no longer seen as an option. Also, control of inflation becomes a necessity if viability of our balance of payments and in particular, the competitiveness of our exports is to be maintained. Hence, the relevant question now is that of the appropriate dimensions of anti-inflationary policy. Regardless of the nature of the inflation, whether it is primarily demand-induced or whether cost push factors are more significant, an important element of policy is the control of monetary expansion. If the goal that is sought to be achieved is one of price stability, obviously, the rate of growth of money and credit over any period of time cannot be far out of line with the increase in real output. However, as a matter of practical policy, a view can be taken on the desirable degree of overall expansion taking into account not only the growth in real output but also some acceptable degree of increase in price level. Since the process of money creation is also a process of credit creation, it is not enough to determine by how much money supply can increase; it is equally necessary to determine how the credit will be allocated among the different users. Therefore, once a view on the desirable expansion is taken, the users of credit both in the Government and in the commercial sectors would have to be subject to the inescapable discipline of minimizing the increase of credit and maintaining total expansion within the limits set. It is only under such conditions that money supply becomes an aggregate truly under the control of the monetary authority.'

The annual report of RBI 1983–84 articulated the same view:

'Credit in the system plays a dual role. Properly channelled, it can help to accelerate production. But at the same time, it adds to the demand pressures through the effect it has on money supply. That is why the rate of growth in money and credit should bear an appropriate relationship to the growth rate in output when reasonable price stability is also an objective to be achieved.'

The annual report of 1984–85 also said,

'While careful supply management could help, aggregate demand is a critical factor in the short run in the management of prices. In view of the direct bearing fiscal deficits have on reserve money and hence on money supply, co-ordination between fiscal and monetary policies is imperative if money supply growth is to be kept within limits and price stability is to ensure with a view to facilitating growth with equity.'

In fact in 1984–85, a serious effort was made by the RBI to engage in a dialogue with the government so that the two could come to an agreed rate of growth of reserve money. RBI feared that the Budget estimates could lead to a situation when money supply growth could exceed 18 per cent. As reported in the *History*, while the government accepted the need to contain monetary growth, it had its own compulsions. The letter from the government said,

'However, you would agree . . . that it is equally important to ensure that urgent development requirements of the country are met as far as feasible. A too narrow and restrictive view would have serious repercussions on the long-term potential of the economy. As you know, our defence requirements are also increasing and obviously, there can be no compromise on this. This year's budget has tried to strike a balance between these pressing commitments and the need to contain the budget deficit.'

At the time of the Golden Jubilee celebrations of RBI on 1 June 1985, Malhotra emphasized the need to strive for price stability even as we sought higher growth. He said, 'While trying to meet the requirements of a growing economy, the Bank must continue to strive for price stability through its monetary and credit policies. Considering the requirements of the Seventh Plan and the difficult resources position, continuing coordination of fiscal and monetary policies and optimal burden sharing between them will be crucially important. Equally necessary will be a policy framework which would encourage savings and investment but discourage speculative activity.' V.P. Singh, who was the then finance minister while endorsing this view, said, 'There is no doubt that in the situation that prevails in our country, price stability is essential not only for promoting growth but also for ensuring social justice and equity . . . Fiscal deficits have a direct bearing on money supply and therefore a high degree of coordination is necessary between fiscal policy and monetary policy so that money supply growth is kept within limits.' It is, however, interesting to see how he perceived the problem from the following interview he had given in April 1985.

Q. Your budget has announced the largest-ever deficit. Can you guarantee that it won't get out of hand like it does each time?
A. I have said again and again (in Parliament). I had three options: cutting plans, increasing taxes, increasing borrowings. We had reached the limit in cutting plans. We reached the limit on borrowings, and we reached the limit in taxes.

Q. Aren't you worried about the possibility of inflation?
A. You feel we should have given more dose of taxation to the economy? Other options were also inflationary.

Q. Would you say it is a calculated risk?
A. Yes it is. You could not have come forward with a riskless budget, no risks whatsoever. Yes, I could have played safe with a non-inflationary budget but with no development, but how would that help?

After the recommendations of the Chakravarty Committee came out, there was another opportunity for discussions between the government and RBI on a wide variety of issues related to monetary policy. The government agreed to indicate in the Budget 'Net RBI Credit to Government' as a memorandum item. It was just a number. It had no operational significance.

As mentioned at the beginning of the chapter, money supply growth was strong during the 1980s. During the period 1980–81 to 1989–90, there was only one year (1981–82) when the growth was below 15 per cent. In all the other years, it was 16 per cent and more. In 1984–85 and 1989–90, it was 19 per cent and more. The average annual rate of growth in reserve money was 16.8 per cent and much of the increase in reserve money was contributed by net RBI credit to the government. Changes in foreign exchange assets had impacted in only one or two years (Table 3.3).

Discussions between RBI and the government were not limited only to the size of the borrowing programme.[2] Two other issues which came up were (a) the rate of interest on government paper and (b) the level of SLR. The government's borrowing programme was facilitated by the SLR prescription and a mandated rate of interest. OMOs ceased to be an instrument of credit control because government securities carried an interest rate that was lower than what a 'genuine' market would have demanded. The government was always keen to keep the interest rate low so as to avoid a high interest burden in the Budget. However, they also realized that keeping the interest very low would damage the balance sheets of banks. RBI had to engage the government every time to raise the rate. SLR prescribes the proposition of time and demand liabilities that have to be kept by banks in the form of

Table 3.3 Net RBI Credit to Government, Net Foreign Exchange Assets of the RBI and Reserve Money—Annual Variation

Year	Reserve Money (M0)	Net RBI Credit to Government	Net Foreign Exchange Assets of the RBI
	1	2	3
1981–82	15.46	39.97	−20.69
1982–83	21.12	23.83	−9.77
1983–84	58.84	39.87	−1.05
1984–85	62.22	75.40	12.75
1985–86	29.49	43.28	8.42
1986–87	66.43	76.07	8.80
1987–88	86.81	64.02	7.95
1988–89	94.69	69.28	7.85
1989–90	146.33	140.68	−1.33

Source: Handbook of Statistics on Indian Economy—Table 44 and 45.

government paper. This was also steadily raised to accommodate the rapid increase in the borrowing programme. By 1988–89, SLR had been raised to 38.5 per cent. A larger pre-emption essentially meant less as a proportion being available for other sectors.

Apart from the monetization of the borrowing, there was also a general concern about the size of borrowing. What constitutes the sustainable level of debt became an issue not only in India but also elsewhere. In India, too, several studies were undertaken to estimate the conditions that must be met to stabilize debt. RBI had made its contributions in this area. One of the early articles was done by A. Seshan in 1985. Later, a comprehensive study of the subject was done by me, along with Anupam Basu and Narendra Jadhav, outlining the consequences of excessive borrowing and the impact on the economy of different modes of financing the borrowing, including resorting to RBI. In fact, this study precedes some of the studies done elsewhere in advanced countries on the behaviour of Debt–GDP ratio.

It should not be mistaken that the RBI in its stance on monetary policy was only focused on money supply growth and prices. The policy announcements during this period were always called credit policy statements. The operating arm was called the credit policy cell and it had detailed discussions with individual banks on the extent of possible expansion in credit and allocation to various sectors. A clear distinction was made between non-food credit and food credit, which was refinanced by RBI. Special efforts to promote rural credit continued. The 'priority sector' credit was expanded even as a proportion. But it is sometimes not understood that because of high pre-emptions in the form of CRR and SLR, what was available for the rest of the sectors was coming down as a proportion.

Recommendations of Chakravarty Committee

Soon after taking over as governor, Manmohan Singh set up several committees to look into various problems faced by RBI. Perhaps the most important among them was the one headed by Sukhamoy Chakravarty to review the working of the monetary system. I was a member of the committee and played a key role in giving shape to the report. Even though the report reflected the ideas that I had been talking about, the most important thing was that a person like Chakravarty had given his endorsement. It was not a passive endorsement but a positive one; his having spoken on several occasions, emphasizing the significance of the recommendations.

The background to the setting up of the committee was clear. The country had seen sharp increases in prices from time to time. Fiscal policy had a direct impact on monetary policy. The financial system needed many changes. The Chakravarty Committee covered a wide area, even though the most important recommendations related to the operation of monetary policy. The committee recognized the existence of multiple objectives for monetary policy. But it was also clear that among the various objectives, price stability was the dominant objective. It also came to the conclusion that regulation of money supply was important, if price stability was to be achieved. Obviously, supply factors are relevant. In an economy like that of India where agriculture has a critical role, supply shocks are frequent. However, a sustained increase in price level could not happen without the money supply facilitating it. Demand management and therefore money supply regulation became critical in controlling inflation. Control of monetary expansion required control over reserve money. It was here that fiscal dominance had become relevant. The committee noted, 'Growth in government expenditure over the last fifteen years has been accompanied by growth in Reserve Bank credit to government' and added, 'A feasible approach to evolving a policy framework for ensuring a desired rate of growth of government expenditure as well as a desired rate of growth of reserve money and money supply involves a certain degree of co-ordination between government and the Reserve Bank in evolving and implementing agreed policies. Such co-ordination is essential and also feasible.'

For the desired level of money supply, it said: 'Therefore, while recognizing the importance of supply factors in framing any policy aimed at price stability, it is necessary also to evolve a framework for ensuring that increases in money supply are not too far out of alignment with year to year growth in output.'

The committee therefore recommended monetary targeting and said:

'It is in the above context that the need for the monetary authority to embark on monetary targeting in the more formal sense acquires importance.

'The successful formulation of monetary policy in terms of money stock as the target rests on three critical assumptions. First, the demand for money is amenable to prediction over the relevant time frame with reasonable accuracy in the context of relationships between money, output and prices which we examined earlier. Second, the money multiplier is reasonably stable and predictable. Third, the monetary base or reserve money is subject to control by the monetary authority.

'The observed relationships between money, output and prices in India over the past two decades suggest a basis for determining the range of targets for monetary growth. The anticipated rise in real output could be taken as the starting point of the exercise. The observed income-elasticity of demand for money and the acceptable rate of increase in the price level during the year will be the other outputs. For example, if anticipated real output growth in the forthcoming year is 5.0 per cent, the income-elasticity of demand for broad money is 2.0 and the acceptable rise in prices is 4 per cent (reflecting changes in relative prices necessary to attract resources to growth sectors), the target for monetary expansion may be set at 14 per cent for the year or a narrow range may be considered around 14 per cent. Having so derived the monetary target for the year, it is necessary to ensure that the monetary target is duly revised upwards or downwards during the year to accommodate revisions if any in the anticipated growth of real output, subject to the situation on the price front being not too much out of alignment with assumptions made earlier. This approach provides the necessary flexibility to the monetary targeting exercise and enhances its effectiveness as a monetary policy tool. What we have in view is not mechanistic monetary targeting un-influenced by the impact of developments in the real sector, but what we might characterize as monetary targeting with feedback which enables changes in the targets to be made in the light of emerging trends in output and prices. The setting of the monetary target has to be in the form of a range rather than a specific magnitude of monetary expansion, and should be altered during relevant period in response to major developments in the real sector. The original target range should be announced in advance and the circumstances under which modifications will be made should also be made clear, the modifications too should be announced in advance. We therefore recommend that the Reserve Bank of India adopt monetary targeting as an important monetary policy tool, subject to the cautions sounded by us. This would bind the Reserve Bank and the Government of India in a common effort to achieve the desired rate of growth in money supply as in the Indian situation, control on monetary growth is impossible without the full support and understanding of the government.'

Apart from the regulation of the money supply, the committee made several interesting suggestions as far as the interest rate structure is concerned. It first examined the administered structure of interest rates that prevailed and said:

'It would be useful to state briefly the major deficiencies in the prevailing system of administered interest rates. These are:

- The administered interest rate system has grown to be unduly complex and contains features which have reduced the ability of the system to promote the effective use of credit.
- The yields on Treasury Bills and government securities are at levels which have led to a considerable monetisation of public debt, leading to high levels of monetary expansion.
- The captive market for government securities and the relatively low return to banks on their holdings of government securities have adversely affected the growth of the capital market on the one hand and profitability of banks on the other.
- Concessional rates of interest appear to have allowed projects of doubtful viability to be undertaken.
- The policy of insulating banks from price competition, and confining competition to customer service has not served to promote high standards of customer service.
- Quantitative credit controls have come under severe stress in the absence of support from any price rationing mechanism.
- The administered interest rate system has been found to be lacking the flexibility necessary for augmenting the pool of financial savings by effecting suitable changes in the deposit rates from time to time as the low profitability of banks mentioned earlier has made banks wary of increasing the average cost of deposits.'

The committee did not recommend free determination of interest rates. It suggested an administered structure that conformed to certain principles. It recommended:

'The level and structure of interest rates that we have recommended here explicitly takes into account the need to make a careful assessment of inflationary expectations in the economy while determining the nominal level of certain crucial interest rates. The interest rates are to be determined by the Reserve Bank in consultation with government as may be necessary. Within the broad framework of administered interest rates which we have recommended, banks will have considerable flexibility to compete among themselves and with the non-bank financial sector by varying their deposit rates and lending rates. The framework of administered rates which we have recommended is presented in the following Table.'

Table The Level and Structure of Interest Rates
Nominal Interest Rates

Treasury Bills (91 days)	**Expected short-term inflation rate** *plus* a marginally positive return.
15 year dated Securities	**Expected long-term inflation rate** *plus* a positive real rate of return of 3 per cent per annum.
Bank deposits with a maturity of 5 years or more	**Expected long-term inflation rate** *plus* a positive real rate of return of not less than 2 per cent per annum: the nominal rate to be determined by the Reserve Bank as the maximum rate payable on bank deposits.
Basic (minimum) Lending Rate of banks	Maximum nominal deposit rate fixed by the Reserve Bank *plus* 3 per cent per annum. Banks being free to adopt higher lending rates.'

In effect, the administered structure was expected to 'mimic' the market.

The Chakravarty Committee's recommendations were generally well received. Governor Malhotra, to whom I handed over the report on behalf of the committee, was enthusiastic. A group was immediately set up in RBI to process the recommendations. The government also generally welcomed the report. One of the recommendations was to indicate in the Budget a separate item called 'Net RBI Credit to Government'. This would clearly bring out the support provided by RBI to the borrowing programme. The government accepted this recommendation. However, this had no operational significance. The Budget at a glance contained a number but with a remark, 'Not independently estimated'. After some years, the item was also dropped. The Economic Survey of 1986–87 on the Chakravarty Committee said:

'The Chakravarty Committee had laid stress on the desirability of developing monetary targets at the aggregative level for securing an acceptable and orderly pattern of monetary growth. The range of the monetary targets needs to be determined in the light of a number of considerations, including expectations regarding the growth in output, the rate of increase in prices and the income elasticity of demand for money. It was also pointed out by the Committee that targets so derived for the year, might need to be revised upwards or downwards during the year to accommodate the impact of developments in the real sector of the economy. The Committee, accordingly, recommended for the setting of overall monetary targets with feedback which enables changes in the targets to be made in the light of emerging trends in output and prices. The recommendation of the Committee has since been accepted by the Government and an exercise to develop operationally meaningful targets and monitor them on an experimental basis has been carried out in consultation with the Reserve Bank of India.'

The Economic Survey of 1988–89 was even more categorical and said:

'Restoration of better balance between Government revenues and expenditures is not only essential for bringing about the desired improvement in public sector savings performance, but also for enhancing future prospects of price stability. Relatively high rates of growth in money supply during the current decade averaging around 16–17 per cent per year have contributed to an average rate of wholesale price inflation of about 8 per cent per annum. As pointed out by the Chakravarty Committee Report on the Monetary System, much of the growth in money supply can be explained in terms of budgetary deficits run by the Central Government. A reduction in underlying average rate of inflation in the medium term is likely to require a reduction in the average rate of growth of money supply, which in turn will entail moderation in the scale of Central Government budget deficits.'

Both Governor Malhotra and I spoke on the report at several places emphasizing the need to implement the recommendations in a phased manner. My presidential address at the Indian Economic Association meeting of 1988 explained in detail the rationale behind the recommendations. I said:

'As each successive Plan came under a resource crunch, there was an increasing dependence on market borrowing and deficit financing which became pronounced in the Seventies and thereafter. The single most important factor influencing the conduct of monetary policy since 1970 has been the phenomenal increase in reserve money contributed primarily by Reserve Bank credit to the Government. It is in this context that the issues of stabilisation and the role of monetary regulation in containing inflation have been raised.

'For regulating money supply, the monetary authority must have a reasonable degree of control over the creation of reserve money. Obviously, there are exogenous factors such as the movements in foreign exchange assets, which affect the level of reserve money. The degree of independence in regulating reserve money depends upon institutional arrangements governing the functioning of monetary authority. Over the years, the practice has grown under which the entire budget deficit of the Central Government has been taken by the Reserve Bank of India, leading to monetisation of deficit.

'The Reserve Bank had, therefore, to address itself to the difficult task of neutralizing, to the extent possible, the expansionary impact of deficits after taking into account the short-term movements in its holdings of net foreign exchange assets. The increasing liquidity of the banking sector resulting from rising levels of reserve money had to be continually mopped up. The instrument of open market operations is not available for this task, given the interest rate structure. The task of absorbing excess liquidity in the system had to be undertaken mainly by increasing the cash reserve ratio. At some point, this can result in crowding out of credit to the commercial sector. With frequent and sharp increases, the cash reserve ratio has almost reached its statutory limit.

'The growing budgetary deficit and their absorption by the Reserve Bank highlight not only the close link between fiscal and monetary policies, but also the need for close co-ordination between the two. The essence of co-ordination between monetary and fiscal policy lies in reaching an agreement on the extent of expansion in Reserve Bank credit to Government year to year. This will set a limit on the extent of fiscal deficit and monetization and thereby provide greater manoeuvrability to the monetary authorities to regulate the volume of money supply. It is in this context that the introduction of a system of monetary targeting mutually agreed upon between the Central Government and the Reserve Bank assumed significance.

'Monetary policy can play a useful role in ensuring growth with price stability. Inflation, it is true, is not purely a monetary phenomenon. Supply shocks of various types can trigger price increases. The regulation of money supply in accordance with the output trends can succeed only if there is close co-ordination between monetary and fiscal policies. Deficit financing or created money is not a resource. It is only a means of transferring resources from one sector to another, which it can accomplish if practiced in moderation. If price stability as an objective has to be achieved, fiscal deficits and, therefore, borrowings from the Reserve Bank, must be limited to levels consistent with the increase in money supply justified by the expected increases in output.'

Chakravarty was not a monetary economist. He was basically a real sector-growth specialist who commanded enormous respect among economists. At the Sir Purushotamdas Thakurdas Memorial Lecture, he took the time to speak extensively on the report. Some quotes from him are extremely appropriate. He said:

'What is the basic conceptual framework that the Committee uses? As I understand it, the Committee does assume that there is a reasonable degree of stability in the demand for money in India in a *functional* sense. If this assumption were to be denied, then many recommendations will lose their significance and it is doubtful whether with a grossly unstable demand function for money, there is a major role left for monetary policy itself from the point of view of inflation management.'

On monetary targeting, he said:

'Even granting that the approach of the Committee represents an acceptable solution to the problems of regulating monetary expansion, the recommendations of the Committee in regard to monetary targeting have occasioned fears that the monetary authority will gain an unintended control over the scale of public expenditures. This impression needs to be dispelled. The phrase monetary targeting is not necessarily to be equated with the rigid targets. Only a pure monetarist might view monetary targeting as being nothing other than an inflexible rule. What the Committee has advocated is "monetary targeting with feedback". It has taken care to specify several qualifications to the monetary target as might be derived from the demand for money function or a more comprehensive econometric model providing for a study of interrelationship between money, output and prices on the one hand, and between credit and output on the other. Keeping in view the limitations of empirical investigations of economic phenomena in the context of policy induced structural changes and strong exogenous supply, institutional and other factors, the Committee has taken as its starting point expansion of M_3 within a targeted "range" rather than a precise targeted increase. Further the Committee visualizes that the "range" will be computed each year. These are major departures from rigid monetary targeting or from an inflexible money supply growth rule. A clear appreciation of this feature of monetary targeting recommended by the Committee is central to the correct interpretation of the Committee's recommendations.'

Bhabatosh Datta, while generally complimenting the report, also says, 'One would not expect a body of experts like the Chakravarty team to be unflinching monetarists but a great deal of attention has been given to the question of monetary targeting.' There were critics who saw the recommendations as 'monetarist'. This comes from a misunderstanding of what monetarism is and what the recommendations said. To label anyone who thinks 'money supply' is an important variable influencing price level as 'monetarist' would mean that all Central banks are monetarists. Monetarists wanted the growth in the money supply to be independent of growth. What the committee recommended was different. Real growth or expected real growth plays a key role in determining the growth target. The relationship between real income and money is an important determining factor. It is predicted on a reasonably stable demand function for money. As output changes, so does the money supply target. Besides, the formula for determination of the money supply target takes into account an acceptable level of inflation. The committee quite clearly did not go with absolute price stability. It came to the conclusion that, in the Indian context, an inflation of 4 per cent may be inevitable and therefore acceptable. The committee did recognize that calculation of the required growth of money supply depended on many behavioural and institutional factors. The choice of money supply as the target was also conditioned by circumstances. The report said:

'Traditionally, regulation of the volume of money and credit in the economy has been a basic function of monetary authorities. The choice of a monetary indicator like money supply, or alternatively, interest rates, has been considered necessary for the effective conduct of monetary policy because changes in key economic variables like output and prices are a result of many complex forces in the economy like the behaviour of entrepreneurs and labour. Further, the transmission mechanism of monetary policy is itself a complex process. Monetary indicators are, therefore, needed to study the immediate impact of monetary policy. In the context of administered interest rates the rate of interest could hardly serve as a target variable. Behaviour of money supply and credit has, therefore, been taken as an important indicator of the stance of monetary policy in India during the past fifteen years.'

The emergence of interest rate as a target had to wait. That stage would come only after the dismantling of the administered structure of interest rate. That happened in the early 1990s, paving the way for the use of interest rate as a policy variable. In the policy framework suggested by the Chakravarty Committee Report, money supply was only an intermediate target. The objectives of monetary policy remained the same—growth and price stability. The target was to be steered to achieve faster growth with reasonable price stability.

Experiment with Freeing Interest Rate

The 1980s saw a number of measures taken by RBI to improve the functioning of the monetary system. After the nationalization of commercial banks in 1969, the banking system went through sweeping changes, which were focused on geographical expansion and allocation of credit. In the process, the system also operated under a complex set of regulations and this led to loss of competition and consequently, efficiency. From the mid-1980s, an attempt was made to streamline the system and bring in greater flexibility in the operations of the financial markets.

One of the significant reform experiments introduced was the freedom given to banks to fix the rate of interest on deposits up to one year subject to a maximum of 8 per cent. This was done through a circular issued in April 1985. It was an experiment that had to be aborted. A narration of the events leading to the promulgation and suspension of this move is interesting, and it throws light not only on the self-confidence, or lack of it, of commercial banks but also the mindset that prevailed in the government at that time. By April 1985, the share of short-term deposits in total deposits had fallen. This was because the rate of interest on short-term deposits was kept much lower than long-term deposits. The range of interest rates in 1980 was 5 per cent to 8 per cent. In 1984, it was between 3 per cent and 11 per cent. A consequence was the sharp reduction in the share of short-term deposits. That was why it was decided that banks should be given the freedom to fix the rate on short-term deposits. Each bank could take into account its own composition of deposits and decide the rate. It was also felt that the discretion relating to the rate of interest could be one element of portfolio management.

When the circular was issued, the Indian Banks' Association (IBA) decided to fix the rate on different maturities below one year and every bank was to follow this prescription. This killed the scope for initiative by individual banks. RBI was substituted by IBA. There was a hue and cry in the newspapers and IBA withdrew its circular. Some private banks, including foreign banks, decided to offer 8 per cent even on fifteen days' deposits. There was immediately a panic among public sector banks and they all decided to follow suit. At the same time, they screamed that their profitability had been affected. This created a piquant situation. Public sector banks were not willing to exercise discretion. They were scared of the consequences of a few private sector banks raising the rate of interest on fifteen days. RBI could have handled the situation. But the government was taking a different view. It wanted RBI to review the situation. I was called to Delhi for a discussion. The government also felt that RBI had taken the decision without fully consulting with it. The government refused to think ahead. The experiment came to an end with a whimper. RBI decided to withdraw the circular and issue a fresh one specifying interest rates on all maturities below one year. As Malhotra and I were sitting down to draft the new circular, I offered to send the new circular under my signature. But Malhotra said 'no' and added, 'I had sent the original circular and let me sign the new circular also.' What were the lessons from the experiment? First, it was obvious that granting partial freedom was difficult. Unless it was part of an overall scheme, it may not have the desired results. Second, banks had neither the intention nor the will to experiment. If public sector banks had stood together, the actions of a few private banks, which were minor players, would not have mattered. They lost their nerve too soon. Third, the government at that time was refusing to move in a new direction. The mindset was still closed. After the second circular was issued, I wrote a letter to the government explaining once again why RBI took the decision it took. I pointed out the argument that it could erode profitability was not correct.

Money Market Reforms

The period 1982–89 saw some important changes in the functioning of short-term money markets. It also saw changes in the government securities market but particularly in the short end. The Chakravarty Committee envisaged an active government securities market despite the operation of SLR and mandated interest rates. The RBI introduced the 182 days treasury bills and these were sold through auction. The auction method was a multiple financing mechanism. The advantage of this type of auction was that bidders were required to pay the price/yield they quoted. This was just the beginning and the early 1990s were to see many more changes. RBI used an implicit maximum coupon rate in accepting or rejecting the auction.

A committee under the chairmanship of N. Vaghul was set up in 1986 to look at the money market and make recommendations for better functioning of its various segments. Based on the recommendations of the committee, the participants in the call money market were expanded and some were restricted to be on the lending side. The ceiling on the call money rate was not removed immediately. It took some years before the ceiling could be removed. Among the new instruments introduced mention must be made of certificates of deposit (CDs) and commercial paper (CP). CDs could be issued by scheduled commercial banks and had a maturity between ninety-one days and one year. CDs were issued at a discount to face value and the discount rate could be freely determined. CDs offered an additional instrument of investment to institutions that had temporary surplus funds. The most important thing was it was a successful experiment and banks exercised the freedom given to them in relation to interest rates sensibly and wisely.

CPs were introduced in January 1990. RBI allowed highly rated corporate borrowers to issue CPs with several conditions. The CPs were unsecured promissory notes not tied to specific transactions; they could be placed with investors through banks or other financial institutions (FIs). Only banks that had a net worth of at least Rs 10 crore were given permission. The issuing company had to obtain an excellent rating from a rating agency approved by RBI every six months. The maturity period of CPs ranged from ninety-one days to six months. There were many other conditions. Basically, CPs were offered to corporates to diversify their source of short-term borrowing. This was also a very successful experiment.

To facilitate the development of the money market, a new institution known as the Discount and Finance House of India (DFHI) was set up in 1985. I was the first chairman of the institution. The purpose of the institution was to provide liquidity to short-term instruments, such as treasury bills and commercial paper. The primary focus initially was on treasury bills. The holders of the treasury bills could get them discounted if they so desired. To facilitate the work of DFHI, apart from capital, it also had access to RBI for refinancing. The DFHI played a very important role in widening and deepening the money market. It was an extremely successful institution.

Even within the limits in which RBI operated, the 1980s saw significant changes in the approach to monetary policy. Till the beginning of the 1980s, RBI's focus was on estimation of credit that was required and its allocation. The two policy statements that RBI issued in a year were called credit policy statements. In the 1980s, an attempt was made to estimate the likely growth of money and to derive from such an estimate the availability of credit. This availability was matched with demand. The emphasis on directed credit, such as priority sector credit, continued. In fact, it was raised from 33 per cent to 40 per cent in 1980. The 1980s was marked by some sharp exchanges with the government on the size of the borrowing programme and the extent of RBI's support.[3] The Chakravarty Committee recommendations marked an important watershed. The ideas that were already taking shape in RBI were articulated in a consistent and comprehensive framework. This became the basis of the dialogue between RBI and the government. The pity is that while the government did not express any serious disagreements on the core recommendations, its actions resulted in a widening fiscal deficit and an increasing proportion of monetization of deficit (Table 3.4). In 1989–90, the proportion of gross fiscal deficit met by net RBI credit to government was 39.5 per cent. In 1984–85, it stood at 43.3 per cent. Though the proportion came down after 1984–85 for three years, it was also marked by sharp increases in SLR, which facilitated government borrowing. By 1989–90, the two pre-exemptions in the form of CRR and SLR amounted to 53 per cent, leaving only 47 per cent of net demand and time liabilities available for credit. The money market underwent some significant changes which made the short end of the market more efficient. By 1989–90, the economy had reached a critical point with the fiscal deficit and current account deficit peaking. At that time, V.P Singh was the prime minister.

Table 3.4 Trends in Budgetary Deficit and Net RBI Credit to Government (Centre and States)

(Rs in crore)

Year	Budgetary Deficit	Gross Fiscal Deficit (GFD)	Net RBI Credit to Government	Net RBI Credit to Government (as percentage of GFD)
1980–81	3,374	8,299	4,038	48.7
1981–82	2,420	8,666	3,997	46.1
1982–83	2,476	10,627	3,368	31.7
1983–84	1,978	13,030	3,987	30.6
1984–85	5,183	17,416	7,540	43.3
1985–86	3,627	21,857	4,328	19.8
1986–87	8,928	26,342	7,607	28.9
1987–88	5,882	27,044	6,402	23.7
1988–89	5,262	30,923	6,928	22.4
1989–90	10,573	35,632	14,068	39.5
1990–91	11,275	44,632	15,165	34.0

4

The Crisis Years: 1990–92

1990–91 was perhaps one of the worst years that the Indian economy had to face. The deteriorating BOP situation got worse because of certain global developments. The possibility of default in our external payments loomed large. Even though policymakers strived hard to avoid such a situation, a contingency plan was still prepared. Eventually, that calamity was avoided. In fact, the end of the crisis saw a new beginning. The break with the past saw a new dawn.

Impact of Gulf War

As mentioned already, the current account deficit of 1989–90 was 2.3 per cent of GDP. The major global shock came with the invasion of Kuwait by Iraq in August 1990. It lasted seven months. Compounding this were the recessionary conditions and slowdown in world trade. On top of these came the break-up of the Soviet Union with which India had a special trade arrangement. The share of Eastern Europe in India's exports was as high as 22 per cent at that time.

The first impact of the Gulf War was on India's petroleum, oil and lubricants (POL) import bill. Crude oil prices doubled initially from $15 per barrel to $30 per barrel. Thereafter, towards the end of the year, it declined to $19 per barrel. The POL import bill during 1990–91 was $6 billion as against $3.8 billion for 1989–90. This amounted to a 58 per cent increase. This was the direct impact and there were many other additional costs. India's exports to West Asia were severely affected. Remittances from Iraq and Kuwait came down. Added to this was the cost incurred in foreign exchange for the repatriation of the people affected. The total estimated impact amounted to $2.987 billion. Details are given in Table 4.1. The current account deficit as a proportion of GDP rose to 3 per cent of GDP in 1990–91, the highest seen so far.

The capital account of the BOP also came under stress. India faced enormous problems to finance this high level of current account deficit. NRI deposits, which were an important source of support, turned negative by September 1990. There were withdrawals instead of receipts. The net inflow for the year as a whole in 1990–91 was $1.5 billion as against an inflow of $2.4 billion in 1989–90. There was certainly a loss of confidence (Table 4.2). The same sentiment was seen with respect to commercial borrowings. This loss of confidence was reflected first in the cost of borrowing and later in the availability itself. Short-term credit by way of banker's acceptance facility, which financed oil purchases, was available at 0.25 per cent over London Interbank Offered Rate (LIBOR) until November 1990. Thereafter the premium went up to 0.65 per cent points over LIBOR in March 1991. It rose further to 1.25 per cent points by May 1991. The credit via this route not only became very expensive but there also were occasions when

Table 4.1 Direct Balance of Payments Impact of the Gulf Crisis during 1990–91

Item	US$ million
Additional POL Import Bill (Net of POL exports)	2,020
Export Loss to West Asia (of which: Iraq and Kuwait)	280 (150)
Non-realization of other Export Dues from Iraq	114
Loss in Remittances from Iraq and Kuwait	273
Foreign Exchange Costs of Emergency Repatriation	300
Total	2,987

Source: Government of India, Economic Survey, 1990–91.

Table 4.2 Key Components of India's BOP

(US$ million)

	1989–90	1990–91	1991–92
Merchandise			
a. Exports (fob)	16,955	18,477	18,266
b. Imports (cif)	24,411	27,914	21,064
I. Trade Balance (a-b)	-7,456	-9,437	-2,798
II. Invisibles (net)	615	-242	1,620
III. Current Account (I+II)	-6,841	-9,680	-1,178
IV. Capital Account (a to f)	6,977	7,188	3,777
a. Foreign Investment	410	103	133
b. External Assistance (net)	1,856	2,210	3,039
c. Commercial Borrowings (net)	1,777	2,248	1,456
d. Rupee Debt Service	—	-1,193	-1,240
e. NRI Deposits (net)	2,403	1,536	290
f. Other Capital	531	2,284	101
V. Overall Balance (III+IV)	+136	-2,492	2,599
VI. Monetary Movements (VII+VIII+IX)	-136	2,492	-2,599
VII. Reserves (increase - / decrease +)	740	1,278	-3,384
VIII. IMF (Net)	-876	1,214	785
IX. SDR Allocation	0	0	0

Note: '—': Nil
Source: Reserve Bank of India, Handbook of Statistics on the Indian Economy, 2008–09.

the maturing amounts could not be rolled over. Borrowing in general became expensive because of the downgrading of India's credit rating by international rating agencies in March 1991. India's rating slipped to the bottom of the investment grade. The only way to manage this situation was to draw down the reserves, which had itself dwindled. The reserve drawdown during the year was $1 billion. This was possible only because of the initial accretion to reserves coming from the use of IMF facilities.

The Government and RBI Interaction

The deteriorating fiscal and BOP situation was known to the government and RBI and there were frequent exchanges of notes and consultations. The BOP situation could not be tackled without the government containing its fiscal deficits. The combined fiscal deficit of the Central and state governments, which was around 8 per cent of GDP during the first half of the 1980s, increased to 10 per cent during the second half and touched 12 per cent in 1990–91. The Central government was aware of this. Attempts were made to raise revenue. At the time of the Gulf crisis, for example, a 'Gulf evacuation' surcharge on airfares was imposed. Petroleum prices were raised and a surcharge on corporate income was levied. But the expenditures, especially defence expenditures, were rising. In substance, growth was bought at a high cost. The rising fiscal deficit could not be met through normal channels of borrowing. RBI had to step in to fill the gap. Thus, the extent of monetization rose. This had the effect of pushing up prices. In the '70s, the Central government had a revenue surplus but the picture changed in the 1980s with the emergence of large revenue deficits. We had dealt with this in an earlier chapter. Suffice to say, the steep rise in the fiscal deficit was a major contributor to the crisis.

There was a continuing exchange of ideas between RBI and the government on the various dimensions of the economy. *History* refers to the detailed letters sent by RBI on 24 May 1989, 19 February 1990 and 13 August 1990. The August 1990 note was explicit in the need to approach international financial institutions to tide over the crisis.

The letter as quoted in the *History* says:

'The advantage of such extraordinary financing would be that adjustment will take place in a more orderly fashion and will be less disruptive of the growth process. Also, arrangements with the aforesaid multilateral institution/institutions will give the right signals to the financial markets and enhance the willingness of the banking community to lend more money to India. However, recourse to the IMF has political overtones and will involve strong conditionality. Such conditionality will, however, involve more or less similar measures that will have to be taken even if there is no recourse to the IMF. One important difference, however, could be that under a Fund programme tightening imports may be more difficult than would be the case otherwise. Adjustment without extraordinary financing will have to be much stronger implying substantial reduction in the current account deficit in a shorter span of time. Either way, the policy with regard to the exchange range of the rupee may not be different from what is being pursued at present.'

The letter also talked about revaluing the gold assets held by RBI to international prices. It also reiterated that it might be advisable to keep 15 per cent of the gold reserves outside India as permitted under Section 33 (5) of the Reserve Bank of India Act.

The Act was subsequently amended to revalue gold at the market price. Equally important was the suggestion to keep 15 per cent gold reserves abroad. The suggestion implied earning an income in good times and using it as a pledge in bad times. Had this suggestion been acted upon, much of the travail we went through later could have been avoided.

To go back to the letter, it made a strong case for approaching international institutions and it also pointed out that the conditionalities would be no different from what we would have otherwise undertaken. No immediate action was taken. This was a failure of political leadership, which was reluctant to act either because it had not recognized fully the seriousness of the situation or because it was ideologically averse to go to IMF. In the September address of the finance minister Madhu Dandavate at IMF, there was no inkling of the crisis that India was facing. The collapse of the V.P. Singh government in November 1990 only worsened the crisis and left the new government headed by Chandra Shekhar, which was also a minority government, with no other alternative but to approach IMF. However, there was a vast difference between the situation in December 1990 when we actually went to IMF and that in August 1990 when the idea was mooted on paper. There was a fast deterioration during this period. In fact, India had withdrawn by 4 September 1990, in three instalments, the reserve tranche of the IMF that amounted to SDR 487 million. The reserves in December 1990 were just equivalent to three weeks' imports. That was really a handicap at the time of the negotiations.

Even as depletion of reserves gathered momentum, attempts were being made to contain imports. In October 1990, RBI imposed a cash margin of 50 per cent on imports other than capital goods. This cash margin was raised to 133.3 per cent in March 1991 and again to 200 per cent in April 1991. A surcharge of 25 per cent on interest on bank credit for imports was levied in May 1991. These were horrendous measures that resulted in a sharp reduction in imports. These measures were taken, even as we were engaged in raising extra funding to augment the reserves.

Other Options

In December 1990, Prime Minister Chandra Shekhar asked me on one occasion, 'What option have you left me?' In fact, at that time there seemed to be no option other than going to IMF, World Bank and other international institutions. Of course, one option was to default on our payments. India had never defaulted on its commitments. It is true some countries, particularly in Latin America, had defaulted and took time to rebuild their strength. But this was a hazardous route to follow. It could bring at best some temporary relief. Default would bring in further downgrading in rating and this could complicate further raising of funds. The import compression which had already reached a breaking point would have to be pushed further, resulting in a serious disruption of the growth process.

Yet another alternative was to raise funds from sources that would not impose any conditions. There were many approaches to the government by various parties offering substantial funds. The government was keen to explore these offers. RBI, as well as many in the Ministry of Finance, were sceptical of these offers. In fact, a deep scrutiny of some of these offers turned out to be without any basis. The motivation for such offers was not clear.

The position at that point was so acute that there was even some talk of selling properties owned by the government abroad. There was some discussion about the sale of our embassy in Tokyo, which was an extremely valuable asset. Of course, the idea was not pursued.

Mood of Negotiations

After the approval by the Chandra Shekhar government, negotiations with IMF started. Deepak Nayyar (who was Chief Economic Adviser at the Ministry of Finance)and I were part of the delegation to negotiate. The executive directors of India at IMF and World Bank were also involved. The initial approach to IMF was in relation to Compensatory and Contingency Financing Facility (CCFF). This facility was mainly created to help countries that were affected by a sudden rise in the price of imported commodities, like oil, or a sudden fall in the price of exports.

This came with very limited conditionalities. However, our objective was not just confined to this facility. We wanted a much larger standby arrangement. The IMF was generally sympathetic to our demands, even though it had its own set of answers for solving chronic BOP problems. Our task was to negotiate an arrangement that was consistent with our own approach. Michel Camdessus as the head of IMF was an extremely pleasant person. Despite the core beliefs of IMF, he really wanted to help India. He had a high impression of Indian bureaucrats and their commitment. While generally the atmosphere was congenial, there were occasions when there was a hardening of positions on either side. As the August 1990 letter of RBI pointed out, many of the conditionalities were what we would have done on our own. Of course, there was a change in our approach as well to which I shall come later. Withdrawals from CCFF started in early 1991 and continued into 1991–92. India withdrew $221 million in August 1991 and $637 million in September 1991 under CCFF. I was part of the negotiating team up to August 1991. Thereafter, I left RBI and joined as a member of the Planning Commission. The standby arrangement for a provision of $2.2 billion by IMF was approved in November 1991. The task of negotiation between December 1990 and July 1991 was greatly handicapped by the political situation in India. In February 1991, the full Budget was not presented. Only a vote of account was taken. Later, the Chandra Shekhar government also fell. All this happened when we were in Washington, negotiating. The task of convincing IMF that the negotiated terms could be implemented took some effort. In December 1990, there was also a change in the governorship of RBI. The departure of Malhotra was shrouded in mystery. Why the new government headed by Chandra Shekhar chose to ask him to leave was not clear. In dealing with the crisis, Governor Malhotra was firm and focused. However, Venkitaramanan, after assuming charge as governor, was equally focused and effective.

As we were negotiating with IMF, there were other efforts made to obtain extraordinary financing from World Bank, ADB and bilateral donors such as Germany and Japan. An arrangement with IMF was, however, fundamental. Other institutions were willing to act, only if we had a settlement with IMF. Governor Venkitaramanan was extremely active. He reignited his old contacts in various international bodies. In the absence of a stable government, the role of RBI and the governor became more important. Governor Venkitaramanan was described by an economic daily as a lone (loan) ranger. He and I went to the Bank for International Settlements (BIS) to find out if our gold could be effectively used. We visited the central banks of several countries, including France and Britain. The extent of exceptional financing raised is indicated in Table 4.3. In 1991–92, the total amounted to $935 million.

Table 4.3 Special Factors Affecting Movement in Foreign Currency Assets

Sl. No.		In USS million	
	Item	1991–92	1990–91
	1.	2.	3.
I.	Change in Foreign Currency Assets	3,395	-1,132
II	Special Factors	3,739	2,328
	Exceptional Financing	935	–
	Germany	60	–
	Japan	295	–
	ADB	125	–
	World Bank	455	–
	Transaction with IMF* (Net SDR Transactions Affecting Foreign Currency Assets)	498	1,636
		923	692
	Other Schemes	304	262
	Foreign Currency (Banks and Others) Deposits	-1,627	168
	Foreign Currency Non-Resident Accounts		
	NRI Bonds and Other Deposits	9	262
	India Development Bonds	1,374**	–
	Immunity Schemes	863	–
	Swaps	1,383	–
III	Change in Foreign Currency Assets (I-II)	-344	-3,460

Source: Annual Report of Reserve Bank of India, 1991–92.

* Represents changes in foreign currency assets arising from drawals from IMF and from sale/purchase of SDRs on government account.

** Of total collection of US$ 1627 million under ID Bond, US$ 1374 million accrued to foreign exchange assets of the RBI during 1991–92.

Pledging of Gold

Even as we were exploring different possibilities for raising resources, one issue that came up was related to the use of the gold RBI had as part of the reserves. It may be recalled that in August 1990, Governor Malhotra had suggested keeping 15 per cent of gold reserves abroad so that it could be utilized at a time of emergency. We supported exploring this possibility. In fact, this was also a hint given by fund managers and international banks with whom we were negotiating.

Several steps were being taken to activate the RBI's gold holdings. The first step was to revalue the gold holdings at market price. This was done by the government through an ordinance in October 1990, which was later approved by the Parliament to become part of the Reserve Bank of India (Amendment Act), 1991. In January 1991, a proposal was mooted by the State Bank of India (SBI) to raise foreign exchange through the lease of gold held by the government. In April 1991, the government agreed to the proposal to pledge 20 tonnes of confiscated gold to raise a foreign exchange loan by SBI and gold was dispatched in four consignments in May 1991. This was actually executed in the form of sale with a repurchase option. RBI was involved totally in this arrangement. This was not enough. But the major issue was the use of gold held by RBI.

In using RBI's gold, there were three sets of issues to be faced and cleared. First, at the policy level, a decision was needed. Given the sentimental attachment to gold, it was felt from the beginning that outright sale of gold was not thought of as an option. Pledging gold and raising a foreign exchange loan was the only thing contemplated. Second whatever was to be done had to be consistent with the provisions of the RBI Act. Under the Act, RBI could borrow only from other currency authorities. The maturity of the loan had to be only for a month. Third, there were issues connected with the physical task of selecting, packing and sending gold out. It bristled with many problems.

The initiative to pledge gold was taken by RBI. It, of course, needed the permission of the government, which was given. It was a bold decision by a government which at that time was only a caretaker government led by Chandra Shekhar. It showed great wisdom and courage. That was the starting point.

Under the RBI Act, RBI can borrow only from a 'currency authority', which is the Central Bank of a country. BIS had to be ruled out because it was not strictly a currency authority. It turned out that Bank of England and Bank of Japan were two central banks who would be willing. But both the institutions insisted that the pledged gold must be kept outside India, despite India being a depository country under IMF. As mentioned earlier, the RBI Act does permit keeping of gold outside India, but with some restrictions. There was also another problem. To conform to the provisions of the Act with respect to borrowing, RBI had to transfer the asset from the issue department to the banking department and this was done before trans-shipping the gold. Since RBI is permitted to borrow only for a month, the borrowing had to be rolled over from month to month.

The third set of issues relating to the shipment of gold turned out to be more arduous than expected. The gold stock of RBI was kept in two places. Since the quantity of gold to be pledged was around 50 tonnes, it was decided to use only the gold that was in stock in Mumbai. Transporting gold from any other place to Mumbai would have been another huge task. However, there was another serious problem. The gold that was in stock was in various forms. Not all of them satisfied London Good Delivery (LGD) specifications in terms of fineness, weight and marks. It was decided to send the pure gold bars as they were and Bank of England was entrusted with the responsibility of converting non-LGD bars into LGD bars. The departments concerned had to weigh a sizeable number of bars to complete the job. Packing, insuring and finally sending the gold through the airlines had to be done in a short span of time without attracting much attention. This was an operation in which various departments of RBI such as External Investments and Operations (DEIO), Issue, Banking Operations and Legal had to come together and act. P.B. Kulkarni, chief of DEIO and his band of devoted colleagues did a tremendous job. In all, 46.91 tonnes of gold were dispatched in four consignments by air beginning 4 July. The largest consignment was the second one, which had to be transported through a chartered carrier. It is interesting to note that the actual dispatch happened after the new government of Narasimha Rao and Manmohan Singh had taken over. The new finance minister raised no objection and he, in fact, defended the action in the Parliament.

The loan raised against the pledging of gold was repaid by November 1991. However, that gold was not brought back but kept abroad and continued to be counted as part of the assets. SBI also repurchased the gold it had sent and this (18.36 tonnes) was sold to RBI by the government. This was also kept abroad.

The entire episode is not without its drama. For example, when any commodity is sent out of the country, the nature of the commodity has to be declared. I spoke with the commissioner of customs and a special authorization from the finance ministry had to be obtained to send gold without such a declaration. I also remember that as one of the consignments had an intermediate stopover, a sudden doubt arose whether this was covered by insurance. On a Sunday, I had the office opened to check the policy and was relieved to find that it was a 'Vault to Vault' insurance cover. Finally, one other incident. When gold was moved from the vault of the Bombay office to the airport, the movement along the road was closely monitored. It so happened in the case of one large consignment, the bullion van had to stop because of a suspected tyre burst of one of the cars in the convoy. Fortunately, before much commotion could happen, the convoy resumed its journey.

The total loan raised against the pledge of gold was US $405 million. In today's reckoning it may look small. It is not even equal to what we get sometimes in the form of capital flows on a single day. But that amount was crucial at that time to prevent a default. There was no intention on the part of RBI or the government to hide the transaction from the public. RBI wanted to make it public once the operation was over. Otherwise, there was some operational risk. The shipment of gold brought out loud and clear the extremely critical situation in which India was placed. It also brought home to everyone the enormity of the crisis. In a sense, it paved the way for the reforms that were to come.

The Decision to Devalue

As the new government took over by the end of June 1991, the BOP situation was staring the government in the face, even though some efforts had been made to augment reserves. Almost the first decisive action of the new government was with respect to the exchange rate. Discussions between the Ministry of Finance and RBI were held at the highest level. As far as I can recall, there was really no opposition to the move. The situation had deteriorated to a point that it had become inevitable. Discussions centred on the extent of the adjustment and the mode. In fact, by a steady day-to-day adjustment, the rupee in terms of the dollar had depreciated by 10.8 per cent between March 1990 and March 1991. However, given the situation, a sharper and one-time adjustment was needed. Of course, every decision to 'devalue' the currency has a political connotation. The task of convincing Prime Minister Narasimha Rao and President Venkataraman was a task that Manmohan Singh as finance minister took on himself.

The decision was to effect a 'downward adjustment', which was to be done in two stages with a gap of two to three days and this was to be done by RBI in the course of the daily fixation of the exchange rate. Technically, the rate was to be fixed in relation to the value of a basket of currencies within a given margin. As mentioned in an earlier chapter, we had long before gone outside the margin. A sharp downward adjustment would take it even further outside the limit. Since the adjustment was to be made in two stages, the code name for the exercise was 'Hop, Skip and Jump'. Why two stages? This was partly to test the market with an initial dose and then to follow it up. In a sense, the first announcement would prepare the market. After the political clearance, the signal was given to Governor Venkitaramanan and me to go ahead. At that time, I was in charge of exchange rate adjustment.

On 1 July 1991, I made the first change. The foreign exchange market, while welcoming the move, was a bit shaken. It took time for the participants to digest it. But then speculation started as to where the process would end. There were editorial comments that talked about devaluation much beyond what we had in mind. It was then we decided to advance the date and not give too much of a gap. So on 3 July, the next adjustment was made according to the plan. The depreciation worked out to 17.38 per cent against the intervention currency, pound sterling. Was there any rethinking on the part of the government during the intervening time? Certainly, I was not aware of it. Somehow, 'devaluation' is always regarded as a 'quasi' political decision. The new government, hardly a few weeks old, could have been subject to various pressures. I did not hear anything from the finance minister. On 3 July however, I got a call from Manmohan Singh at around 9.30 a.m. He put to me a neutral question asking how the situation was and I simply said, 'I have jumped.' He said 'fine' and that was the end of that episode. However, there have been subsequent reports that Narasimha Rao had some second thoughts. It was good that RBI was given the full responsibility to implement the decision. This was an important change which, in retrospect, turned out to be fully justified. It must be noted that in all previous cases of devaluation, it was announced by the government. Manmohan Singh gave interviews as well as spoke in the Parliament about why the decision to devalue had to be taken. After the announcement on 3 July , the market had to be assured that there would be no further sharp downward adjustment. This was necessary to prevent exporters from postponing bringing in receipts or NRIs postponing sending deposits. Our action in the next week in terms of the adjustment of the value of the rupee reassured the market. In fact on 2 August 1991, I addressed a gathering in Bombay providing a detailed account of the reasons behind the adjustments in the value of the rupee and reiterated that there would be no further sharp change. The lecture, entitled 'Recent Exchange Rate Adjustments: Causes and Consequences', was later published in the RBI Bulletin in September 1991.

The decision to make the downward adjustment was a bold decision. It required a lot of courage. But devaluation has been done in the past also. What was in fact bolder was the ushering in of reforms in general and particularly in the external sector.

5

At the Planning Commission

It was in August 1991 that I was invited to become a member of the Planning Commission. The initiative was taken by Manmohan Singh to recommend my name and, of course, it had to be approved by the prime minister. My earlier contact with P.V. Narasimha Rao was when he, as education minister, met the Economic Advisory Council of which I was a member. But the Planning Commission that was constituted was unwieldy. Besides the minister members, there were seven others. After an initial exchange of views, I was given the responsibility for financial resources and perspective planning besides a host of other charges. In fact, railways was also with me and I played some role in the introduction of a uniform gauge system. I was keen that the phasing of the programme was done in such a way that maximum benefit was obtained. The major task before the new planning commission was to formulate the Eighth Five-Year Plan, which had to be done under radically changed circumstances. The government had decided to make a break with the past and move on a different path. The planning exercise had to reflect this radical shift.

The break with the past in terms of policy came in three important directions. The first was to dismantle the complex regime of licences, permits and controls that dictated almost every facet of production and distribution. Barriers to entry and growth were dismantled. The second change in direction was to reverse the strong bias towards state ownership and proliferation of public sector enterprises in almost every sphere of economic activity. Areas once reserved exclusively for the state were thrown open to private enterprise. In substance, the objective was to improve the productivity and efficiency of the system by injecting a greater element of competition. The third change in direction was to abandon the inward-looking trade policy. By embracing international trade, India signalled that it was abandoning its export pessimism and was accepting the challenge and opportunity of integrating with the world economy. The Budget presented in July 1991 outlined the stabilization and structural reform measures which the government had in mind. However, the speech as such had more to say on stabilization measures rather than structural reforms. Manmohan Singh ended his speech with the following stirring words:

'I do not minimize the difficulties that lie ahead on the long and arduous journey on which we have embarked. But as Victor Hugo once said, "No power on earth can stop an idea whose time has come." I suggest to this august House that the emergence of India as major economic power in the world happens to be one such idea. Let the whole world hear it loud and clear. India is now wide awake. We shall prevail. We shall overcome.'[1]

Planning as an exercise has to undergo a change in the context of the paradigm shift in economic policy. Before going into that, a few words about the nature of change and the reasons behind it are necessary.

One question that keeps popping up is what made policymakers change their views and adapt to a new approach. After all, all those involved in effecting the new transition were part of the older view and were, in fact, champions of that approach at one time. Take for example, the South Commission Report,[2] the main architect of which was Manmohan Singh and which was published in 1990. The report had a section on state, planning and the market and had said:

'The roles of the State and the market will necessarily vary, and depend on the country's developmental stage and experience as well as its inherited set of social institutions. In countries that have yet to industrialize, or where the private sector is weak, the State's role may have to go beyond macroeconomic policy to launching and managing productive enterprises. In countries that have advanced in industrialization and have a dynamic private sector, the State, besides setting broad economic policies, may confine itself to charting the path of development, identifying and promoting sectors for new investment, encouraging entrepreneurship, and preventing unacceptable inequalities in economic power and in income.'

The report elsewhere too talked about a change in approach to industrialization and trade policy. But on dispensing with controls, the report was lukewarm and not categorical. It must be said to the credit of Manmohan Singh that even in the days when he was an advocate of industrial licenses and controls, he was in favour of freer trade. That, in any case, would have imparted some efficiency in the system. But what then explains the radical change? Two things were relevant. First, the world was changing. Many East Asian countries had moved fast with a different philosophy. China had also moved following Deng's approach and was talking more in terms of social marketing. The Soviet Union had disintegrated and Eastern Europe turned its face against regimented economies. Second, India had been experimenting in the 1980s with greater liberalization. The attempts were good beginnings. But they remained sporadic and were focused on easing the controls rather than doing away with controls. However, the movement was in the right direction. It was really the enormity of the problem that we faced that brought about the sudden shift. Policymakers finally felt that the old style of dealing with the crisis would not be adequate. It was quite possible to take a limited view and solve the BOP problem alone. But then India would have remained a low-growth economy. One question that is frequently asked is how far were IMF and other international financial institutions responsible for changing the approach. It may be recalled that the August 1990 letter of RBI clearly pointed out that many of the conditionalities that IMF might impose would be the ones we would ourselves impose. It is true that the so-called 'Washington Consensus' wanted countries to adopt a more competitive economy and lessen the direct role of the state in economic activity. This was a view towards which we were gravitating. The intensity of the crisis and the need to find immediate answers resulted in a quantum jump. The change did happen and that was good for the economy. The political leadership comprising the prime minister, finance minister and Mr Chidambaram, minister of State for Commerce, and the bureaucrats at the front formed a good team to deliver results. Sweeping changes were introduced covering fiscal policy, trade policy, industrial policy, exchange rate management and the financial and banking sector. There was a common thread running through all these measures and that was to introduce a competitive system.

The Eighth Five-Year Plan was the first document that spelt in full the implications of the new economic policy. In the writing of the document, I had a major responsibility because I was the chairman of the drafting committee. Prof. Hashim, who was the head of the Perspectives Planning Division, did most of the writing. Pranab Mukherjee was the deputy chairman of the Planning Commission and, in the innumerable conversations I had with him, I had never seen him differing from the tenets of the new policy. Of course, he did not disown the past. His views are well expressed in the preface to the report.

He begins by saying,

'We are launching the Eighth Five Year Plan in the backdrop of widespread changes which have altered the international social and economic order. Centralized economies are opening up to free market forces and competition. We are also witnessing an eventful release of people's power for creative freedom and active involvement in restructuring the economic order for human development. This tidal wave of change has not left India untouched. In these trying and turbulent times, we have to respond and adjust to the changes quickly and creatively.'

Later he says, 'The Eighth Plan has been formulated in the face of these challenges. This makes it a plan with a difference. It is a plan for managing the change, for managing the transition from centrally planned economy to market-led economy without tearing our socio-cultural fabric.'[3]

He further adds, 'In line with the changed circumstances, we have redefined the role of the Planning Commission. From a highly centralized planning system, we are gradually moving towards indicative planning.'

P.V. Narasimha Rao, as prime minister was chairman of the Planning Commission. Sometimes his role in reforms is not fully understood. He was not a reluctant reformer. He strongly believed in changes. In fact as prime minister, he also held the portfolio of industry and was directly responsible for dismantling the licences and controls that characterized our industrial system.

He begins his foreword to the Eighth Plan with the following,

'The Eighth Plan is being launched at a time of momentous changes in the world and in India. The international political and economic order is being restructured everyday, and as the 20th Century draws to a close, many of its distinguishing philosophies and features have also been swept away. In this turbulent world, our policies must also deal with changing realities.'

He adds,

'It is thus not a choice between the market mechanism and planning; the challenge is to effectively dovetail the two so that they are complementary to each other.'

Narasimha Rao couched his views in such a way that it appealed to the old guard of his party. He always talked of 'continuation' when there was really a 'break'. That was his style. However, he was genuinely concerned with the conditions of the poor and vulnerable. When the draft of the report was sent to him, he made no changes. He only wanted social expenditures to be increased. This, however, was not a simple arithmetic. It required adjusting many variables such as savings. But we complied. He, in fact, wrote elsewhere,

'There is, however, one danger which we must recognise and guard against in the "opening up" process. This could lead to wider disparities within the society. To meet this situation, we have to enable the under-privileged sections also to derive the benefit of the new opportunities. This process would naturally need some time to fructify. Until that happens, there has to be a by-pass arrangement whereby benefits reach the lowest rungs of the social pyramid directly from the State. We are doing this.'

In fact, Narasimha Rao was fond of his expression 'bypass'. He mentioned it to me several times. The full meeting of the Planning Commission that approved the plan was a disappointment. It did not discuss any of the major issues.

The Eighth Plan contains the usual elements, such as the projected economic growth, trends in savings and investment, and the pattern of financing the Plan. But the special element was the discussion on the nature of planning and the policy framework under the changed circumstances. The Plan first draws attention to the changing world scenario.

'The Eighth Plan is being launched at a time which marks a turning point in both international and domestic economic environment. All over the world centralised economies are disintegrating. On the other hand, economies of several regions are getting integrated under a common philosophy of growth, guided by the market forces and liberal policies. The emphasis is on autonomy and efficiency induced by competition. We cannot remain untouched by these trends . . . It also needs to be guided by its own experience, gained during the last four decades. If planning has to retain its relevance, it must be willing to make appropriate mid-course corrections and adjustments. In that process, it may be necessary to shed off some of the practices and precepts of the past which have outlived their utility and to adopt new practices and precepts, in the light of the experience gained by us and by other nations.'

On the nature of the Plan, it says,

'So long as public sector investment is a significant proportion of the total investment, planning in so far as it relates to the public sector has to be detailed, setting forth not only the objectives but also examining the alternatives and identifying specific projects in the various sectors. Besides, the plan of the Centre will have to be appropriately linked with the State Plans as both the Centre and the States have responsibilities in almost all areas. All this is analogous to corporate planning. For the rest of the system, however, the Plan will be indicative outlining the broad directions in which the economy should be growing.'

On the role of the public sector, the report makes certain pertinent points:

'The public sector plan will have to become very selective in the coverage of activities and in making investments and should clearly define its objective principles. The following principles will have to be followed:

i.   The public sector should make investments only in those areas where investment is of an infrastructural nature which is necessary for facilitating growth and development as a whole and where private sector participation is not likely to come forth to an adequate extent within a reasonable time perspective;

ii. The public sector may also withdraw from areas where no public purpose is served by its presence. The public sector should come in where the investment is essentially for preservation and augmentation of basic resources of the country, like land, forest, water and ecology, science and technology or for running key infrastructural activities. The public sector will have responsibility for meeting social needs or for regulating long-term interests of the society like population control, health, education, etc.

iii. In large parts of public sector operations where commodities or services are produced and distributed, unless it is necessary for protecting the poorest in the society, the principle of market economy should be accepted as the main operative principle. It means charging as per cost and costing with full efficiency in operations.'

The Plan had a separate chapter entitled 'Policy Framework' wherein it detailed not only the steps that have already been taken but also the steps that should be taken in the future. It set out the broad policy framework in the following words:

'In general, the following macroeconomic policies need careful consideration during the Eighth Plan period:

a.   The policy regime governing trade, technology and transborder capital flows,
b.   Industrial deregulation and administered price policy,
c.   Financial sector reforms, and
d.   The stance of demand management as reflected in monetary and fiscal policies.

Broadly speaking, the first three of these policies taken together constitute what has now come to be known as "structural" policies, i.e. policies by and large aimed at improving the supply-side of the economy. The last one corresponds to what has traditionally been covered under "stabilisation" policies, i.e., policies aimed at controlling aggregate demand in accordance with the long run growth path of an economy. Recently, Government has initiated significant policy changes on both these areas of economic policy. However, the process of reforms initiated recently represents only a beginning. We have to carry it farther if we want to reap the full benefits of these reforms. Therefore, sustaining the pace of economic reforms will be the major challenge during the Eighth Plan period.'

While much of my time at the Planning Commission was spent on drafting the contours of the Eighth Plan, an attempt was made to streamline the financial allocations to states. Ultimately, the size of the states' plan was heavily influenced by the allocation of plan grants and loans. In fact, before the discussion with the state's delegates, an attempt was made to determine, in conversation with the chief minister and finance minister of the states, the financial allocation. Thereafter, the formal discussions were a formality. One important issue that came up for a decision by the National Development Council (NDC) during this period was the modification of the Gadgil Formula that had been in force for determining the allocation of funds among states out of plan transfers. Narasimha Rao, as chairman of the Planning Commission, announced in a full planning commission meeting the constitution of a committee comprising the deputy chairman, finance minister and me to consider this issue. It was the recommendations of this committee that formed the basis for further discussions at NDC. An important change in the formula was the inclusion of performance by states as a criterion. The position taken by a state during the discussions depended on which formula benefited it most! If we look at the criteria that finally emerged, they did not differ very much from what Finance Commissions used for horizontal allocation.

During my stay at the Planning Commission, I continued to take an interest in what RBI was doing. Both Governor Venkitaramanan and Deputy Governor Tarapore met me often. I was broadly in sync with the measures that were announced from time to time. I held the view that tightening had reached its limits and therefore some softening was required. I was also involved in designing the NRI bonds to raise resources. I travelled to the US and addressed several gatherings of NRIs, emphasizing the far-reaching changes in economic policy that were afoot. During my stay at the Planning Commission that lasted for fifteen months, I chaired two committees, one on BOP and the other on disinvestment, both of which had an impact on policy. The report of the High Level Committee on Balance of Payments of which I was the chairman, was set up by the Ministry of Finance to look particularly into the capital account of the BOP. The committee submitted an interim report in February 1992. The purpose of this report was to make a recommendation regarding the exchange rate system, which could be announced in the Budget and implemented by RBI from March 1992. After the devaluation of the rupee, the Exim Scrip was introduced in August 1991 as an important reform in the trade policy, replacing a complicated system of incentives. Several options were considered and the committee recommended introducing what it called a 'partially convertible rupee system' involving two channels. These were the official channel that would be used for meeting priority requirements at the official exchange rate and the market channel for the rest of the transactions where the exchange rate would be determined by the market forces, replacing then existing Exim Scrip. The Committee presented in its report a very detailed list of actions to be taken. The ratio of the official market was set at 40 per cent and the balance 60 per cent was through the market. Arvind Virmani had prepared a technical appendix for the report. The scheme was later named the Liberalized Exchange Rate Management System (LERMS) and the RBI very successfully implemented it. The final report of the committee comprised many recommendations, including the move to the unified market determined exchange rate system. Some of the recommendations are mentioned below. The report was a very detailed and careful analysis of India's BOP and covered almost all aspects of the BOP policy. For the record, it must be noted that the members of the committee were Montek Singh Ahluwalia, A.V. Ganesan, Ashok Desai, S.S. Tarapore and Y.V. Reddy, who also acted as the Secretary to the committee.

Favouring a realistic exchange rate, the committee recommended the unification of the exchange rates as an important step towards full convertibility on current account. In pursuance, the unified exchange rate system was introduced with effect from 1 March 1993. More will be said on this later.

The committee recommended that a reserve target range should be fixed from time to time taking into account the need to accommodate three months of imports and other short-term payments obligations. Thus, this measure goes beyond the traditional way of looking at only imports. In the committee's view, reserves should not be allowed to fall below the floor level. The committee also recommended that the option of RBI converting gold into foreign currency resources should be constantly reviewed, though an immediate case for exercising such an option was not established. Additionally, the committee recommended that a part of the gold reserves should be available for conversion at short notice into currency resources to meet contingencies.

With regard to external assistance, the committee suggested that 100 per cent of external assistance might be passed on to states for all sectors. It considered that commercial borrowings with a maturity period of less than five years should not be encouraged and favoured a cautious approach to public guaranteeing of external borrowings. It suggested an annual limit of US $2.5 billion in the case of disbursements of external commercial borrowings. Furthermore, the committee concluded that debt–equity conversion is not a desirable option for debt management in India. The committee recommended launching of gold bonds as an experiment.

To reduce the volatility and cost of NRI borrowing, the committee recommended a minimum maturity period of one year in the case of Foreign Currency Non-Resident (FCNR) deposits and gradual reduction in the differential between the international interest rates and FCNR rates. The committee has also favoured development of markets for NRI bonds to attract medium-term investment by NRIs.

The committee observed that short-term debt should be permitted only for trade-related purposes. The committee also recommended the setting up of a monitoring system for short-term debt for ascertaining the extent of outstanding short-term debt at any point of time. With a view to attracting foreign investment, the committee favoured a National Investment Law for codifying the existing policy and practices relating to dividend repatriation, disinvestment and employment of foreign nationals.

For the medium-term, the committee considered it necessary to achieve an annual growth in exports of at least 15 per cent in dollar terms. Furthermore, it felt that a current account deficit of 1.6 per cent of GDP could be maintained through a sustained level of net capital receipts.

The Ministry of Finance set up a committee in 1992 under my chairmanship to look at what it called disinvestment of shares in public sector enterprises. The committee submitted its report in April 1993. It looked at (a) the criteria for selection of public sector enterprises for disinvestment, (b) the criteria to determine the percentage of equity to be disinvested, (c) the target clientele, (d) the modus operandi for disinvestment, and (e) the criteria for valuation of equity shares. The committee observed that there was a need to broadly indicate the objectives of disinvestment in public sector equity. The limits to the level of disinvestment in the committee's view were derived from the target level of government ownership in each enterprise in the medium term. In respect of units reserved for the public sector, 51 per cent could be retained, which would enable control over management. In certain cases, the government's hold could be limited to 26 per cent. In all other sectors, the government would have to justify its continued holding of equity on considerations as an investor. The committee recommended that once a reasonable market price was established in a normal trading atmosphere over a reasonable period of time, the fixed price method would be the most appropriate. Where this was not possible, the auction method with wide participation could be adopted. The committee also recommended that 10 per cent of the proceeds could be set apart by the government for lending to the public sector enterprises concerned on concessional terms to meet their expansion. Regarding target clientele, the committee recommended that it should include the general public, mutual funds, NRIs and foreign investors, as well as employees of public sector enterprises, with a ceiling on the number of shares that could be purchased at a discount on the market price. It recommended the setting up of a standing committee on public enterprises disinvestment. The committee proposed that part of the proceeds could be utilized for reducing government debt. The report thus constituted the first blueprint for disinvestment. The committee included as members K.P. Geetha Krishnan, M.S. Ahluwalia, Suresh Kumar, Ashok Desai, S.S. Nadkarni and Y.V. Reddy.

My association with the Planning Commission goes back to 1965 when I was professor at the planning unit of the Indian Statistical Institute (ISI). This unit was located on the fifth floor of Yojana Bhavan. At that time, the planning unit had a galaxy of distinguished economists, including B.S. Minhas, T.N. Srinivasan, Mrinal Datta Chaudhuri, N.S. Iyengar and others. Pitambar Pant, who was heading the perspective planning division and who was, in fact, the main driving force in the Planning Commission, was also associated with ISI and looked after the planning unit. Pant was a man of great vision and dedication. Those were the heydays of planning. There was a near consensus on the need for planning among intellectuals. Of course, there were a few distinguished exceptions. Pant was a great optimist. I recall his Kale Memorial Lecture wherein he said, 'What cannot be achieved today can be done tomorrow. Today is confined but tomorrow can be defined.' This unbounded optimism had one disadvantage. It clouded the need to look at what had gone wrong. The return to the Planning Commission in 1991 was welcome. The Planning Commission, of course, had grown. In fact, it was a bit unwieldy. There was abundant expertise and knowledge in the Planning Commission. Those who were recruited directly had excellent domain knowledge. Some of the civil servants opted to be in the Planning Commission but many others were dumped into it. There were two schools of thought on the nature of planning. One view was that planning should be from 'bottom up' and therefore there was a need for decentralized planning. It was this line of thought that led to drawing up district plans and local level plans. The other school of thought mostly emphasized the need for centralized decision-making on key matters of strategy. There was a growing uneasiness about the proliferation of centrally sponsored schemes. These schemes designed by the planners at the Centre had a bait of financial assistance. Several committees were set up to reduce the number of centrally sponsored schemes. But there was not much success. The Planning Commission performs three sets of functions. The first was to outline the broad strategy of development. The second function was one of allocating plan funds among states and the third function was to evaluate the projects and give approvals. The second and third roles are debatable. However, the first function is critical. A growth commission charged with the mandate to prepare a blueprint with goals and objectives to be achieved over a definite period is still a need of the hour. It is necessary to have a powerful think-tank in government that identifies the concerns and problems that would emerge over time and offer advice on how to deal with such problems. The success of the Planning Commission in its new avatar will depend upon how well this function is performed.

PART II

At RBI between 1992 and 1997

6

The Beginnings of Autonomy

Monetary Developments: 1992–97

The 1990s saw a significant change in the institutional framework in which monetary policy operated. In fact, it can be claimed that RBI could operate as a normal central bank only after these changes were put into effect. While these will be spelt out in detail later, some of the salient changes may be pointed out here as a prelude to the discussion on the stance of monetary policy between 1992 and 1997. First and foremost, the relationship between RBI and the government underwent a change with the phasing out of the system of the issue of ad hoc treasury bills. This practice of using ad hoc treasury bills implied automatic monetization of the fiscal deficit and it had greatly whittled down the ability of RBI to regulate the money supply. In effect, RBI acquired some independence which was badly needed. Second, there was a sea change in the manner of government borrowing. The SLR was brought down drastically. It came down from 38.5 per cent of net demand and time liabilities in 1990–91 to 25 per cent in 1996–97. The interest rate on government bonds and treasury bills was not fixed but determined by the market. The borrowings were raised through auctions and thus government borrowings came under market discipline. More importantly, OMOs by RBI became feasible and RBI gained an important tool of control. In most countries, OMOs are a major instrument of control. Even though RBI held a large stock of government paper in its portfolio, they could not be used as a policy instrument because the interest rates on those securities were way below market rates. With interest rates on government paper market-determined, the RBI's armoury of control got strengthened. The third important institutional change was the dismantling of the administered structure of interest rates that the banking system and other institutions had to abide by. Even as of March 1992, there was an elaborate system of prescription of lending rates and deposit rates. As mentioned earlier, a big effort was made in September 1990, to reduce the complex interest structure and bring it down to five slabs. Even then, broadly speaking, interest rates were prescribed than determined by the market. It took almost five years to dismantle the administered interest rate structure. With the dismantling of administered rates, the interest rate was market-determined and emerged as a policy variable. Initially the focus was on the bank rate; later it shifted to the repo rate. Coupled with this was the development of the money market and government securities market. The various measures taken to develop these markets helped to make OMOs and bank rates instruments of control. The markets acted as the transmission channels.

The table below and the chart provide a picture of the behaviour of the three major macroeconomic variables—inflation, money supply and GDP. Inflation figures relate to wholesale prices, since by and large in those days this was the index that was monitored. The money supply continued to remain high except in two years when it was below 15 per cent. Inflation remained high in these years but fell sharply in the last three years, if we take year-end inflation.

GDP growth picked up steadily and touched 8 per cent in 1996–97. In 1997–98, GDP growth fell below 5 per cent.

Table 6.1 WPI Inflation, Money Supply Growth and GDP Growth Rates of Indian Economy

Year	WPI Inflation (Average of Weeks)	WPI Inflation Y-O-Y (as on 31 March)	Money Supply Growth*	GDP Growth
1991–92	13.7	13.6	19.3	1.4
1992–93	10.0	7.1	14.8	5.4
1993–94	8.3	10.6	18.4	5.7
1994–95	12.6	16.9	22.4	6.4
1995–96	8.0	4.5	13.6	7.3
1996–97	4.6	5.4	16.2	8.0
1997–98	4.4	4.3	18.0	4.3

Source: Handbook of Statistics on Indian Economy, RBI.

*Growth rates are based on end-March outstanding amounts.

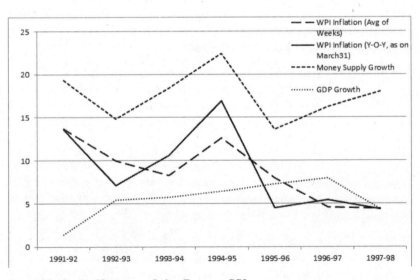

Source: Handbook of Statistics on Indian Economy, RBI.

I) Reforms in the Institutional Framework
  Phasing out ad hoc treasury bills

The autonomy of central banks has been a recurring theme in the literature on monetary policy and central banks. The legal status of central banks in terms of their relationship to the government varies from country to country. However, the exact relationship between the central bank and the government in any country is determined by historical circumstances as well as by the practices that have developed over time. At one end of the spectrum are central banks which are almost viewed as being subordinate to the government—in the sense that the stance of monetary policy is primarily determined by the government. At the other end of the spectrum are the countries where central banks remain independent of the government and take monetary policy decisions on their own. The concept of the autonomy of central banks has essentially been discussed in terms of the independence a central bank enjoys in taking monetary policy decisions. The issue of independence obviously arises only in a system where the central bank has 'discretion' in the determination and conduct of monetary policy. The institutional independence of a central bank may not really mean much under a system where the monetary authority is compelled to follow a prescribed rule—such as a fixed rate of growth in the money supply, or as the ones under the gold standard.

The argument in favour of the independence of central banks rests on the premise that monetary stability—essential for the efficient functioning of the modern economic system—can be best achieved only if the task is entrusted to professional central bankers who can take a long-term view of the monetary policy stance. Too much concern with the 'short term' can result in 'stop-go' policies. While the independence of the RBI did not become an issue in the reform process, the critical question that came up was: How can one make the RBI more independent in its operations? It was in this context that the system of issuing ad hoc treasury bills to replenish the cash balance of the government became an issue.

The genesis of the practice of automatic monetization lay in an administrative decision which appeared, prima facie, to be innocuous. Under section 17(5) of the RBI Act, RBI is authorized to grant to the government advances repayable not later than three months from the date of taking the advance. These provisions are enabling and not mandatory, and the provisions of the Act did not require the RBI to finance unlimited deficits of the government. What historical documents reveal is that in early 1955, as a matter of operational convenience, an official of the RBI and an official of the Ministry of Finance agreed that whenever the cash balance of the government fell below Rs 50 crore, ad hoc treasury bills would be created to restore the Central government's cash balance to Rs 50 crore. This seemingly innocuous operational arrangement opened up the floodgates of automatic monetization of deficits, which impacted the course of monetary policy over the next forty years.

The consequences of the arrangement of the issue of ad hoc treasury bills did not go unnoticed. H.V.R. Iyengar, governor of RBI, took up the issue with the finance minister. He wrote on 5 July 1957:

'Ever since I came to the Reserve Bank, I have been exercised over the fact that under the arrangements in force for the last 5 years or thereabouts, currency is expanded against the creation of ad hoc Treasury Bills as a merely mechanical process depending on the weekly closing balance of the Central Government. There is no check against the volume of currency that could be so expanded. If Government want to go on increasing their expenditure without regard to the available resources, there would be nothing to stop them, so far as ways and means are concerned; the currency would be provided automatically. The process is in fact so mechanical that it is operated by my Calcutta Manager and I hear about this action subsequently.

'The Reserve Bank, under the Statute, is charged with the responsibility of regulating "the issue of bank notes and the keeping of reserves with a view to securing monetary stability in India." (Please see the preamble to the Act.) As matters now stand, with an automatic expansion of currency at the will of Government, the Bank in my judgment, is not really in a position to discharge its responsibility.'

The finance minister (T.T. Krishnamachari) replied:

'Please refer to your letter of the 5th of July on the subject of the creation of ad hoc Treasury Bills. While I appreciate your concern in this matter, I feel that it would be a mistake to lay down any rigid procedure such as is followed in France. That does not appear to have helped France in keeping away from difficulties. What to my mind is necessary is to ensure that Government policy is formulated in this respect after very full discussion with the Reserve Bank and that the latter is kept informed from time to time of any changes that Government feel called upon to make before they are made.'

The tone of the finance minister's letter is clear. He was prepared for discussions. But the final say was with the government. There is an element of 'disdain' in that letter. Even though the Budget is approved by the Parliament, most often the actual deficit of the government was higher than what was indicated in the Budget. Indeed, the control of liquidity is a major concern of RBI.

The issue remained dormant for two decades. It was, however, seen in the 1980s that the fiscal deficit was rising fast and the extent of monetization of that deficit was also rising. The Chakravarty Committee in 1985 strongly advocated, as mentioned in an earlier chapter, a system of monetary targeting that could bind the government and RBI to a mutually agreed level of RBI credit to government consistent with the appropriate level of money supply. Elaborating on this, I said at the seventy-first Annual Conference of the Indian Economic Association in 1988:

> 'The essence of coordination between fiscal policy and monetary policy lies in reaching an agreement on the extent of expansion in Reserve Bank credit to the government, year to year. This will set a limit on the extent of fiscal deficit and its monetization and thereby provide greater manoeuvrability to the monetary authorities to regulate the volume of money. It is in this context that the introduction of a system of monetary targeting mutually agreed upon between the government and the central bank assumes significance.'

The problem with the system of the issue of ad hoc treasury bills was that it provided for an unlimited amount of credit to the government from RBI. In fact, what was taken in the form of ad hocs was never returned. What took place was the government's conversions of the outstanding ad hocs into dated securities, commonly known as 'funding'. Such funding was in the range of Rs 50–100 crore a year. With the large accumulation of ad hocs with RBI and the attendant problems of rolling over large amounts of short-term paper since 1982, there was not only a spurt in the amount of funding but also a fundamental change in the basic characteristics of the conversion. Whereas the earlier conversions were in the form of government-dated security with some specific maturities, at varying rates of interest, in the post-1982 period, the conversions were into 4.6 per cent special securities, with no specific date for redemption. RBI drew attention to the consequences of the system on several occasions during the 1980s. In its annual report for 1989–90, RBI also provided an alternative to the system of ad hoc treasury bills. In the recent period, there has been a worldwide debate, including in India, on the question of greater autonomy for central banks. Autonomy in the Indian context would mean that RBI should be able to effectively discharge its role as a monetary authority and as a regulatory body over the financial system. To enable RBI to discharge its role more effectively as a regulator of the financial system, the existing overlap of functions and responsibilities between the government and RBI over commercial banks needs to be minimized. The persistent and growing budgetary deficits have, over the years, led to an erosion of monetary stability. The increasing reliance on automatic monetization of the budgetary deficit of the Central government is reflected in a sharp rise in the monetized deficit to an estimated 3 per cent of GDP in 1989–90. RBI has advocated that the automatic monetization of the budgetary deficit of the Central government should be phased out over time. An interim objective could be to have a specific understanding on the amount that the Central government can borrow from RBI. Over the medium term, such automatic monetization should be phased out and a system of ways and means advances should be established to enable the Central government to meet temporary mismatches between receipts and payments. An implication of this approach is that the Central government would need to increasingly raise its borrowings at market rates of interest. Such a development would also enable RBI, as already indicated, to carry out effective OMOs. While these steps require a fundamental change in the system of financing the government, the statutory provisions regarding RBI lending to the government are enabling and not mandatory and as such, a reform of the present system can be undertaken within the current framework of the Reserve Bank of India Act.

As part of the reform process initiated in 1991, it was felt that the relationship between the RBI and the government should also undergo a change. The system of issue of ad hoc treasury bills that put no limit on the extent and monetization of deficit was inconsistent with the reform process. Therefore, in order to draw attention to this problem, I dwelt on this subject in the Kutty Memorial Lecture in September 1993. After tracing the evolution of the system and its consequences, I said:

'In the last few years, there has been a conscious effort to contain fiscal deficit and budget deficit. This has facilitated the efforts of the Reserve Bank to moderate the growth in money supply. However, the system is far from perfect. So long as the practice of the issue of ad hoc treasury bills continues, there is no immediate check on the expansion of RBI credit to the Government. Even in the last few years, when year-end deficits have been moderated, deficits during the year have been large. It is, therefore, necessary to move away from the system of issue of ad hoc treasury bills and the consequent monetization of the budget deficit. The latest Annual Report of the Reserve Bank has suggested that the proportion of the auction bills in the total creation of 91-day treasury bills should be raised in a phased manner so that by 1996–97 the system of ad hoc treasury bills is totally discontinued. At that point, the Central Government can be provided with a ways and means advance limit from the Reserve Bank for meeting temporary requirements with the limit being liquidated by the end of the financial year. In effect, this will mean that the borrowing requirements of the Government will have to be met outside the Reserve Bank. This, however, does not imply that the Reserve Bank of India will not hold any Government paper. It may and will. As part of its open market operations, it will decide on the extent of Government paper it wants to hold. With the moving away from automatic monetization of the deficit, monetary policy will be determined by the overall perception of the monetary authority on what the appropriate level of expansion of money and credit should be, which, in turn, will depend on how the real factors in the economy are evolving.'

I added:

'Autonomy in any case is not unrestrained. In a democratic set-up it can always be subject to policy directives either from the Government or the legislature. In the Indian context, perhaps the first step should be to move away from the system in which the deficits that are incurred by the Central Government automatically get financed by the Reserve Bank through the issue of ad hoc treasury bills. This is distinct from the question of setting limits on the Government's borrowing.'

Formally, I took up the issue with the finance minister (Manmohan Singh). I had no problem in convincing the finance minister. He readily agreed to bring to an end the earlier agreement. Discussions only centred on the time period over which the system should be phased out and the alternative arrangement that must be put in place to enable the Central government to tide over temporary mismatches between receipts and payments. The formal announcement was made in the Budget for 1994–95. The finance minister, referring to the issue, said:

'Turning to the need to strengthen fiscal discipline, I have long felt that Government should not be able to finance its deficits by creating money, through unlimited recourse to the Reserve Bank, by issue of ad hoc Treasury Bills. This practice has also weakened the Reserve Bank's capacity to conduct effective monetary policy. As a corrective measure, I propose to phase out the Government's access to ad hoc Treasury Bills over a period of three years. In 1994–95, the budget deficit is being limited to about two-thirds of one per cent of expected GDP, or Rs 6000 crore. Normally, net issue of ad hoc Treasury Bills for the year as a whole should not exceed this amount. It has also been agreed with the Reserve Bank that the net issue of ad hoc Treasury Bills should not exceed Rs 9000 crore for more than ten continuous working days at any time during the year. If this happens, the Reserve Bank will automatically sell Treasury Bills in the market to reduce the level of ad hoc Treasury Bills. This is a historic step which will in due course contribute to a significant improvement in fiscal and monetary discipline, and give the Reserve Bank greater scope for effective monetary management. In subsequent years, the recourse to ad hoc

Treasury Bills will be progressively reduced and by 1997–98, the Government will cease to have direct recourse to the Reserve Bank for financing its deficit and will have to meet its entire requirements through borrowing from the market.'

The actual agreement was signed on 9 September 1994, by Montek Singh Ahluwalia on behalf of the government and Dr Rangarajan on behalf of RBI. Appendix I reproduces the agreement. The details of the agreement are spelt out in the finance minister's speech. The implementation of the agreement ran into difficulties during the next two years. In 1995–96, the fiscal year average increase in ad hoc treasury bills at Rs 10,280 crore was well beyond the year ceiling of Rs 9000 crore. In 1996–97, even though net issue of ad hoc treasury bills remained within the level at the end of the fiscal year, the fortnightly average levels remained quite substantial during the first half of the year. There had to be 'forbearance'. However, both the government and RBI decided to go ahead and implement the original programme. There was a change in the finance minister. P. Chidambaram had taken over in 1996. He was quite categorical on the need to abide by the original programme. His observations in the Budget speech of 1997–98 were reassuring and showed his commitment to the reform agenda. He said:

'Hon'ble members will recall that in my last Budget speech I had promised to present concrete proposals in this Budget to phase out the system of ad hoc treasury bills by 1997–98. I am glad to announce that the government and the RBI have worked out the specific measures in this regard.

'The system of ad hoc treasury bills to finance the budget deficit will be discontinued with effect from April 1, 1997. A scheme of ways and means advances (WMA) by the RBI to the Central government is being introduced to accommodate temporary mismatches in the government's receipts and payments. This will not be a permanent source of financing the government's deficit. Besides ways and means advances, RBI's support will be available for the government's borrowings programme. Details of the scheme are being separately announced by the RBI.

'What I am effecting today is a bold and radical change which will strengthen fiscal discipline and provide greater autonomy to RBI in the conduct of the monetary policy. With the discontinuance of ad hoc treasury bills and tap treasury bills, and the introduction of ways and means advances, the concept of Budget deficit, as currently defined, will lose its relevance either as an indicator of short-term requirement of funds by the government or the extent of monetization. Therefore, it is proposed to discontinue the practice of showing the "Budget deficit"; instead Gross Fiscal Deficit (GFD) would become the key indicator of deficit. The extent of RBI support to the Central government's borrowing programme will be shown as "Monetized deficit" in the Budget documents.'

The Agreement was formally signed on 1 April 1997. Appendix 2 reproduces the agreement. It replaced the system of ad hoc treasury bills by ways and means advances to the Government of India. It set the limit for ways and means advances at Rs 12,000 crore in the first half of the year and Rs 8000 crore for the second half. The rate of interest on these advances was to be calculated as rate minus 3 per cent when they were within the limit and an additional 2 per cent on overdrafts. The calculated rate was linked to the cut-off price of ninety-one-day treasury bills. The agreement was signed by M.S. Ahluwalia on behalf of the government and by me on behalf of RBI. Dr Y.V. Reddy was also present on behalf of RBI.

The phasing out of the system of ad hoc treasury bills helped to enhance the operational autonomy of RBI in the conduct of monetary policy. Equally, it had implications for fiscal discipline. This, however, does not constitute monetary policy. This is, at best, the first step. Both the stance and content of monetary policy depends on multiple factors.

The reforms of the institutional framework relating to monetary policy were in three directions. Besides phasing out the system of ad hoc treasury bills, these were: first, related to the dismantling of the administered structure of interest rates. Second, the set of reforms included the reduction of pre-emptions in the form of CRR and SLR. The third related to the restructuring of the government securities market, which made OMOs possible. In this process, RBI gained an important tool of credit control.

Dismantling the Administered Structure of Interest Rates

Interest rates on deposits and loans had been fixed by RBI for a long time, almost since 1964. Initially, for some time, the Indian Banks Association fixed them. But later, RBI took over the task. Basically, one major function of commercial banks was 'outsourced'. What is the logic behind entrusting this function to a central bank? After the nationalization of major banks, it was felt that the system was one and the central bank might as well determine the interest rate on deposits and loans rather than sending out signals to commercial banks to pick up. This essentially implied that there were no differences among banks with regard to the economic environment they faced. The individual characteristics of banks insofar as they related to raising funds and disbursement were ignored or were treated as non-existent. The net effect was that RBI ended up prescribing a detailed structure of interest rates on deposits and loans which ran into several pages. This also meant that rates like bank rate, which were associated with a central bank, ceased to have any importance, since the central bank directly determined the lending rates of commercial banks. The system of administered interest rate also offered an opportunity to discriminate among borrowers and offer concessional rates to certain sectors, such as small-scale industries or agriculture, and to some borrowers, such as small- or medium-size retailers. The cross-subsidization of rates was implicit in this arrangement.

A typical interest rate structure prescription that was in operation in the 1980s is given in the Appendix. One of the attempts made during the 1980s was the simplification of the complex administered structure. Of course, the primary purpose of setting the level of interest rates is to regulate inflation and promote growth. When the interest rate structure was prescribed, it had other elements. It was determining the maturity structure as well. The Chakravarty Committee offered some key suggestions for prescribing interest rates. It wanted the deposit rates to be linked to the expected inflation rate. The basic minimum lending rate was to be prescribed as a premium over the maximum deposit rate. In September 1990, a major effort was made to reduce the complex lending structure to six slabs. The circular signed by me indicated the rationale for the restructuring. The circular said:

'The present structure of lending rates of scheduled commercial banks, as it has evolved over time, is characterized by an excessive proliferation of rates. There are not only a number of rate prescriptions for each activity but also borrowers are charged vastly different rates for the same loan amount. It has, therefore, become necessary to undertake a rationalization of the present lending rate structure of scheduled commercial banks.

'2. Accordingly, a new structure of lending rates of scheduled commercial banks linking interest rate to the size of loan is being prescribed and this significantly reduces the existing multiplicity and complexity of interest rates. In the case of the Differential Rate of Interest Scheme under which credit is provided at a rate of 4.0 per cent and export credit which is subject to an entirely different regime of lending rates supplemented by interest rate subsidies, the existing lending rate structure would be continued.

'3. The revised structure of the lending rates (other than for DRI advances and export credit) for scheduled commercial banks, effective September 22, 1990, will be as follows:

Interest Rate Structure for Advances of Scheduled Commercial Banks (Other than DRI Advances and Export Credit) Effective September 22, 1990.

Size of Limit	Rate of Interest (per cent per annum)
a. Upto and inclusive of Rs 7,500	10.0
b. Over Rs7,500 and upto Rs 15,000	11.5
c. Over Rs15,000 and upto Rs 25,000	12.0
d. Over Rs25,000 and upto Rs 50,000	14.0
e. Over Rs50,000 and upto Rs 2 lakhs	15.0
f. Over Rs 2 lakhs16.0 (minimum)'	

The critical point to note is that the revised structure linked the interest rate only to size of the loan. It recognized the need to support small borrowers but did not see the rationale for adopting any sector-wise criteria except in the case of exports. The circular therefore said:

> 'Under the new structure of lending rates it may be noted that in the case of short-term agricultural advances upto Rs 25,000 there will be no change over the present concessional rates while for advances over Rs 25,000 and upto Rs 2 lakhs, there will be some reduction in the rate depending on the amount of advances. In the case of short-term advances to a small-scale industry, the new rates though related only to the size of the loan will not be materially different from the existing rates for most borrowers.'

The circular did not deviate from the need to prescribe lending rates. It only simplified it.

As the reforms were launched in 1991, one of the areas taken up for reform was the structure of interest rates. The general direction of monetary reforms was to move away from direct to indirect controls and also to let the commercial banks take their own decisions on deposits and loans. Consistent with this approach, attempts were made step-by-step to move away from fixing deposit rates and lending rates. The movement was much faster with lending rates. While the level of the rate was determined by the stance of monetary policy, the reform of the structure was determined by long-term reform considerations. The 1990 circular had six slabs. In 1992–93, the number of slabs was reduced to four. In April 1993, the slabs were further reduced to three. In October 1994 came the big change when the minimum lending rate for advances over Rs 2 lakh was withdrawn, leaving the banking system virtually free to prescribe lending rates except for two categories of small borrowers, that is, borrowers with less than Rs 25,000 and those between Rs 25,000 and Rs 2 lakh. This brought to an end the process of rationalization of the lending rate structure. This marked the beginning of the process of price discovery and the opening up of the interest rate channel of monetary transmission.

The deregulation of the deposit rate structure took much more time. For example, the rate on savings deposits was deregulated only recently. In the first stage, an attempt was made to link deposit rates to the bank rate. But by October 1997, banks were given the freedom to determine the interest rate on term deposits of thirty days and over.

While in general deposit rates and lending rates were freed, there were prescriptions relating to export credit on the lending side and on savings and various types of external accounts on the deposit side. Looking at the reform of the interest rate structure, two points need to be noted. First, in transferring back to commercial banks the function of fixing interest rates on deposits and loans, they have been restored with a legitimate function of theirs. Second, while the lending rates were freed, the prescription relating to allocation of credit, such as those in relation to priority credit, were retained.

Reduction in CRR and SLR

We had indicated earlier while dealing with the 1980s how CRR and SLR were raised steadily to almost 'unbearable' levels. CRR was introduced originally to serve as an instrument of credit control. CRR is the proportion of net time and demand liabilities to be kept by commercial banks in the form of cash balances with RBI. The higher the ratio, the less is the ability of banks to expand their loans. As the ratio was being raised to higher and higher levels, the question of paying interest on the balances by RBI also arose. The payment of interest somewhat offsets the impact of CRR since it is an outflow from RBI. CRR was raised from the statutory minimum of 3 per cent of net demand and time liabilities to 15 per cent by July 1989.

SLR is the proportion of net demand and time liabilities to be kept in the form of certain securities, mostly government securities. Originally, this was intended as a liquidity shield for commercial banks because government securities were liquid and could be bought and sold in the market. But over time, it had transformed into something else. It became a means to support the borrowing programme of the government. In certain circumstances, raising SLR may serve as a credit control measure. In situations where in the absence of higher absorption by commercial banks, the alternative was for the central bank to absorb it, SLR increase serves to dampen expansion of credit. Since the interest rate on government paper was usually fixed at a low level, this put a financial burden on the commercial banks. SLR had increased from the original level of 25 per cent to 38.5 per cent by September 1990. By

March 1991, the pre-emptions in the form of CRR and SLR out of incremental deposits amounted to over 60 per cent. One element in the reform process was to bring down the pre-emptions in the form of CRR and SLR to reasonable levels and serve their original functions.

The reduction in CRR had to proceed in steps because inflation was still a problem. As of 1 July 1989, there was a uniform CRR of 15 per cent. In May 1991, an incremental CRR of 10 per cent over the increase in the May 1991 level was imposed. In January 1992, deposits mobilized through India Development Bonds were exempted from incremental CRR. The first reduction came in April 1992, when the incremental CRR was dropped. CRR was lowered to 14.5 per cent in May 1992 and further to 14 per cent in May 1993. In 1994, there was a reversal in the context of rising inflation. RBI had to work out a compromise between short-term compulsions and medium-term objectives. CRR was raised in two stages to 15 per cent in 1994. In November 1995, CRR was brought down to 14.5 per cent and further to 14 per cent in December. Thereafter, there were sharper reductions. In July 1996, it was 12 per cent and by January 1997, it was brought down to 10 per cent. CRR pre-emptions on external deposit accounts, which came under a separate regime, were also reduced from time to time.

CRR in January 1997 was still high. It was so since CRR continued to remain the major instrument of credit control. OMOs were just emerging as an additional instrument with rates of interest on government securities getting market determined.

The reduction in SLR had to contend with the continuing high level of the fiscal deficit. Certainly one of the reform objectives was to reduce the fiscal deficit as a per cent of GDP. While the correction process was on, there were years in which the government found it difficult to contain it. The opening up of the external sector also meant a reduction in customs revenue. The reduction in SLR started with incremental deposits. In 1992, SLR was reduced to 30 per cent on deposits over the level in April 1992. Thereafter, SLR on the base level as of April 1992 was also reduced. The big change came in October 1993 when SLR over incremental deposits was set at 25 per cent. The final change came in October 1997, when SLR was brought down to 25 per cent. This was indeed a substantial change and set a new tone to the government securities market.

The road travelled in reducing the pre-emptions was not easy. In the case of CRR, as inflation had not fully abated, on occasion, CRR had to be raised. But the medium-term objective was always kept in view. It is interesting to note that several developed countries had abolished the requirement of commercial banks to keep deposits with the central bank. On SLR, while the Central government was focused on reducing the fiscal deficit as a percentage of GDP, the path was not smooth. While it was easy to bring down the SLR on incremental deposits, reducing the rate on the base was difficult as it would have made the borrowing programme of the government very difficult. By 1997, the objective with respect to SLR was achieved.

Reforms in Money Market and Securities Market

A strong and sound financial system is a necessary companion of a strong and growing economy. The financial system comprises institutions, instruments and markets. The financial system helps to transfer surplus funds of savers to investors who want to invest more than they save. Wide and deep financial markets are a prerequisite for effective functioning of a central bank. The signals sent out by the central bank reach the various segments of the economy through the markets. Markets serve as transmission channels. One of the elements in the reform process was to widen and deepen the money market and government securities market. Certain steps had been taken in the late 1980s itself to create an active money market. With the dismantling of the administered structure of interest rates, the move towards widening the money market became possible. The government securities market remained mostly inactive as the interest rate was fixed by the government and that too at a low level. The holders were mostly captive institutions that were required to hold government securities. With the steady freeing of interest rates on government papers, an active market started emerging. An active secondary market in government securities is a precondition for the use of OMOs as an instrument of credit control. OMOs involve buying and selling of securities by RBI. Several significant steps were taken between 1992 and 1997 to widen and strengthen the primary and secondary markets in government securities. This section will give a brief presentation of these measures.

Changes in the Money Market

In the late 1980s, new instruments such as certificates of deposit (CDs) and commercial paper (CP) were introduced. The participants in the call money market were widened to include financial institutions that could only lend. The Discount and Finance House (DFHI) was set up to provide liquidity and thereby strengthen the market. The ceiling on the rate in the call money market was removed. All these measures brought about a 'metamorphosis' as Governor Malhotra said. These measures were taken forward in the 1990s.

During 1990–91, the call money market was widened to include FIs such as the Industrial Development Bank of India (IDBI), the National Bank for Agriculture and Rural Development (NABARD), etc. These institutions could only lend. In 1992, an important step taken was to allow the setting up of money market mutual funds by commercial banks. The objective was to provide additional short-term avenues to investors and to bring money market instruments within the reach of individuals. 364-day treasury bills were sold through fortnightly auctions from April 1992. These were issued without support from RBI and without a predetermined amount.

In 1993, FIs which were permitted to lend on the call money market were also allowed to borrow from the money market with some stipulations.

In January 1993, ninety-one-day treasury bills were introduced on an auction basis with a predetermined amount and with RBI support at the cut-off yield. The conditions attached to the issue of CDs and CPs were liberalized from time to time. In October 1994, it was stipulated that whenever CP was issued, the bank had to effect pro tanto reduction in the cash credit limit of the company. In April 1995, a scheme for the funding of treasury bills into dated securities through auction was introduced. In December 1995, changes were made to make money market mutual funds more flexible and attractive. One important change was allowing the entry of the private sector in 1997. Treasury bills of different maturities were issued to facilitate cash management needs of different requirements of the economy. Of course, it facilitated raising of funds by the government as well. Thus, a whole gamut of measures was introduced to create an active treasury bills market. These comprised institutional changes as well as induction of new instruments.

Creating active primary and secondary markets for government securities was a major goal of RBI. This could happen only when the government moved away from determining the rate on government paper. Thus, two decisions of the government and RBI—one of reducing SLR and the second of letting the government paper be sold through auction—led to the creation of an active market. April 1992 saw the auction of dated securities, heralding a new era. In October 1992, a new refinance arrangement called government securities refinance facility was introduced. Repos auctions in central government securities commenced with a view to even out the liquidity within the fortnightly make-up period. RBI set up an Internal Debt Management Cell in October 1992. Together with the changes introduced with respect to treasury bills, the measures taken in relation to dated securities constituted an important transition towards a market-determined system. In fact, in 1992–93, the Central government raised its entire market borrowing through the auction system. RBI wrote to the government in January 1993 and said,

'During 1992–93, a number of measures have been taken to evolve an active debt management policy and the measures include the introduction of 364-day Treasury Bills on an auction basis, auction of Central Government dated securities, Repos auctions, the recently announced auction of 91-day Treasury Bills and the raising of the maximum interest rate on Government dated securities. We admittedly have a considerable amount to traverse before open market operations become the principal instrument of Reserve Bank's intervention. Hence, we need to reinforce the measures taken in 1992–93 by further measures in 1993–94 and in particular, we need to give attention to the institutional structure necessary for developing the secondary market in securities.'

In September 1993, SLR on incremental deposits was fixed at 25 per cent. In January 1994, the government floated zero coupon bonds of five-year maturity on an auction basis for the first time. Steps were also taken to fund treasury bills into dated securities with a view to changing the maturity pattern of debt and avoiding frequent turnovers.

In order to develop an active secondary market, the Securities Trading Corporation of India was set up in May 1994 and it started operations in June 1994. This was similar to the DFHI which was set up in 1988 to take care of the short end of the market.

Continuing the efforts to improve the institutional infrastructure relating to government securities, RBI announced in March 1995 the scheme of primary dealers. Primary dealers help placement of government securities in the primary market by committed participation or what is normally called underwriting in auctions. They help the secondary market in giving two-way quotes. Thus, primary dealers act as market makers. They are not final investors but dealers in securities. This institutional arrangement has taken deep roots and is functioning very well.

A Delivery Versus Payments System (DVP) was introduced in July 1995. The DVP system synchronizes the transfer of securities with the cash payment and this reduces the settlement risk in securities transactions. Liquidity support was given to mutual funds dedicated exclusively to investment in government securities. In 1996, a system of satellite dealers was introduced as part of the efforts to broaden the market. In 1997, the government decided to permit foreign institutional investors (FIIs) in the category of 100 per cent debt funds to invest in government securities in both primary and secondary markets. The initiative for this was taken by RBI. In a letter in November 1995, the governor wrote to the government:

'Given the high level of requirement of the Central Government in the current year and the difficulties faced in raising funds, my view is that we should permit FIIs to invest in the Government dated securities market subject to the condition that the FIIs will not be allowed to sell these securities in the secondary market for a minimum period of six months after acquisition. The earlier concern that such an opening will lead to a large inflow of funds appears unlikely under the present market conditions.'

This narration only highlights some of the key changes. For a more detailed account, one has to go to the annual reports of RBI and *History*. However, a few concerns that arose during implementation need to be noted. While introducing the auction system, a choice had to be made between two types of auction methods—the multiple price auction and the uniform price auction. Under the multiple price auction, bidders were required to pay the price or yield they had quoted. Under the uniform price auction, every bidder was allocated securities at the cut-off yield or price. At that time, the multiple price auction was adopted, since it could maximize the revenue to the government. However, over time several changes have occurred. Both commercial banks as well as other bidders were new to the system of auctions and it took time to understand fully the implications of the auction system and get prepared for it. There were lessons to be learnt by RBI as well. It must also be noted that all these auctions were conducted with a ceiling on the interest rate. This was done with a view to reduce the burden on the government. RBI realized that this was inconsistent with pure auctions. The net result was that there were occasions when the government came with a fixed amount for borrowing, and there was a devolution on RBI to declare the flotation as fully subscribed. For most of the period between 1991 and 1997, the system of ad hoc treasury bills continued. That disturbed the price discovery mechanism. The issue of treasury bills of varying maturities also created problems because of their short maturity. There was bunching of repayments and that is why the system of funding treasury bills into dated securities was resorted to. Of course, this was also done through auction. Here comes in the debt management policy. While the government was committed to reducing the fiscal deficit, there were some years when deficits were large. For example in 1993–94, the gross fiscal deficit as a percentage of GDP rose to 6.87 per cent from 5.69 per cent in the previous year. Even in that year, RBI succeeded in selling most of its initial subscriptions in the market later. It must be noted that the monetized deficit showed a steady decrease.

Gross Fiscal Deficit, Primary Deficit, Budgetary Deficit and Monetized Deficit of the Central Government

Year	Gross Fiscal Deficit	Net Primary Deficit	Budgetary Deficit	Monetized Deficit
(1)	(2)	(3)	(4)	(5)
1990–91	8.53	3.35	2.12	2.75
1991–92	5.89	1.45	1.11	0.89
1992–93	5.69	1.65	1.74	0.60
1993–94	6.87	2.77	1.25	0.03
1994–95	5.56	1.16	0.09	0.21
1995–96	4.95	0.89	0.81	1.63
1996–97	4.73	0.64	0.94	0.14

Notes:
1. Ratios for the period 1993–94 onwards are based on new GDP series (1993–94 = 100).
2. With the discontinuation of ad hoc treasury bills and ninety-one-day treasury bills from April 1997, the concept of conventional budget deficit lost its relevance.
3. GFD is the excess of total expenditure including loans net of recovery over revenue receipts (including external grants) and non-debt capital receipts.
4. Primary Deficit means GFD minus net interest payments.
5. The conventional deficit (Budgetary Deficit) is the difference between all receipts and expenditure, both revenue and capital.
6. Monetized Deficit is the increase in net RBI credit to the government, which is the sum of increases in RBI's holding of Central government dated securities, treasury bills, rupee coins and loans and advances from RBI to the Centre since 1 April 1997, adjusted for changes in the Centre's cash balances with RBI in the case of the Centre.

Source: Reserve Bank of India, Annual Report, various issues; Handbook of Statistics on the Indian Economy, 1999.

Taken from *Reserve Bank of India Volume 4*, 1981–97.

The weighted average rate of borrowing by the Central government showed a rise. In 1990–91, it stood at 11.41 per cent. In 1996–97, it touched 13.69 per cent.

Coupon Rates on Government Dated Securities

Fiscal Year	Weighted Average Rate	Range
(1)	(2)	(3)
1980–81	7.03	6.00–7.50
1985–86	11.08	9.00–11.50
1989–90	11.49	10.50–11.50
1990–91	11.41	10.50–11.50
1991–92	11.78	10.50–12.50
1992–93	12.46	12.00–12.75
1993–94	12.63	12.00–13.40
1994–95	11.90	11.00–12.71
1995–96	13.75	13.25–14.00
1996–97	13.69	13.40–13.85

Source: Reserve Bank of India, Annual Report, 1996–97.

Taken from *Reserve Bank of India Volume 4*, 1981–97.

The finance minister at one time was unhappy with it. He did express his feelings to me. But we realized that this was the price we had to pay, if the borrowing programme remained high. However, the monetized deficit came down sharply and had a favourable effect on prices. It will be appropriate to conclude this section with what I had said in 1996:

'The groundwork has been laid to expand investor base gradually towards the non-traditional investors. Auctions have contributed to a new treasury culture and a progressive development of bidding and portfolio management skills among market agents. The yield curve has become flexible showing shifts according to market conditions and expectations. The increase in the secondary market activity combined with the improvements in payment and settlement system has brought about greater integration between money and capital markets and a better alignment of interest rates. The market aligned interest rates have enabled the Reserve Bank to use active open market operations to partly sterilize the liquidity impact of foreign exchange inflows in 1993–94 and 1994–95.'

II) Monetary Policy Measures

The stance of monetary policy during the period 1992–97 was not a fixed one. It kept on changing from year to year. There were broadly four considerations influencing monetary policy. First was the need to contain inflation, given that crisis years showed a sharp rise in prices. It was done in the context of the emerging growth trends. After GDP growth dipping to the low of 1.4 per cent in 1991–92, the average growth rate over the next six years was 6.2 per cent. It was only in 1997–98 the growth rate fell below 5 per cent for reasons explained later. The second consideration was the medium-term goal of bringing down the pre-emptions in the form of CRR and SLR. In fact, the drastic reduction in CRR by five percentage points over five years enabled the banks to provide larger credit to the commercial sector. Ipso facto, the space for the priority sector credit also expanded. The reduction in SLR also provided a larger space for provision of credit. Thus, there was an underlying expansionary trend. Third, while there was a persistent effort to bring down the fiscal deficit as a percentage of GDP, there were some years when net RBI credit to government was large as in 1995–96 and 1997–98. In other years, it was modest. Monetized deficit as a percentage of GDP came down from 2.75 in 1990–91 to 0.21 in 1994–95. It rose to 1.63 in 1995–96. Fourth, for the first time capital inflows from abroad played a major role in injecting primary liquidity. This happened in two years and in one year there was substantial outflow, putting pressure not only on the value of the rupee but also on the overall stance of monetary policy.

1992–93

1992–93 saw a move away from the extremely tight policy put in place in 1991–92. The annual report of RBI for 1992–93 said:

'Monetary policy in 1992–93 and the early months of 1993–94 can be broadly grouped under five major heads. First, a conscious effort was made to gradually reduce interest rates in the system as inflation rates declined and macroeconomic situation improved. The opportunity was also taken to progressively rationalize the lending rate structure. Second, as the macroeconomic crisis situation had eased, a quick move back to lower level of reserve requirements was felt to be an appropriate policy response. Measures were taken to allow a more liberal flow of refinance to banks and institutions to augment lendable resources. Third, 1992–93 was a landmark in that there was a cautious attempt to move from direct to indirect instruments of monetary control and an attempt is being made to develop the tool of open market operations as an effective instrument of monetary control. As part of this strategy, attempts are being made to develop an adequate institutional framework to facilitate an active secondary security market. Fourth, a number of policy measures were undertaken to improve the flow of credit to sectors such as exports, priority sector including agriculture and small-scale and large-scale industry. Finally, as part of the endeavour to strengthen the financial system, considerable attention was paid to introducing measures to improve the working of the banks, financial institutions and non-bank financial companies.'

The gross fiscal deficit of the Centre came down to 5.69 per cent of GDP in 1992–93. It was still high, but certainly a great improvement over the level of 8.33 per cent in 1990–91. Monetized deficit came down to 0.6 per cent of GDP. The important policy measures during the year were twofold. First, with the abatement of inflationary pressures, the minimum lending rate for credit limits over Rs 2 lakh was brought down by four percentage points from 20 per cent to 16 per cent. Simultaneously, the maximum deposit rate was brought down by one percentage point. Second, since April 1992, there were significant modifications in respect of both SLR and CRR. Against this background, bank credit expanded by 21 per cent as against 8 per cent in the previous year. The money supply growth moderated to 14.3 per cent. WPI inflation stood at 7.3 per cent.

1993–94

With a moderation in inflation and money supply growth in 1992–93, RBI projected a further moderation in the money supply in 1993–94, but this was not to be. Overall growth in GDP in 1993–94 turned out to be 5.7 per cent but money supply growth was 18.4 per cent, way above the initial projection. The year also ended with inflation in double digits at 10.6 per cent. In the first half, it looked as if inflation was coming down. That was why the minimum lending rate was brought down. However, the second half turned out to be different with a large inflow of capital. The foreign exchange reserves during the year doubled from $9.8 billion to $19.2 billion. This completely altered the picture .The reserve money growth during the year was 25.2 per cent .The growth in net RBI credit to government was modest. The primary liquidity injection was because of the increase in foreign exchange assets. RBI undertook OMOs to partially neutralize the impact of an increase in forex reserves. But its capacity in this area was limited, as government paper with market-determined interest rates was only of recent origin.

The capital inflows were far in excess of the current account deficit. As it will be explained later, for various reasons, it was not found to be prudent to let the rupee appreciate.

1994–95

1994–95 continued to witness rising capital inflows. Foreign exchange reserves increased from $19.2 billion at the end of March 1994 to $25.1 billion at the end of March 1995. Fresh OMOs could not be undertaken because of a lack of adequate market-determined securities. To meet the challenge of rising money supply because of the injection of primary liquidity induced by capital inflows, RBI raised the CRR from 14 per cent to 15 per cent, an increase of one percentage point. In October 1994, the prescription of a minimum lending rate for credit limits over Rs 2 lakh by RBI was given up. However, RBI retained its power to prescribe the maximum deposit rate. This rate was raised by one percentage point in October 1994 and the prime lending rate of the five largest banks went up to 15 per cent from 14 per cent in February 1995 and to 15.5 per cent in April 1995.

The year 1994–95 experienced an unusually high rate of growth of the money supply of 22.4 per cent even though there is some exaggeration because the last reporting Friday fell on 31 March 1995. There is also some window dressing on 31 March. Real rate of growth was good at 6.4 per cent. Monetized deficit as a percentage of GDP was low at 0.2 per cent. The huge expansion in the money supply enabled banks to subscribe substantially to the government borrowing. The current account deficit was 1 per cent of GDP. As mentioned earlier, the year saw a reversal of the trend in relation to CRR. Even though the medium-term goal was to reduce it, because of the special situation that prevailed, it had to be raised. Despite the control measures taken, this was the second year in succession when inflation was in double digits.

1995–96

1995–96 experienced a combination of several influences which made it stressful. The annual report of RBI for 1995–96 said,

> 'The year 1995–96 was one of the most difficult years for the management of monetary policy. There was a strong demand for

funds from both the Government sector as well as the commercial sector; the legitimate demands for these sectors had to be met without losing sight of the objectives of maintaining price stability and also maintaining the exchange value of the rupee. Monetary policy interventions, therefore, had to be frequent particularly in the second half of the year in the light of changes in the domestic money and capital markets and the foreign exchange market.'

This was a difficult year for three reasons: First, the gross fiscal deficit showed a rise. Second, while during the two previous years when the country had to face the consequences of rising capital inflows, this year RBI had to face the impact of sudden capital outflows. Third, the combination of measures taken to meet the increasing fiscal deficit and to offset capital outflows had an impact on money supply growth and prices, which were subject to different interpretations.

While large capital inflows had the impact of pushing up the money supply, capital outflows had the contrary effect. The capital outflows started in October 1994 and continued with varying intensity for the next four months. RBI's intervention in the foreign exchange market through spot sales of US dollars resulted in the absorption of rupees, leading to stringency in the domestic money market. This was inevitable. However, as will be explained later in another section, it was offset by several measures taken by RBI to provide liquidity.

The initial stringency was more than adequately compensated for. In fact, during the year, the borrowing programme of the Central government resulted in RBI picking up one-third of the borrowing. This was a reversal of the trend seen in the previous years. The monetized deficit was previously showing a steady decline. Of course, this had an expansionary effect. CRR was lowered in November 1995 by half a percentage point to 14.5 per cent. It was further reduced to 13.5 per cent in April 1996. The money supply growth came down sharply to 13.6 per cent, even though there were some problems of measurement. If measured correctly, the money supply growth in 1994–95 would come down a little bit and the money supply growth in 1995–96 would be slightly higher. On a year-on-year basis, the WPI inflation came down to 4.5 per cent. However, on the basis of average of weeks, it came down to 7.7 per cent. RBI came under severe criticism from some quarters because of the sharp decline in prices. This aspect will be discussed in a separate section.

1996–97

The approach to monetary management in 1996–97 was well brought out by the annual report of RBI for 1996–97. It said,

> 'There were two immediate concerns which needed specific attention of monetary policy during the early part of 1996–97, viz., the high rates of interest and decline in credit. To effectively address these concerns, it was necessary to strengthen the lendable resources of banks. Accordingly, there was a sharp scaling down of the cash reserve ratio (CRR) by as much as 4 percentage points to 10 per cent during April 1996–January 1997. This, coupled with strong growth in time deposits led to a substantial easing of the liquidity situation. Subsequently, i.e. in the second half of the year, as capital inflows recovered, with relatively low demand for credit, particularly from the corporate sector, nominal interest rates at the shorter end declined sharply. Interest rates at the longer end, however, experienced marked stickiness partly because inflationary expectations have not come down. The consequent increase in term spread, particularly in the second half of 1996–97, warranted active liquidity management by the Reserve Bank with a view to ensuring that the overall liquidity in the system does not build up inflationary pressures and that interest rates and exchange rate remain relatively stable.'

The year 1996–97 was significant for one major reason and that was the complete phasing out of ad hoc treasury bills from the system. The final agreement between RBI and the government was signed in March 1997. From April 1997, the government was entitled only to ways and means advances from RBI.

Among the monetary measures, the most important was the reduction in CRR from 14 per cent to 10 per cent. This was a massive reduction and released Rs 17,850 crore to the lendable reserves of the banks. In addition, there was a reversal in the trend in capital flows. Much of the turmoil in 1995–96 was caused by the capital outflows.

The contraction in the current account deficit and resurgence of capital inflows resulted in an accretion to foreign exchange assets of the order of $7.8 billion (Rs 27,000 crore). The market borrowing programme of the government went through smoothly. RBI support was small, unlike in 1995–96. The bank rate, which was reactivated to serve as a signal rate from RBI, was reduced first from 12 to 11 per cent and then later to 10 per cent in June 1997. Banks were given full freedom to fix the interest rate on domestic deposits of over one year. The prime lending rate of banks came down by 100 to 150 basis points. Despite the increase in lendable resources, the pickup in non-food bank credit was low at 10.9 per cent. One of the reasons could be the higher level of the real interest rate because of the sudden drop in inflation. The nominal interest rate did not come down as fast as inflation. Besides, the fall in the nominal interest rate was more at the short end of the market than at the long end. For the long-term interest rates to come down, inflationary expectations had to come down, which could happen only when lower inflation was sustained over a period of time. The real GDP rate of growth was high at 8 per cent. The money supply grew by 16.2 per cent. Year-on-year inflation at the end of March 1997 was 5.4 per cent. This was according to the WPI index based on 1980–81=100. Manufacturing growth in 1996–97 was still high at 8.6 per cent even though it was lower than 13.6 per cent in 1995–96.

1997–98

1997–98 showed a decline in GDP growth mainly because of a negative growth in agriculture. Manufacturing growth was 5.8 per cent, which was lower than 7.4 per cent in the previous year. Monetary policy during the year had to reckon with two conflicting situations between the three quarters of the year and the last quarter. Capital inflows were strong and comfortable in the first half. RBI purchased $5.4 billion during April–August 1997. Post November 1997, the impact of the East Asian crisis resulted in the weakening of the rupee and strong action had to be taken to contain it. Money supply growth was 18 per cent, and WPI inflation remained below 5 per cent for the second year in succession.

The two monetary policy announcements in April and October 1997 in a sense completed the programme of reform in the monetary framework. Without going into specific measures taken, the broad features of the new monetary policy framework that had emerged were: Banks were given the freedom to fix the lending rates and deposit rates. The ambit of prescription by RBI in these areas was severely limited. The bank rate was reactivated to serve as a reference rate as well as an effective signalling mechanism to reflect the stance of monetary policy. The interest rates on various refinance facilities were linked to the bank rate. The bank rate was steadily brought down until November 1997. Thereafter, the direction had to be reversed to deal with the impact of the East Asian crisis. A general refinance facility was established to enable commercial banks to tide over temporary liquidity shortages. The interest rate on this facility was linked to the bank rate. The money market was widened to include more participants. Several changes were made in the money market instruments to make them more attractive. The pre-emption in the form of CRR was brought down and it, however, continued to be an operative credit control instrument. That is why, while it was planned to bring it down to 8 per cent in 1997, it was not fully implemented in the wake of the East Asian crisis. The system of payment of interest on eligible CRR balances was rationalized. The SLR prescription was made uniform at 25 per cent on the entire net demand and time liabilities. This was the minimum stipulation under the Banking Regulation Act. The system of primary dealers and satellite dealers became well established. The repo market emerged as an equilibrating force in the money market. With the introduction of treasury bills of fourteen days maturity, the maturity spectrum of treasury bills was widened. By 1997–98, the auction system in the government securities market was stabilized. Ready forward transactions were extended to cover Public Sector Undertakings' (PSU) bonds and private corporate debt securities. There was a growing integration of the various markets and more particularly between the domestic money market and the foreign exchange market. Our experience in 1995 and in post November 1997 clearly showed that it was not possible to contain one market without containing the other. In fact, the two credit policies put together amounted to a big change in the monetary policy enumerated.

Despite a high level of money supply growth at 18 per cent, WPI inflation remained highly subdued. In fact, most of the measures taken before the East Asian crisis hit us were expansionary. In the first half, capital flows were strong and this was also expansionary.

The Episode of 1995–96 and 1996–97

The turmoil in the foreign exchange market in October 1995 had its impact on monetary policy. The actions taken at that time affected interest rates and flow of credit, which led to much controversy. It is best to explore this episode in some detail as such incidents are likely to occur even now.

The nominal exchange rate of the rupee started falling steeply in October 1995. The factors responsible for the fall and the speculative forces that were in operation will be discussed in a subsequent chapter. In this section, we focus only on the impact on the economy of the interventions undertaken to meet the problem.

The exchange market intervention to prevent the depreciation of the rupee meant the sale of dollars out of the reserves by RBI. This led to the withdrawal of liquidity in October 1995 to the tune of Rs 2780 crore from the money market, which resulted in a sharp increase in call rates. The intervention continued in a limited way in November and December. However, there was a pickup in sales in January 1996 and February 1996. Thus, in all, dollar sales resulted in a total withdrawal of liquidity to the extent of Rs 5995 crore. As mentioned earlier, there were steep rises in interest rates particularly in the call rates. However, intervention became essential because of the need to contain rupee depreciation. The speculators' hopes had to be belied. It must be noted that there was no intention to reduce liquidity. It was just a one-off intervention. Faced with this situation, RBI began injecting liquidity through a reduction in the CRR. In fact, by December 1995, the negative impact of the intervention was

fully offset by injection. The following table taken from the annual
report of RBI for 1995–96 set out the impact of all the measures
taken. In fact, by March 1996 capital inflows resumed and there was
no need for intervention.

Table 6.2 Release of Resources through CRR Reduction during the period 11 November 1995 to 6 January 1996

		(Rs crore)
1.	Reduction in average CRR by one-half of 1 per cent with effect from fortnight beginning 11 November 1995	2000
2.	Reduction in CRR from 14.5 per cent to 7.5 per cent up to outstanding level of FCNR (B) deposits as on 24 November 1995 with effect from fortnight beginning 9 December 1995	1050
3.	Reduction in average CRR by one-half of 1 per cent with effect from fortnight beginning 9 December 1995	2000
4.	Exemption from CRR of 7.5 per cent on FCNR (B) deposits outstanding as on 24 November 1995 with effect from fortnight beginning 6 January 1996	1200
5.	Exemption from CRR of 7.5 per cent on NRNR deposits outstanding as on 27 October 1995 with effect from fortnight beginning 6 January 1996	715
6.	Reduction in CRR from 14 per cent to 10 per cent on outstanding NRE deposits as on 27 October 1995 with effect from fortnight beginning 6 January 1996	560
	Total Release of Resources	7525

Source: Annual Report 1995–96.

The various policy measures taken to release resources are given in
Table 6.3.

Table 6.3 Liquidity Impact of RBI's Domestic Monetary and Exchange Rate Management

(Amount in Rupees crore)

Year / Month	Liquidity Impact of RBI Foreign Exchange Intervention		Release of Resources through Reduction of CRR		Net Impact	
	During Month	Cumulative	During Month	Cumulative	During Month	Cumulative
1	2	3	4	5	6	7
1995						
October	−2,780	−2,780	0	0	−2,780	−2,780
November	−392	−3,172	+2,000	+2,000	+1,608	−1,172
December	−199	−3,371	+3,050	+5,050	+2,851	+1,679
1996						
January	−1,426	−4,797	+2,475	+7,525	+1,049	+2,728
February	−1,198	−5,995	0	+7,525	−1,198	+1,530
March	+3,247	−2,748	0	+7,525	+3,247	+4,777
April	+1,192	−1,556	+3,300	+10,825	+4,492	+9,269
May	+304	−1,252	+1,900	+12,725	+2,204	+11,473
June	+2,653	+1,401	0	+12,725	+2,653	+14,126

Source: Annual Report 1995–96

The concern expressed at that time was that RBI's actions had led to a sharp reduction in the money supply and that had a negative impact on the economy. It also happened that inflation came down sharply, leading to a rise in the real rate of interest, particularly in the long end. It is true that the money supply in 1995–96 came down to 13.6 per cent. The lower growth is partly due to the high base since the last reporting Friday fell on 31 March 1995. As indicated earlier, there was always some window dressing of deposits on 31 March. However, even after allowing for it, the money supply growth was below trend. But non-food credit did expand. Between 17 March 1995 and 31 March 1996, the absolute increase in non-food credit was Rs 54,684 crore as compared to an increase of Rs 45,775 crore between 18 March 1994 and 31 March 1995. Such a large credit expansion was facilitated in part by reductions in CRR, which led to an expansion in the lendable resources of commercial banks. There was, nevertheless, sharp criticism that growth had been impeded by a restrictive monetary policy that gave primacy to price stability. In fact, growth did not slow down in 1995–96. The GDP growth rate in 1995–96 was 7.3 per cent as compared to 6.4 per cent in 1994–95. Industrial production in 1995–96 was 12.1 per cent compared to 9.4 per cent in 1994–95. In fact, industrial production was above the trend. In 1996–97, GDP growth was 8 per cent, partly helped by strong agricultural growth. Industry grew by 6.6 per cent. To recall, the money supply grew by 16.2 per cent. It was only in 1997–98 that GDP growth fell to 5.1 per cent. Manufacturing growth was 5.8 per cent and agricultural growth fell by 1.5 per cent. But both in 1996–97 and in 1997–98 (until November 1997) monetary policy measures were highly expansionary. It is true inflation fell sharply. The average inflation for the three years beginning 1992–93 was 11.5 per cent. It came down to an average of 4.7 per cent in the three years beginning 1995–96. In the comparable periods, money supply growth in the first period was 18.5 per cent while in the latter period, it was 15.9 per cent. Thus, the fall in the inflation rate was much steeper than the fall in the growth rate of the money supply. It took time for real rates of interest to get adjusted to the new situation. But the sharp decline in the growth rate came only in 1997–98. The possible reasons for this decline lie beyond monetary factors.

III) Stance of Monetary Policy

The stance of monetary policy in any year had been determined by the larger objectives of monetary policy and the circumstances prevailing in that year. The annual reports of RBI between 1992 and 1997 talked extensively of the objectives that guided monetary authorities. The 1995–96 report said:

'The broad objectives of monetary policy have remained the same over years. These are (a) to ensure adequate expansion in credit to assist growth and (b) to moderate monetary expansion to maintain a reasonable degree of price stability. The emphasis as between the two objectives in any given year depends upon the objective conditions prevailing in that year. However, the aim of monetary policy over the medium-term is to ensure growth with price stability.'

On the objective of price stability itself, the 1993–94 report said:

'The objective of price stability, however, is not an end in itself; it is a means to achieving sustainable growth. Except in very short periods, there cannot really be a conflict between the objectives of price stability and growth. Even on considerations of social justice, inflation control is important as inflation hurts the poorest segments of society the most.'

The 1994–95 report explained the multiple factors influencing inflation and the role of monetary policy:

'Monetary policy must be seen as an arm of economic policy. All the objectives of economic policy would as a result become the objectives of monetary policy. Some policy instruments are, however, better suited to fulfil certain objectives than others. Monetary policy in this context is perhaps best suited to meet the objective of price stability. This, however, does not mean that inflation is purely a monetary phenomenon. Prices are a result of a complex set of factors operating on the supply and demand side. The level of output, and more particularly of essential commodities, imports and the distribution system, all have a bearing on the price situation. Inflation, which is best described as a continuing price increase cannot happen unless there is sustained increase in money supply. That is the reason why controlling overall monetary demand is pivotal to any programme of combating inflation. It is the change in money supply, taken in conjunction with the change in real output, which ultimately impacts on prices. Historical experience suggests that if, over a period of time, money supply increases at a rate disproportionate to the increase in real output, then prices tend to rise. It is misleading to think that there is a trade-off between growth and inflation. Over the medium term growth can occur vigorously only if there is a stable price environment. Controlling inflation has thus to remain a major objective of monetary policy.'

Between 1992 and 1998, RBI had used money supply as an intermediate target. Money supply was not an indicator. RBI looked at several variables, such as inflation at the wholesale and retail levels, overall bank credit, non-food credit, etc., before taking a decision. Money supply was chosen as the variable to be manipulated. RBI did so for two reasons. First, RBI found the demand function for money was reasonably stable. It is this reason which prompted RBI to adopt flexible monetary targeting as a means to achieving price stability and allow the money supply to grow adequately to favourable expected growth. Second, as the administered interest structure was still to be dismantled, interest rate was not available as a target variable. But RBI hoped it could emerge as a target variable in the years to come. It is worth quoting the following passage from the annual report of 1996–97:

'The fundamental question in the conduct of monetary policy relates to the approach to money supply and interest rate. An issue that comes up frequently for discussion is whether there should be a targeted rate of growth in money supply. The answer to this issue lies in the inter-relationship among money, output and prices. Most empirical exercises in respect of India point out that the demand for real money is reasonably stable function of a select set of variables. Financial innovations and cross border movements of funds which have contributed to instability of demand function for money in the advanced economies are yet to have the same impact in India. In fact, in the absence of stable demand function for money, the role of monetary policy itself becomes negligible in inflation management. With a stable function, it becomes possible to estimate the appropriate growth in money supply given the expected increase in real output and acceptable level of price increase. An increase in money supply results in an increase in demand; it also influences output through the availability of credit. Targeting money supply would, therefore, have to be flexible, taking into account the various feedbacks. Monetary aggregate as an intermediate target is useful since it helps to predict price movements with reasonable accuracy over a period of time. It is also easily understood by the public at large as indicative of the stance of monetary policy. In India, the approach to targeting money supply has been eclectic in that a number of aggregates including aggregate credit are continuously monitored. In fact, with a substantial reduction in the Cash Reserve Ratio, a given order of increase in money supply can result in a much larger expansion in credit than before.'

As an alternative to monetary targeting, interest rates are often considered as an intermediate target in developed economies where interest rates play an important role in equilibrating markets. The various segments of financial markets are closely integrated in developed economies, with interest rates in various markets mutually influencing one another. This is not the case in India yet, even though the beginnings of such an integration of markets are discernible in recent years. With the demand function of money reasonably stable, the quantity of money plays an important role in determining prices in India. Under these circumstances, it is better to target money than interest rates. However, the monetary authority must watch the behaviour of interest rates in various markets and must be willing to intervene and smoothen the volatility. This is not necessarily inconsistent with an overall monetary target. In fact, with the inflation rate coming down and remaining in a narrow range, it becomes possible to focus on the interest rate along with overall monetary growth.

The 1996–97 report also talked about how monetary policy should react to capital inflows:

'Another aspect of conduct of monetary policy which has assumed importance in the last few years has been monetary management under conditions of large capital inflows. With large capital inflows, the domestic currency begins to appreciate. Such an appreciation can be prevented if the central bank intervenes and buys the excess supply of foreign currency at the market rate. The consequent accretion to reserves will, however, lead to an expansion in money supply with implications for inflation. Exchange rate management will have to balance the needs of the exporters to have a favourable exchange rate and the need to prevent monetary expansion from going beyond what is considered appropriate for maintaining price stability. Obviously, yet another objective of exchange rate management will be to contain volatility in the exchange rate and ensure orderly conditions in the market. Containment of domestic price increase is important since it has the same beneficial effect as the depreciation of the nominal exchange rate in so far as exporters are concerned. If the nominal exchange rate is stabilized at a certain level by letting the foreign currency assets of the Reserve Bank to increase, it may have an adverse effect on the exporters through price increase arising from more than the desired increase in money supply. There can, therefore, be no rigid formula governing exchange rate determination. While to some extent, the expansionary impact of the increase in foreign currency assets resulting from capital flows can be sterilized, there are limits to such sterilization both in terms of cost and the impact on interest rate. It can be argued that in a situation of a free mobility of funds, the rise in interest rate because of sterilization would only offset the fall in the interest rate arising from the initial expansion in money supply. However, in a real life situation, there can be overshooting of interest rate. On the whole, a balance will have to be struck so that the overall monetary growth remains at the targeted level.'

Getting back to the objective of monetary policy and the mandate for RBI, the 1996–97 report added:

'Autonomy or independence of central banks is an issue that is being debated widely the world over. Autonomy has many dimensions, of which the most important relates to the conduct of monetary policy. History shows that successful monetary policy requires not only a high degree of operational freedom for the central banks but also a clear enunciation of the dominant objective of policy. In industrially advanced countries, inflation control has become the dominant if not the only objective of monetary policy. With the discontinuation of the automatic monetization of Central Government deficit, a major step towards functional autonomy has already been taken. However, there has to be a general consensus on the need to keep the inflation rate around a certain level. In the recent period, the conduct of monetary policy has been criticized by a few as being obsessed with achieving a lower inflation rate. Emphasis on inflation control was not meant to lower the importance of the growth objective. On the other hand, it is the sustained reduction in inflation rate which will pave the way for attaining all the broad macroeconomic objectives including higher economic growth. Monetary policy in India is emerging as an independent policy instrument. However, there is need for clarity as to what the dominant objective of monetary policy should be. It is this clarity that will enable the reserve bank as a central monetary authority to function more effectively.'

We see here the beginning of inflation targeting as a possible model for India adapted to suit Indian conditions. But as the 1993–94 report said: 'It is here that there is a need for a broader national consensus before prescribing a mandate for a central bank.'

The monetary policy measures were generally well received. The industry was happy as long as RBI was expanding lendable resources and widening the money market and bond market. The industry was unhappy in 1996 because of the rise in interest rates. It, however, welcomed the April and October 1997 monetary measures wholeheartedly. Economic dailies were normally supportive of the measures taken. A typical headline in these papers after October 1997 was 'Reformer Rangarajan unveils Big-Push Policy'. One correspondent wrote in April,

'The monetary and credit policy for the first half of 1997–98 announced by the Reserve Bank of India (RBI) Governor, Dr C. Rangarajan on April 17, should do its bit in putting back the economy on the recovery path. The policy has been so packed with measures of far-reaching significance that it would stand out in much the same way as Mr. P. Chidambaram's Budget (provided it is passed by Parliament).'

The monetary policy measures were, however, heavily criticized by one set of critics who were, in general, uncomfortable with liberalization and the economic reforms launched in 1991. *Economic and Political Weekly* (*EPW*) in its editorials was largely critical of monetary policy measures during the period 1991–97. In fact, it was critical even of the changes that were in process in the 1980s. In 1988, they had an editorial entitled 'Monetarist Blinkers'. After the April 1997 measures, N.A. Majumdar wrote a piece in *Business Line* with the title 'Time for Rip Van Winkle to wake up'. It is important to understand why some of the critics were unhappy. The main argument of these critics was that RBI was focused exclusively on price stability and ignored other objectives. More particularly, these critics wanted direct intervention in credit allocation and distribution. From 1996, there was a decline in industrial growth. As already pointed out, because of the sudden decline in inflation, the real interest rates rose. These critics wanted a more activist policy in credit disbursal. It is true that maintaining price stability was a major objective of monetary policy. As indicated earlier, RBI regarded price stability not as an end itself. It was seen as a means to maintaining sustained growth. In fact, between 1992 and 1997, there was only one period when money was tightened. The primary cause of this was the fall in the value of the rupee and the need to correct a difficult exchange market situation. Selling of dollars sucked in liquidity and the money market became tight as already explained. But this phase lasted only four months. Money supply growth was low only in one year. In fact, the monetary sector reforms, which included a reduction in CRR and SLR, were expansionary in their impact. The lendable resources actually expanded. Direct interference in credit allocation is usurping the power of commercial banks. However, the prescription of the priority sector was maintained. With the enlargement of lendable resources because of the lowering of CRR and SLR, the actual flow of credit to priority credit sectors also expanded. More will be said about this when we discuss banking sector reforms. The best that monetary policy could do was to increase availability. Supply should not be a constraint. Demand for credit depends on the overall economic environment. In fact, the average growth rate in the period 1992–93 to 1997–98 was 6.2 per cent. The Eighth Five-Year Plan period saw the highest rate of growth for any plan period until then.

The description of the policy that was pursued as 'monetarist' is incorrect. It betrays an ignorance of what 'monetarism' means. Pure monetarism essentially follows a fixed rate of growth of the money supply.

On the other hand, the policy stance in the early 1990s was to regulate the money supply, taking into account the expected rate of growth of the real economy. The average rate of growth of the money supply was 17.2 per cent and it varied from 13.6 per cent to 22.4 per cent. In fact, the money supply growth was far in excess of real growth. Monetary policy was very much in support of real growth while keeping a watch on inflation. It is, however, a fact that inflation was finally brought under control. It fell to about or below 5 per cent for three years consecutively.

POLICY ENVIRONMENT

Box 1.1
Supplemental Agreement between the Reserve Bank of India and the Government of India

An Agreement made this ninth day of September 1994 between the President of India acting through the Ministry of Finance, Government of India (hereinafter referred to as "the Government") of the one part and the Reserve Bank of India (hereinafter called "the Bank") of the other part.

2. Whereas the erstwhile Secretary of State for India in Council and the Bank have entered into an agreement dated fifth day of April 1935 (hereinafter referred to as "the principal agreement").

3. Whereas under clause 5 of the principal agreement it is provided that the Bank shall not be entitled to any remuneration for the conduct of ordinary banking business of the Governor General in Council (now Government of India) other than such advantage as may accrue to it from the holding of his cash balance free of obligation to pay interest thereon.

4. Whereas it has been further agreed in November 1937 and January 1955 by exchange of letters that the Government shall maintain with the Bank a cash balance of not less than Rs.50 crore on Fridays and Rs.4 crore on other days free of obligation to pay interest thereon and further whenever the balance in the account of the Government falls below the minimum agreed to, the account be replenished by the creation of ad hoc Treasury Bills in favour of the Bank.

5. Whereas it has been announced by the Union Finance Minister in his budget speech for financial year 1994-95 the intention to phase out the Government's access to ad hoc Treasury Bills over a period of three years beginning financial year 1994-95.

6. Whereas it has been agreed between the parties that at the end of the financial year 1994-95, the net issue of ad hoc Treasury Bills should not exceed Rs.6,000 crore. It has also been agreed that the net issue of ad hoc Treasury Bills should not exceed Rs.9,000 crore for more than ten continuous working days at any time during the financial year 1994-95. It has further been agreed that, if the net issue of ad hoc Treasury Bills exceeds Rs.9,000 crore for more than ten continuous working days at any time during the year, the Bank will automatically reduce only the excess beyond the prescribed level of ad hoc Treasury Bills, by auctioning Treasury Bills or floatation of Government of India dated securities. Similar ceilings for the net issue of ad hoc Treasury Bills will be stipulated for 1995-96 and 1996-97. From 1997-98 the system of ad hoc Treasury Bills will be totally discontinued.

7. Whereas it has been agreed between the parties that a suitable monitoring mechanism would be put in place by the Bank so as to furnish the Government up-to-date position about the net issue of ad hoc Treasury Bills.

8. Whereas the parties have agreed on certain changes in the matters referred to above, it is now hereby agreed and declared as follows :

(1) This agreement shall be supplemental to the principal agreement and the subsequent letters exchanged and shall come into force with effect from the date of this agreement.

(2) The Bank would monitor, on a daily basis, the position in regard to the net issue of ad hocs over the level at the end of the financial year 1993-94; similar monitoring will be provided for each of the financial years 1995-96 and 1996-97. The Bank will advise the Government of the net increase in ad hocs on a daily basis; and furthermore, the number of consecutive working days when the net issue of ad hocs exceeds the limit prescribed in paragraph 6 hereof. Central Government holidays at New Delhi and bank holidays at Nagpur will be excluded from the computation of the number of consecutive working days. On receipt of the advice, Government could convey to the Bank its views and instructions in regard to regularisation or the extent to which the Bank may raise market borrowing on behalf of Government.

9. In witness whereof Finance Secretary to the Government of India acting for and on behalf of and by the order and direction of the President of India has hereunto set his hand and the common seal of the Reserve Bank of India has been hereunto affixed in the presence of its subscribing officials the day and year first above written.

Signed by the said Shri Montek Singh Ahluwalia, Finance Secretary, Government of India for and on behalf of President of India in the presence of Shri N.P. Bagchee, Additional Secretary (Budget) to the Government of India.

Sd.
(Montek S. Ahluwalia)
Sd.
(N.P. Bagchee)

The Common seal of the Reserve Bank of India was affixed hereto in the presence of its Governor Dr. C. Rangarajan who has signed in the presence of Shri S.S. Tarapore, Deputy Governor of Reserve Bank of India.

Sd.
(C. Rangarajan)
Sd.
(S.S. Tarapore)

2

ECONOMIC *REVIEW*

Box 1.2

Supplemental Agreement between the Reserve Bank of India and the Government of India

An agreement made this twenty sixth day of March 1997 between the President of India acting through the Ministry of Finance, Government of India (hereinafter referred to as "the Government") of the one part and the Reserve Bank of India (hereinafter called "the Bank") of the other part.

A. WHEREAS the erstwhile Secretary of State for India in Council and the Bank have entered into an agreement dated fifth day of April 1935 (hereinafter referred to as "the Principal agreement").

B. WHEREAS it has been agreed in November 1937 and January 1955 by exchange of letters that the Government shall maintain certain minimum cash balance and further that whenever the balance in the account of the Government falls below the minimum agreed to, the account be replenished by the creation of ad hoc Treasury Bills, in favour of the Bank.

C. WHEREAS the President of India and the Bank have entered into a Supplemental Agreement dated ninth day of September 1994 (First Supplemental Agreement) regarding phasing out of ad hoc Treasury Bills, and in terms of paragraph 6 of First Supplemental Agreement, the system of ad hoc Treasury Bills to replenish the balance of the Government to the agreed minimum level as laid down is to be totally discontinued with effect from 1997-98.

D. WHEREAS the Union Finance Minister in his budget speech for Financial year 1997-98 has presented concrete proposals setting out modalities for phasing out ad hoc Treasury Bills from April 1, 1997.

E. WHEREAS It has been agreed between the parties that a suitable mechanism would be put in place so as to enable the Government to manage its cash balance position with the Bank.

F. AND WHEREAS the parties have agreed on certain changes in the maters referred to above.

NOW IT IS HEREBY AGREED AND DECLARE AS FOLLOWS:

(1) This agreement shall be supplemental to the principal agreement and the First Supplemental Agreement dated September 9, 1994.

(2) The practice of issuing ad hoc Treasury Bills to replenish the

(Contd. . .)

cash balance of the Government to the agreed minimum level will be discontinued with effect from April 1, 1997.

(3) The outstanding ad hoc Treasury Bills as on March 31, 1997 would be funded into special securities without any specified maturity at an interest rate of 4.6 per cent per annum on April 1, 1997. The outstanding Tap Treasury Bills as on March 31, 1997 will be paid off on maturity with an equivalent creation of special securities without any specified maturity at an interest rate of 4.6 per cent per annum.

(4) From April 1, 1997, the Bank shall make Ways and Means Advances to the Government, if so required, at such rate of interest as many be mutually agreed from time to time, provided such advances outstanding at any time shall not exceed the limit, as may be mutually agreed upon from time to time. The advances shall be fully paid off within a period not exceeding three months from the date of making such advance. Interest shall be calculated on daily balances and debited to the account of the Government with the Bank at such intervals, as may be decided by the Bank.

(5) In the event of Government's account as at the close of business on any working day emerging and remaining overdrawn beyond the agreed limit for Ways and Means Advances, the Bank may charge interest on the daily balances overdrawn at such rate or rates, as may be mutually agreed upon from time to time, by debit to the account of the Government with the bank at such intervals, as may be decided by the Bank.

(6) When 75 per cent of the Ways and Means Advances is utilized, the Bank would trigger fresh floatation of Government securities.

(7) Ways and Means Advances and Overdraft would be monitored and regulated on such terms as may be mutually agreed from time to time.

(8) If the Government runs surplus cash balances beyond an agreed level, the Bank will make investment, as may be mutually agreed from time to time.

(9) Subject to the terms hereinabove, the arrangements for the fiscal year 1997-98 have been mutually agreed as under:

(i) The limit for Ways and Means Advances will be Rs. 12,000 crore for the first half of the year (April to September) and Rs. 8,000 crore for the second half of the year (October to March).

(Contd. . .)

POLICY ENVIRONMENT

(Contd. . .)

(ii) The interest rate on Ways and Means Advances and Overdraft for the Government will be the following:

    (a) Up to the Ways and Means: Calculated Rate Advance Limits

                minus 3 per cent

(b) For Overdraft :The rate at beyond the   (a) **plus** Ways and   2 per cent on the and Means   Overdraft amount Advances limits

NOTE: The "Calculated Rate" for any quarter beginning April 1, 1997 will mean the average of the implicit yield at the cut-off price of 91-day Treasury Bill auctions held during the previous quarter

(10) The arrangement for the fiscal year 1998-99 with regard to limits for Ways and Means Advances, as also interest rate on Ways and Means Advances and Overdraft will be through exchange of letters.

(11) (a) The arrangements after fiscal year 1998-99 in respect of limits for Ways and Means Advances and interest rate on Ways and Means Advances and overdraft will be through exchange of letters.

(b) Overdraft will not be permissible for periods exceeding ten 'consecutive' working days, after March 31, 1999.

NOTE: For the purpose of computation of the number of 'consecutive' working days. Central Government holidays at New Delhi and bank holidays at Nagpur will be excluded.

(12) In witness whereof Finance Secretary to the Government of India acting for and on behalf of and by the order and direction of the President of India has hereunto set his hand and the common seal of the Reserve bank of India has been hereunto affixed in the presence of its subscribing officials the days and year first above written.

Signed by the said
Shri Montek Singh   }
Ahluwalia,
Finance Secretary,   }
Government of India for
and on behalf of   } sd/–
President of India   } 26.3.97
in the presence of
Shri J.S. Mathur,   } sd/–
Additional Secretary
(Budget) to the   } 26.3.97
Government of India   }

(Contd. . .)

(*Contd...*)

The Common seal of the }
Reserve Bank of India   }
was affixed hereto in the
presence of its Governor } sd/–
Dr. C. Rangarajan who   }
has signed in the presence
of Dr. Y.V. Reddy, Deputy } sd/–
Governor of Reserve
Bank of India   }

7

External Sector Management 1992–97

Coping with an Open Economy

The external sector management was a success story of liberalization. India's BOP between 1992–93 and 1996–97 remained stable. Indeed, India was able to meet the East Asian crisis from a position of strength.

After the successful handling of the 1991 BOP crisis, the government and RBI went on to unleash a host of measures to liberalize India's foreign trade and finance. Import tariffs were brought down steadily and quantitative controls were also being withdrawn. The capital account of India's BOP was liberalized with permission given to foreign institutions to invest in the Indian stock market. FDI was encouraged with many of the restrictive measures being withdrawn. Above all, the exchange rate regime underwent a big change. The value of the rupee was allowed to be determined by and large by market forces. This, of course, did not preclude RBI's intervention in the market to maintain orderly behaviour. This chapter will discuss these fundamental changes and it is divided into three sections. Section I will discuss the BOP scenario over the years 1992–97. Section II will provide an account of measures undertaken to deepen and widen the foreign exchange market. Section III will describe the behaviour of the Indian rupee as it was allowed to float and the actions taken when there was turbulence.

I) Balance of Payments Situation

The broad picture that emerges of the BOP situation between 1992–93 and 1996–97 is one of a strong external sector. The current account deficit over the five-year period averaged 1.14 per cent. With the opening of the capital account, the strong inflow of capital raised the foreign exchange reserves from $9.8 billion at the end of March 1993 to $26.4 billion at the end of March 1997. At one point, the total foreign exchange reserves stood at 8.6 months of imports. Export growth remained sturdy. The average rate of growth during the years 1993–94 to 1995–96 was 19.6 per cent. The foreign debt stock to GDP ratio came down from 37.5 per cent as at the end of March 1993 to 24.8 per cent as at the end of March 1997. A year-by-year analysis is given below. Table 7.1, 7.2 and 7.3 provide data on salient components of BOP.

Table 7.1 India's Balance of Payments

Year	1992–93	1993–94	1994–95	1995–96	US$ million 1996–97
I. Merchandise					
A) Exports, f.o.b.	18869	22683	26855	32310	34133
B) Imports, c.i.f.	24316	26739	35904	43670	48948
Trade balance (A-B)	-5447	-4056	-9049	-11360	-14815
II. Invisibles, net	1921	2897	5680	5447	10196
III. Current account (I+II)	-3526	-1159	-3369	-5912	-4619
IV. Capital account (A to F)	2936	9694	9156	4690	11412
A) Foreign Investment	557	4233	4922	4803	6154
B) External assistance, net	1859	1901	1526	884	1109
C) Commercial borrowings, net	-358	608	1030	1275	2848
D) Rupee debt service	-878	-1054	-983	-952	-727
E) NRI deposits, net	2001	1207	172	1104	3350
F) Other capital	-245	2800	2489	-2425	-1321
V. Overall balance (III+IV)	-590	8535	5787	-1222	6793

Table 7.1 (Continued)

					US$ million
Year	1992– 93	1993– 94	1994– 95	1995– 96	1996– 97
VI. Foreign Exchange Reserves (as of 31 March)	9832	19254	25186	21687	26423

Source: Handbook of Statistics on Indian Economy 2017–18 (Table 137).

Table 7.2 Key Ratios of India's Balance of Payments

Year	Trade		Invisibles			Current Account		Capital Account			Import cover of reserves (in months)
	Exports / GDP	Imports / GDP	Receipts / GDP	Payments / GDP	Net / GDP	Current Receipts / GDP	Current Receipts / Current Payments	CAD / GDP	Foreign Investment / Exports	Foreign Investment / GDP	
1992–93	7.7	9.9	3.8	3	0.8	11.3	87.7	-1.4	3	0.2	4.9
1993–94	8.2	9.7	4.1	3.1	1	12.2	95.6	-0.4	18.7	1.5	8.6
1994–95	8.3	11.1	4.8	3.1	1.8	13	91.7	-1	18.3	1.5	8.4
1995–96	9.1	12.3	5	3.4	1.5	13.9	88.8	-1.7	14.9	1.3	6
1996–97	8.8	12.6	5.5	2.9	2.6	14.2	91.6	-1.2	18	1.6	6.5

Source: Handbook of Statistics on Indian Economy 2017–18 (Table 238).

Table 7.3 Annual Growth of Exports and Imports (in per cent)

Year	Exports Growth	Import Growth
1992–93	3.76	12.7
1993–94	19.97	6.5
1994–95	18.4	22.9
1995–96	20.75	28
1996–97	5.27	6.7

Source: Handbook of Statistics on Indian Economy 2017–18 (Table 120).

1992–93

In 1992–93, export performance was subdued. Exports grew by 3.7 per cent. Import growth was stronger at 12.7 per cent. This was to be expected after the severe compression on imports in the previous years. Net invisibles were positive. The current account deficit was 1.4 per cent of GDP. The annual report of RBI for 1992–93 records:

> 'Following the liberalization in baggage rules for persons of Indian nationality or origin returning from abroad, which was effected in the Union Budget 1992–93, there was an estimated inflow of about 132 tons of gold valued at approximately US$1.4 billion during 1992–93. In February 1993 similar liberalization was extended to the import of silver, as a result of which, about 650 Kgs. of silver were brought into the country during 1992–93. However, this inflow of bullion is not reflected either under imports or under private transfer receipts in the balance of payments data for 1992–93.'

The capital account benefitted from purchases from IMF. Net purchases from IMF amounted to $1.3 billion in 1992–93. Foreign exchange reserves as at the end of March 1993 stood at $9.8 billion, an increase of $612 million over the previous year. India Development Bonds floated to attract funds from persons of Indian origin resident abroad fetched $189 million.

1993–94

1993–94 was very different from 1992–93. Export growth was 20 per cent. Import growth was relatively modest at 6.5 per cent. Invisibles were also more buoyant. The current account deficit shrank to 0.4 per cent of GDP. This was the first full year after the new system exchange rate regime came into operation. One of the reasons for the fall in non-oil imports was that the need for imports for building up large inventories had diminished. Oil imports benefited from softening of crude oil prices. The accretion to foreign exchange reserves was staggering. The foreign currency assets rose to $15.1 billion as at the end of March 1994, an increase of $8.6 billion. Foreign exchange reserves were equivalent to 8.6 months of imports. At that point in time, this was a historic high.

There were other important features to be noted. Net capital inflows were of the order of $9 billion. The change in the capital account is significant and it is worth quoting what the annual report of 1993–94 said:

'The inflow of foreign investment during 1993–94 was the most significant development in the capital account of the balance of payments. It represented the coming into fruition of reforms instituted in trade, industrial and foreign investment policies in the last three years. Foreign investment through direct equity participation embodying transfer of technology registered an increase from US$341 million during 1992–93 to US$620 million during 1993–94. Investment in Indian stock markets by foreign institutional investors amounted to US$1,665 million. Some Indian corporate entities tapped international capital markets through new instruments like the GDRs and FCCBs to the tune of US$1,460 million and US$914 respectively. Foreign investment, direct and portfolio taken together, but excluding FCCBs amounted to US$4,110 million during 1993–94 as against US$433 million in 1992–93.'

Thus, the opening of the capital account was an important part of liberalization. It was, however, done with great caution, recognizing the volatility of some of these flows.

1994–95

The BOP continued to remain robust. Export growth was strong at 18.4 per cent. Import growth was even stronger at 22.9 per cent. The net result was a rise in trade deficit. But net invisibles doubled. The current account deficit rose but was still low at 1 per cent of GDP.

The current account continued to remain manageable with a small financing demand on the capital account, which could be met by normal capital flows. The criterion of sustainability recommended by the High Level Committee on Balance of Payments was met.

In view of the comfortable situation in BOP, India on 20 August 1994 accepted the obligations under Article VIII of the IMF Agreement by removing restrictions on current account transactions. Thus, the current account convertibility of the Indian rupee was achieved. This was an important step forward.

Since 1993, consequent upon the liberalization of the capital account and worldwide trend of surge in capital flows, India's capital account was flooded with inflows.

The stable exchange rate was an important step. With a low current account deficit and strong capital inflows, the foreign currency assets of RBI rose by $5.7 billion during 1994–95. Thus, the foreign currency reserves of RBI as at the end of March 1994–95 at $25.2 billion was equal to 8.4 months of imports. The total foreign investment flows, including both direct investment and portfolio investment, were $4.9 billion.

1995–96

During the year, while the BOP situation was generally comfortable, there was, however, a rise in the current account deficit, which touched 1.7 per cent of GDP. It, however, posed no financing problem. The turbulence witnessed in the exchange rate of the rupee during the second half of the year necessitated RBI intervention and sale of dollars. While at the end of the year normality was restored (more will be said in the last section of this chapter), there was a decline in the level of foreign exchange reserves during the year. Export growth continued to remain buoyant and the export growth rate peaked at 20.7 per cent. Import growth at 28 per cent was stronger, leading to a widening of the trade deficit. The surplus on invisibles remained at the same level as in the previous year. The current account deficit at 1.7 per cent was slightly higher than what the High Level Committee on Balance of Payments had indicated as the sustainable level.

The capital account flows that financed the current account deficit and added to the reserves declined in comparison to the previous year. Volatility and depreciation of the rupee had an effect on capital flows. The level of foreign currency assets at the end of the year stood cover for about six months of imports, which was a deep drop from the previous year.

1996–97

Export growth was subdued at 5.3 per cent. Part of the explanation for this low growth was the slowdown in world trade coupled with sluggishness in manufacturing goods prices globally. The volume growth of world trade came down from 9.7 per cent in 1995 to 5.4 per cent in 1996. Imports rose by 5.1 per cent during 1996–97, which was also lower than in the previous years. Trade deficit widened. The surplus in invisibles rose sharply and brought down the current account deficit to a reasonable level of 1.2 per cent of GDP. Pointing to the sharp rise in invisibles, the annual report for 1996–97 said:

'The buoyancy imparted to net invisible earnings with the institution of the market determined exchange rate system and the establishment of current account convertibility was sustained during 1996–97. A surge in the surplus on the invisibles account was led by burgeoning private transfers, partly reflecting the conversion of India Development Bonds (IDBs), and a noteworthy improvement in software and other technology related exports. Provisional information indicates an increase of about 46 per cent in exports of software which stood at US$1,100 million in 1996–97. The increase in gross invisible receipts more than offset the increase in net investment income payments. Underlying the growing surplus under net invisibles was the relatively stable growth in outflows under travel payments, as well as profits and dividends, contrary to expectations in the aftermath of current account convertibility. The net surplus under invisibles estimated at US$8,688 million in 1996–97 was significantly higher than that of US$5,460 million in 1995–96. As a result, net invisible receipts financed nearly 70 per cent of the trade balance as compared with 48 per cent in 1995–96.'

The capital account was comfortable. Foreign investment comprising direct and portfolio investment rose and stood at $8.6 billion. India's foreign exchange reserves rose by $4.7 billion during 1996–97 to $26.4 billion as of March 1997. This happened despite large payments on account of redemption of IDBs and net outflows under the FCNR(A) scheme. During the first quarter of 1997–98 alone, reserves rose by $2.9 billion to a level of $29.8 billion by end-June 1997.

This depiction of the BOP position brings out the strengths and vulnerabilities of the external sector. What strikes us most is the low current account deficit, strong capital inflows and the consequent accumulation of reserves. As mentioned earlier, at one point, the foreign exchange reserves were equivalent to 8.6 months of imports. The vulnerability is the probable sudden attack on the rupee and its impact on monetary policy and the economy. Some of the capital inflows that contributed to the accumulation of reserves, such as portfolio investment, could be volatile and needed to be watched. The opening of the capital account was done with caution. For instance, Indian residents were not given the freedom to invest abroad in foreign stock markets. External commercial borrowings above a certain level required prior approval.

A continuous monitoring of the external debt and its composition had become extremely important. In fact, the non-debt-creating flows (foreign investment) were at one time double of debt-creating flows. This is depicted in the graph below.

Graph 1

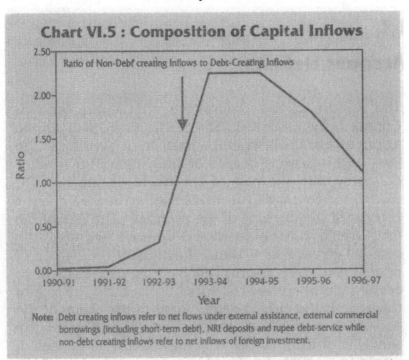

Note: Debt-creating inflows refer to net flows under external assistance, external commercial borrowings (including short-term debt), NRI deposits and rupee debt-service while non-debt-creating inflows refer to net inflows of foreign investment.
Source: RBI Annual Report, 1996–97.

Table 7.4 provides a picture of India's external debt over the years 1992–93 to 1996–97. Net debt stock as a ratio of GDP came down from 37.5 per cent as at the end of March 1993 to 24.5 per cent as at the end of March 1997. Short-term debt to total debt, which was a crucial variable for judging vulnerability, remained at the end of the period more or less at the same level as it was in the beginning, even though it declined substantially in some of the years in between. Debt service ratio also declined over the period.

Table 7.4 India's External Debt (End–March)

(US$ million)

	1993	1994	1995	1996	1997
Total Long-term Debt	83,683	89,068	94,739	88,696	86,744
Short-term Debt	6,340	3,627	4,269	5,034	6,726
Total External Debt	90,023	92,695	99,008	93,730	93,470
Concessional Debt as per cent of Total Debt	44.5	44.4	45.3	44.7	42.2
Short-term Debt as per cent of Total Debt	7.0	3.9	4.3	5.4	7.2
Debt Stock-GDP Ratio per cent	37.5	33.8	30.8	27.0	24.5
Debt-Service Ratio per cent	27.5	25.4	25.9	26.2	23.0

Notes:
1.   Short-term debt does not include suppliers' credit of up to 180 days from 1994–97.
2.   Debt-service is calculated on cash payment basis except for NRI deposits for which accrual method is used. The estimates, therefore, differ from BOP data compilation methodology.
3.   Debt to GDP ratio derived from figures
Source: Government of India, *India's External Debt: A Status Report*, 2001.

While the BOP was well managed, there were many key issues on which decisions had to be taken. The first major decision was with respect to the exchange rate regime. More will be said in the next section. A related decision was in relation to liberalization of the trade regime. The two were interrelated. A market determined exchange rate cannot coexist with a controlled trade regime. In terms of sequence, first came the liberalization of the trade regime. While a controlled exchange rate regime can go with a liberalized trade regime, it could not continue forever. The second important decision was in relation to capital flows. Should the country be open to capital flows in terms of direct investment and portfolio investment? While the decision on the entry of direct investment was that of the government, it was discussed with RBI at all stages. The decision on portfolio investment was discussed with the Securities and Exchange Board of India (SEBI) and RBI by the government. These rules needed fine-tuning because some of these flows could become volatile in times of stress on the rupee. Portfolio investment can be both in equity and debt. Investment in debt instruments is highly sensitive to interest rate differentials. Permitting FIIs to invest in government securities was first mooted by RBI. After discussion, in which the government and RBI exchanged many letters, it was allowed, subject to certain restrictions on the quantum. Investment in short maturity government paper was not allowed. Questions have been raised whether a nation gains by capital inflows. Answers may differ depending on how each country uses such inflows. Capital inflows integrated with an investor-friendly environment can lead to economic growth. Mere substitution of local investment by foreign investment does not lead to additional investment. But there is evidence as far as India is concerned that this is not the normal case. While RBI and the government were broadly on the same wavelength, on details there was a considerable exchange of views between them.

II) Changes in Foreign Exchange Market Regulations

Exchange market regulations needed changes under the new environment of liberalization. In the foreign trade area, quantitative controls on imports were being withdrawn. Tariffs on imports were being brought down substantially. In the area of exchange rate management, we first adopted a dual exchange rate system and finally moved to a market-determined exchange rate system. In 1994, we accepted Article VIII of IMF which essentially meant that all restrictions on current account transactions had to be removed. The capital account of BOP underwent a change with new sources of capital flows being permitted. With a larger quantum of foreign exchange transactions entering the market without much restriction, the foreign exchange market had to be deepened to enable the market to function efficiently. The number of changes that had to be made was very large. Every year saw new announcements to respond to the new situation. In fact, the Foreign Exchange Regulation Act (FERA) had to be modified significantly. Work had begun on that and by 1997 a new bill was almost ready. It was, however, passed by the Parliament subsequently. It is not possible to list all the changes and most of them were technical in character. But it is important to indicate some of the changes to appreciate the change in philosophy.

From March 1992, banks were allowed to offer forward cover, not merely for trade transactions, as was permitted earlier, but also for other genuine transactions as long as the amounts and maturity dates were identifiable. To enable customers greater flexibility in hedging decisions, RBI permitted covering of exposure in currencies other than US dollars. In view of the volatility of the foreign exchange market, corporate entities were permitted to cancel and rebook forward contracts. The earners of foreign exchange were allowed to retain 25 per cent of their foreign currency earnings with the banks, which could be used for certain approved purposes. In November 1993, RBI introduced a scheme of pre-shipment credit in foreign currency to enable Indian exporters to avail of credit at competitive international rates. However, this scheme was withdrawn in February 1996 in view of the pressure on the rupee. Bankers were empowered to negotiate bankers' acceptance facilities with either overseas banks or other institutions without prior approval of RBI for the purpose of rediscounting export bills abroad. Bankers were permitted to release foreign exchange for higher studies abroad in all cases where students had secured admission in an overseas educational institution. (This eliminated the need for students to stand in long queues before RBI in the month of July.) These are some measures that were introduced. But the list is really long.

The annual reports of RBI for 1994–95 and 1995–96 made specific reference to market developments. They reflect the thinking at that time. The 1994–95 report said:

'The growing importance of forward foreign exchange market in an environment of economic liberalization underscores the need to have a well developed market for foreign exchange derivatives. In India, the main instruments of hedging are the forward contracts, the swaps and in the recent period, the cross currency options. In the absence of international quotes for the rupee, it has not been possible to introduce rupee based options.'

The 1995–96 report said:

'The Reserve Bank persevered with institutional measures directed towards widening and deepening of the exchange market and providing market constituents with a greater degree of functional autonomy during the year. Debt service payments on Government account were increasingly routed through the market from July 1995 in an effort to augment the volume of market transactions which, in turn, would enable the determination of a stable and representative exchange rate. With a view to minimizing its influence on the process of rate formation in the market, the Reserve Bank discontinued quoting its buying and selling rate with effect from October 1995. The limit of Rs 15 crore on the aggregate overnight positions of the authorized dealers (ADs) was removed with effect from January 1, 1996 and the ADs were advised to review their own open position limits taking into account the capital base, volume of merchant transactions, dealing expertise and infrastructure available with them, subject to their meeting the 5 per cent capital adequacy requirement on the open position approved by the Reserve Bank in addition to the capital requirements for credit risks. Banks were permitted to fix their own Aggregate Gap Limits instead of restricting themselves to regulations that were in force earlier, depending upon their foreign exchange operations, risk taking capacity, balance sheet size and other relevant parameters. Banks seeking approval from the Reserve Bank for higher limits were required to be in a position to continuously monitor their exposures by marking to market the maturity mismatches. This measure is expected to enhance the liquidity position in the swap market and ensure better management of foreign currency assets and liabilities by the banks. ADs mobilizing deposits under the FCNR(B), EEFC, FCON, and RFC were permitted earlier to invest these funds in short term deposits with banks abroad, rated high by international rating agencies. The rating stipulation was dispensed with from April 1996 onwards for investments by ADs in their own branches abroad. Furthermore, the restriction on ADs with regard to initiating cross-currency positions overseas was relaxed with effect from April 1996 for

ADs having the requisite infrastructure, risk control mechanism and satisfying the capital adequacy norms. A Foreign Exchange Market Technical Advisory Committee is also expected to be constituted shortly which would make recommendations to the Reserve Bank and prepare policy papers on issues specific to the exchange market.'

To prevent ad hoc changes, RBI set up in November 1994 under the chairmanship of O.P. Sodhani, an expert group to recommend measures for the growth of an active and efficient foreign exchange market. The expert group made several recommendations concerning the removal of market constraints, induction of new derivative products, risk management accounting and disclosure standards. These recommendations were implemented in stages so that the twin objectives of encouraging capital flows and ensuring orderly conditions in the foreign exchange market were met.

III) Management of the Rupee

The devaluation of the rupee in July 1991 was followed by the introduction of the exim scrip scheme under which exporters of goods got certain entitlements to imports. However, this was not considered the appropriate model from a long-term point of view. The High Level Committee on Balance of Payments also examined the possible alternatives and recommended in its interim report the introduction of a dual exchange rate system under which the authorized dealers were required to sell 40 per cent of their receipts to RBI at a fixed rate. They could sell the balance in the market. Essential imports, as defined by the government, were allowed to be imported at the fixed rate. This scheme was thoroughly discussed between the government and RBI and there was an exchange of papers between them. Finally, the dual exchange rate system was christened the Liberalized Exchange Rate Management System (LERMS) and was announced in the Budget of 1992–93. Contrary to expectations and fears, the new regime performed well right from the beginning and the gap between the official and market rate remained stable. The market exchange rate in most of the months was only around 16 per cent over the fixed official rate (Table 7.5). The official rate was itself modified in December 1992. The higher spread in February 1993 was because of anticipated changes in the exchange regime.

Table 7.5 Spread between Official and Market Exchange Rates

(Rupees per US Dollar)

Month	Official Rate	Market Rate	Spread	Weighted Rate
1	2	3	4	5
March '92	25.8901	29.4551	13.77	28.0291
April '92	25.8900	30.9253	19.45	28.9112
May '92	25.8900	30.3407	17.19	28.5604
June '92	25.8900	30.2361	16.79	28.4977
July '92	25.8900	30.2524	16.85	28.5074
August '92	25.8900	30.0885	16.22	28.4091
September '92	25.8900	30.0584	16.10	28.3910
October '92	25.8900	30.0471	16.06	28.3843
November '92	25.8900	30.0824	16.19	28.4054
December '92	26.1540	30.7005	17.38	28.8819
January '93	26.1986	30.8833	17.88	29.0094
February '93	26.1986	32.6456	24.61	30.0668

Source: RBI Annual Report, 1992–93.

Right from the beginning, the shortcomings of the dual exchange rate system were known. As long as part of the export earnings was to be sold at an officially determined exchange rate, the tax on exports continued. Talking about LERMS and the unified market exchange rate, the High Level Committee on Balance of Payments in its final report said:

'The option of unified rate implies that exporters and other earners of foreign exchange will convert all their earnings at market rate and all imports will, correspondingly, take place at one market rate. The exchange rate for all transactions would thus be determined by market forces. Foreign exchange would, however, continue to be available only for purposes approved or authorized by Reserve Bank of India. The RBI would continue to have the option at its discretion of buying or selling foreign currency from the authorized dealers (who will continue to be subjected to FERA discipline). The advantages of such a system are:

a.   The justifiable demand of exporters that they should have the benefit of market rate (and not subject to a tax) can be met.

b.   The cumbersome procedures of claiming a part of import needs at official rate through Advance Licence mechanism can be eliminated to help exporters.

c.   The large number of workers who make remittances to India would have the full benefit of market rate.

d.   The existing contradictions in rates applicable to remittances and payments through NREA account would be removed.

e.   Similarly, contradictions between dual exchange rate system and transactions in respect of ACU and erstwhile USSR will also be removed.

f.   There will be an end to uncertainties and anticipatory actions on this account.

g.   A clear signal would be emitted to inspire the confidence of the international community, and

h.   There could be a distinct psychological impact on our people which should help reverse capital flight and further reduce hawala transactions.

As against these advantages, there are some risks and disadvantages that should be assessed. These are:

a.   If the international prices of POL harden during the course of the year, some of the anticipated surplus on "OCC account" may not come about, if all and not a part of imports are paid for at unified rate. Thus, there is need to monitor the developments and consider review of POL prices during later part of the year.

b.   There would be additional cost of importing fertilizers, affecting both prices for farmers and amount of subsidy needed.

c.   Additional budgetary provisions would be needed, depending on where unified exchange rate settles, for debt servicing and import needs of defence.

d.   Import of life saving drugs would be more expensive than at official rate.

e.   There are possible risks of inflation on account of prices of essential commodities and, strains on containing fiscal deficit. But these would be offset by possible liberalized imports that would be afforded.

In weighing the advantages and disadvantages, the Committee took into account the following factors.

a. Under LERMS, market rate has proved to be reasonably stable and within the range of anticipated levels. Hence, the unified rate, in the normal course, should be in alignment with the market rate established in the past few months. Technically, unified rate should settle between the ruling official and market rates.
b. Measures have already been taken to transmit changes in the exchange rate to domestic prices in respect of POL.
c. The macroeconomic environment in terms of rate of inflation, anticipated growth rate and sustainable fiscal deficit inspires confidence to effect changes.

The Committee, after weighing advantages and disadvantages of the options, as described above, recommends that a decision be taken to unify the exchange rate, as an important step towards full convertibility.'

While the report of the High Level Committee was formally submitted only in April 1993, its contents were known to the government since most of the members of the committee were from the government. Also in November 1992, I came back to RBI as governor. The implications of various alternatives were discussed thoroughly with the government. While continuing with LERMS as it was introduced in March 1992 was one alternative, it was thought to be not acceptable. The two serious alternatives were (1) to shift 40–60 proportion to 20–80 and (2) to move to a fully market-determined exchange rate system. The advantage of the first alternative was that it was a gradual movement. There were also concerns about dealing with rupee debt to Russia. The then finance secretary (Geetha Krishnan) was inclined towards this alternative. In line with the views expressed by the High Level Committee, Montek and I were supporting the shift to a market-determined exchange rate. Finally, Manmohan Singh and I met and the decision was to go for a market-determined exchange rate. I also assured him that RBI would be able to manage the transition. The Budget for

1993–94 made the announcement and the new system came into effect on 1 March 1993. As a result, while all foreign exchange transactions were put through authorized dealers (primarily banks), they had no obligation to surrender the receipts to RBI. This did not exclude RBI intervening in the market to buy or sell. Thus, India entered an era of floating exchange rate subject to intervention by RBI. That is why IMF and others still put India under the managed floating regime.

There were a lot of speculations as to where the rupee would settle down. There were grim forecasts of a steep fall in the value of the rupee. Some had moved into the dollar hoping to make a big kill when the rupee experienced a steep fall. We were, however, strong in our view that it could settle down around the market rate under LERMS. The transition in fact turned out to be smooth. RBI was ready to intervene if the value of the rupee fell because of speculative factors. There was some intervention and sometimes even in anticipation of a fall in the value of the rupee.. But the market settled down as can be seen from Table 7.6. As the rupee strengthened, there were threatening calls to me. One day there was a bomb threat and I had to vacate my office. However, the squad did not find any bomb and it was discovered to be an empty threat. The shift to a market-determined average rate system was nothing short of a silent revolution.

Table 7.6 FEDAI* (Indicative) Exchange Rates—Weekly Average
(January 1993 to June 1993)

Week ended	Rupees per US$	
1 January	30.8072	
8 January	30.7901	
15 January	30.7626	
22 January	30.8139	
29 January	31.2650	
5 February	31.8733	
12 February	32.9878	
19 February	32.8364	
26 February	32.9244	
5 March	31.8706	(31.86)
12 March	31.5610	(31.56)
19 March	31.4634	(31.46)
26 March	31.4482	(31.45)
2 April	31.2257	(31.23)
9 April	31.2256	(31.23)
16 April	31.3211	(31.32)
23 April	31.3195	(31.32)
30 April	31.3687	(31.37)
7 May	31.3190	(31.32)
14 May	31.3034	(31.32)
21 May	31.3209	(31.32)
28 May	31.3382	(31.34)
4 June	31.3714	(31.37)
11 June	31.4209	(31.42)
18 June	31.4643	(31.46)
25 June	31.3854	(31.39)

Figures in parentheses are RBI Reference Rates.
* Foreign Exchange Dealers' Association of India.
Source: RBI Annual Report, 1992–93.

1993–94 was the first full year after we moved to the market-determined exchange rate. As already mentioned, the year began with a stable exchange rate and continued through with a stable exchange rate anchored to a level of Rs 31.37 against the dollar (Table 7.7, Graph 2). It was the 'passive' intervention of RBI that led to the stability around this level. A consequence of this policy was that while the nominal effective exchange rate at the end of March 1994 depreciated by 0.2 per cent, that is, almost negligible, the real effective exchange rate appreciated by 5.4 per cent because inflation differentials between India and her major trading partners widened adversely. This posed a problem for exporters.

Graph 2

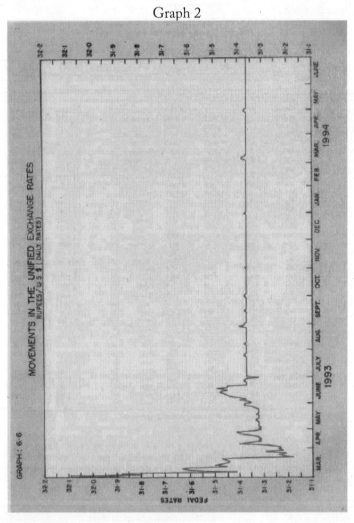

Source: RBI Annual Report, 1993–94.

Table 7.7   Exchange Rate of the Rupee—Weekly Average

(Rupees per US dollar)

Week ended		RBI Reference Rate	FEDAI Rate	Week ended		RBI Reference Rate	FEDAI Rate
1		2	3	4		5	6
1993 February	26	–	32.9244	November	5	31.3700	31.3708
March	5	31.8625	31.8706	November	12	31.3700	31.3705
March	12	31.5600	31.5610	November	19	31.3700	31.3716
March	19	31.4640	31.4634	November	26	31.3700	31.3698
March	26	31.4467	31.4482	December	3	31.3700	31.3703
April	2	31.2300	31.2257	December	10	31.3700	31.3705
April	9	31.2300	31.2256	December	17	31.3700	31.3703
April	16	31.3200	31.3211	December	24	31.3700	31.3700
April	23	31.3200	31.3195	December	31	31.3720	31.3710
April	30	31.3700	31.3687				
May	7	31.3200	31.3190	1994			
May	14	31.3220	31.3234	January	7	31.3700	31.3715
May	21	31.3220	31.3209	January	14	31.3700	31.3705
May	28	31.3380	31.3382	January	21	31.3700	31.3700
June	4	31.3700	31.3714	January	28	31.3700	31.3700
June	11	31.4160	31.4209	February	4	31.3700	31.3700
June	18	31.4560	31.4643	February	11	31.3700	31.3700
June	25	31.3840	31.3854	February	18	31.3700	31.3700
July	2	31.3650	31.3627	February	25	31.3700	31.3700
July	9	31.3700	31.3705	March	4	31.3800	31.3790
July	16	31.3700	31.3686	March	11	31.3725	31.3725
July	23	31.3700	31.3676	March	18	31.3700	31.3700
July	30	31.3760	31.3755	March	25	31.3700	31.3700
August	6	31.3720	31.3713	April	1	31.3700	31.3706
August	13	31.3700	31.3707	April	8	31.3700	31.3705
August	20	31.3700	31.3697	April	15	31.3700	31.3700
August	27	31.3775	31.3763	April	22	31.3700	31.3700
September	3	31.3750	31.3747	April	29	31.3720	31.3735

Table 7.7 Exchange Rate of the Rupee—Weekly Average   (*Continued*)

(**Rupees per US dollar**)

Week ended		RBI Reference Rate	FEDAI Rate	Week ended		RBI Reference Rate	FEDAI Rate
1		2	3	4		5	6
September	10	31.3700	31.3713	May	6	31.3700	31.3705
September	17	31.3700	31.3720	May	13	31.3700	31.3700
September	24	31.3700	31.3708	May	20	31.3700	31.3705
October	1	31.3700	31.3733	May	27	31.3700	31.3713
October	8	31.3700	31.3715	June	3	31.3720	31.3720
October	15	31.3700	31.3708	June	10	31.3700	31.3700
October	22	31.3700	31.3700	June	17	31.3700	31.3700
October	29	31.3700	31.3713	June	24	31.3700	31.3700

FEDAI: Foreign Exchange Dealers' Association of India.
Source: RBI Annual Report, 1993-94.

The remarkable stability of the rupee vis-à-vis the US dollar witnessed in 1993–94 continued during 1994–95. RBI's buying rate was unchanged at Rs 31.37 per dollar till the end of February 1995. The rupee was subject to temporary volatility during March 1995, when it touched the level of Rs 31.97 per dollar. However, since April 1995, the rupee hovered around Rs 31.40 per dollar. It must, however, be noted that while the rupee generally remained steady against the dollar, it depreciated sharply against other major currencies. Between March 1994 and March 1995, the rupee depreciated by 14.5 per cent, 17.6 per cent and 7.6 per cent against the yen, the deutsche mark and the pound sterling because of the weakness of the dollar against these currencies. Because of this trend, the REER as of March 1995 showed a depreciation unlike in 1993–94.

The continuing surge in capital flows during 1993–94 and 1994–95 posed several problems. One related to the exchange rate and the other to the monetary impact of capital flows. The two were in fact interrelated. One question raised by critics was why did RBI choose to maintain a stable rate of Rs 31.37 per dollar. The alternative would have been to let the rupee appreciate. There were compelling reasons to maintain a stable rate. First, India's exports had just begun to show an increase. In fact, the growth rate was substantial, exceeding 18 per cent. We did not want this trend to be reversed. Even though what finally counted was the real effective exchange rate, we did not want even the nominal rate to appreciate. Second, we also needed to build up the reserves. After finalizing the arrangement with IMF, India's exchange reserves started to rise. But these, however, had to be repaid. Our reserves at the end of March 1993 stood at approximately $10 billion. This was equivalent to 4.9 months of imports. This was not adequate if we took into account other short-term liabilities. Third, a possible consequence of letting the rupee appreciate to the full extent would have meant a monetary contraction, which might not have been desirable. But allowing the accumulation of reserves had its own other side effects that had to be handled. The sheer accumulation of reserves had an expansionary monetary effect. The money supply rose by 18.4 per cent in 1993–94 and by 22.4 per cent in 1994–95. This was despite RBI engaging in OMOs involving sale of government securities from its portfolio to neutralize the liquidity created by the inflows. The outright open market sales amounted to Rs 9047 crore during 1993–94. This was equivalent to what would have been achieved by a 2.8 percentage increase in the CRR. RBI's OMOs were severely constrained by the fact that more than 80 per cent of RBI's holdings of government securities were non-marketable. In 1994–95, OMO sales were minimal. Our decision to keep the rupee–dollar exchange rate at a fixed level was prompted primarily by the need to accumulate reserves. We had, however, to bear the consequences of a rise in the money supply and in prices. For the first time in the history of RBI, the question of how to deal with large capital inflows arose.

There are several possible policy responses to surges in capital flows. Most often, central banks intervene in foreign currency markets and buy foreign currency to prevent a nominal exchange rate appreciation. The subsequent policy responses can be of two types: sterilized and non-sterilized. While the non-sterilized responses will allow the monetary impact to filter through the system, sterilized intervention, sometimes described as the 'first line of defence', seeks to curb the monetary effect of the inflows. In both cases, there is a build-up of foreign exchange reserves which can serve as a cushion that is available when there is a reversal of the capital inflows.

Sterilization as an instrument has associated costs. The net cost to a central bank per bond sold by it is the difference between the interest on domestic bonds and the return on foreign reserves. Sterilization has certain other consequences. A tight monetary policy might keep domestic interest rates high, making the capital inflows even more attractive. Maintaining high domestic interest rates also deprives the economy of the benefits of higher domestic investment and growth.

In October 1994, while addressing the Global Asset Management Conference at Hong Kong, I referred to the problem of the impact of capital flows and said:

'The lessons from the experience of countries which have faced a surge in capital flows must relate to both the nature of responses and their sequencing.

1. First is to identify, as far as possible, even though it is difficult to do so *ex ante* to what extent the flows are temporary or permanent. The nature and the cause of the flows can provide a clue. Sterilization is particularly warranted if the flows are deemed temporary. This helps avoid the adjustment costs associated with an initial rise and a subsequent fall.

2. Pure market determination of the nominal exchange rate (i.e., a clean float) in the presence of capital flows can lead to undesirable dynamic behaviour. In particular, the much faster adjustment of financial markets than goods markets can lead to an excessive appreciation (overshooting) of the nominal (and real) exchange rate above its equilibrium level. In turn, such overshooting can be harmful to the tradable sector of the economy, in due course creating a need for excessive depreciation of the nominal exchange rate. Particularly in less developed financial markets, this tendency for dynamic instability creates a case for smoothening the exchange rate path. Over the medium term, the real exchange rate of the relative price of tradable and non-tradable in the local economy will reflect the state of aggregate demand, the stance of trade policy, and the degree of competitiveness in the economy. Intervention in the exchange market to influence the nominal rate

will affect the real rate in a durable way to the extent that overall demand management policies are consistent and supportive.

3. Sterilization as a policy response is intended to neutralize the expansionary monetary impact of capital flows. The extent of sterilization required depends not only on the size of the capital flows but also on the size of the economy. A larger economy may be able to absorb a more substantial quantum of capital inflows than a smaller one, as the money supply expansion arising from such capital inflows may still be consistent with the desired rate of growth in money supply. In a number of situations, what may be required is only partial sterilization. When the acquisition of reserves is greater than that warranted by the monetary programme, then only the central bank will have to act and take measures to control the money stock, be they through open market operations or reserve requirement changes.

4. The need for sterilization also gets moderated by the stance of fiscal policy, as what is relevant is the aggregate demand. If fiscal policy is tight, it may enable the absorption of larger capital inflows without producing an inflationary impact. If the Government draws less from the central bank in the form of credit, it provides more scope to absorb capital inflows without generating larger high-powered money.

   i. Allowing the exchange rate to appreciate may come in as a last resort. Such an appreciation will not have an adverse effect on exports only if the economy is not otherwise overheated and the price situation is under control. The likely impact on competitiveness of exports has made most countries reluctant to use appreciation. There is also the fear that nominal appreciation leading to reduction in the price of imported goods need not necessarily have a favourable impact on general prices, since the overall price level is the result of a complex set of factors.'

The Attack on the Rupee

The prolonged stability in the exchange rate of the rupee witnessed from March 1993 came under attack in the second half of 1995–96. The widening of the current account deficit despite impressive growth in exports, decline in capital flows and the pronounced appreciation of the US dollar against major international currencies triggered market expectations and put pressure on the rupee. In August 1995, an initial weakening of the rupee to Rs 31.95 happened primarily because of the strengthening of the US dollar. The downward pressure on the rupee got intensified in October 1995 when the exchange rate fell to Rs 35.65 per dollar. The annual report of 1995–96 describes the developments as follows:

> 'Unidirectional expectations of a "free fall" of the rupee reinforced the normal leads and lags in external receipts and payments, vitiating orderly market activity. A panic demand for cover by importers and cancellations of forward contracts by exporters created persistent mismatches of supply and demand in both the spot and forward segments of the market. Forward premia rose sharply in October 1995 particularly for shorter maturities with the highest rise being recorded in the cash-spot range. The premia were far out of alignment with interest rate differentials. The high cost of foreign exchange cover prevented banks from mobilizing foreign currency deposits and employing them to fund domestic assets. Accordingly, large dollar balances were held in *nostro* accounts.'

What was the response of RBI? It was a combination of intervention in the market and monetary measures aimed at curbing imports. RBI recognized that the rupee was overvalued. But it wanted the correction to be orderly and calibrated. Simultaneous actions were taken both in the foreign exchange market and money market because of the new scenario in which both markets were interrelated. To prevent speculation, liquidity was withdrawn from the money market even as sales of the dollar continued. This action was supported by measures, such as the imposition of an interest surcharge on import finance and the tightening of concessionality in export credit for longer periods. RBI thus had to face the twin problems of arresting the depreciation of the rupee and curbing soaring interest rates because of the withdrawal of liquidity. In fact, on 3 November 1995, the call money rate had touched 85 per cent. In the foreign exchange market, RBI intervened both in the spot and forward markets.

Table 7.8 RBI's Exchange Market Operations

(US$ million)

Month	Purchases	Sales	Net Purchases (+) / Sales (−)	Cumulative Net Purchases (+) / Sales (−)	Outstanding Forward Liabilities (Month-end)
1	2	3	4	5	6
1995					
October	7	792	−785	−785	20
November	290	401	−111	−896	248
December	272	328	−56	−952	456
1996					
January	1368	1770	−402	−1354	2236
February	140	468	−328	−1682	2316
March	1135	175	+960	−722	2216
April	577	209	+368	−354	2007
May	336	235	+101	−253	2058
June	1150	365	+785	+532	1799
Total	5275	4743	+532		

Source: RBI Annual Report, 1995–96.

Table 7.8 gives details of RBI's exchange market operations. As can be noted from the table, initially the large sales were in October and this continued till December. It brought some stability to the market and the rupee traded within the range of Rs 34.28 and Rs 35.79. But in the second half of January 1996, there was sudden pressure again on the rupee and there was sharp depreciation towards the end of January and in the first week of February 1996. The rupee touched a low of Rs 37.95 for the dollar in the spot market and the three-month forward premia rose to around 20 per cent. This called for further action. In January 1996, sales of the dollar amounted to $1.7 billion followed by a sale of $468 million in February. To curb imports and speed up the repatriation of export proceeds, the following actions were taken. The interest rate surcharge on import finance was raised from 15 per cent to 25 per cent. The scheme of post-shipment export credit in foreign currency was discontinued. Exporters were reminded of the statutory obligation to realize export proceeds within six months from the shipment of goods. Cancellation of forward contracts booked by authorized dealers for amounts of $1,00,000 and above was required to be reported to RBI on a weekly basis. These measures coupled with intervention in the market enabled the rupee to stage a strong recovery in March–April 1996 and the rupee remained in the range of Rs 34–Rs 35 per dollar. Thus, as of March 1996, the rupee had depreciated by only Rs 3 per dollar from 1993. As of March 1996, REER had appreciated by 4 per cent. It was only in January 1996, when the rupee came under record attack, the REER was zero. We have in an earlier chapter described how the withdrawal of liquidity necessitated by intervention was more than offset by reduction in CRR and other measures.

Summarizing the situation between October 1995 and June 1996, the annual report 1995–96 said:

'Although the Reserve Bank intervened actively in the spot, forward and swap markets since October 1995, and the transactions did have an impact on the exchange market and the domestic liquidity situation, two significant developments stand out. First, the net sales in the foreign exchange market between October 1995 and June 1996 have broadly evened out and as such the intervention has helped in smoothening the volatility rather than in propping up the exchange rate. Second, while the intervention impinged quite sharply on domestic liquidity in the initial stage, the overall impact has been broadly balanced with a small net injection of liquidity.'

It is quite clear that in a floating exchange rate system, there can be occasions of sudden pressure on the rupee. Some of these factors responsible for the pressure may originate in causes totally external to India, such as strengthening of the dollar or other factors. Our ability to handle such situations is strengthened by the availability of reserves. But our own experience shows that intervention may have to be supplemented by other measures that may be temporary. We also need to ensure that the rupee does not appreciate too much in real terms even in normal times, which may be difficult to maintain in times of capital surges. The annual report of RBI for 1995–96 written at the time as events were happening said:

> 'The experience of 1995–96 showed that while intervention signals the policy stance, the "testing" of the commitment to the stated policy by the market could be best addressed by supportive measures such as the ones unveiled in February 1996. The Reserve Bank would persevere with its stance of allowing the fundamentals to be reflected in the external value of the rupee and would not hesitate to take actions to quell persistent volatility or misalignment. The broad objective of the exchange rate policy will be to ensure a reasonably stable real effective exchange rate. Monetary policy instruments would be an important means through which policy influences would be transmitted to all the markets including the exchange market, with direct intervention playing a reinforcing role.'

Return to Stability

1996–97 turned out to be in many ways different from 1995–96. Export growth fell sharply to 4.1 per cent. Imports growth was also subdued at 5.1 per cent. The net invisibles rose strongly. As a result, the current account deficit fell to 1 per cent of GDP. There was a resurgence of capital flows, which reached a peak of $10.5 billion. A consequence of these developments was stability in the value of the rupee. The large capital inflows enabled RBI to purchase foreign currency from the market and the foreign currency assets of RBI rose by $4.8 billion. On 29 March 1996, the exchange rate of the rupee was Rs 34.35 per dollar. On 31 March 1997, it was Rs 35.91 per dollar. This meant a depreciation of 4.4 per cent. Taking all currencies into account, export-weighted NEER in March 1996 was 38.58 and it appreciated marginally to 38.94 as of March 1997. REER appreciated by 5.8 per cent. To summarize, the authorities did not face in 1996–97 the kind of challenge they had to address in 1995–96. The nominal exchange rate was bound in a narrow range of Rs 35 to Rs 36 per dollar. With the restoration of exchange rate stability that was sustained throughout the year and significant moderation in short-term interest rates, forward premia declined in the second half of the year and remained within 6 to 8 per cent for forward transactions of three-month and six-month maturities.

The East Asian Crisis

1997–98 was the year when India had to face the impact of the East Asian crisis. However, this happened only in the last four months of the year. From April to September, excess supply conditions prevailed in the foreign exchange market. It was an extension of 1996–97. Buoyant capital inflows pushed up the value of the rupee. RBI had to intervene in the market to prevent excessive appreciation of the rupee. RBI purchases amounted to $5.4 billion during April–August 1997. While there was no nominal appreciation of the rupee, there was a real appreciation. With abundant supply, there was a steady decline in the forward premia up to July 1997.

September 1997 saw a reversal. RBI had to sell $978 million. As the exchange rate falls after a period of stability, importers rush for cover as exporters cancel forward contracts. This phenomenon made its appearance in September 1997. However, in October 1997, there was a resumption of capital flows. RBI purchases amounted to $189 million. From November 1997, market sentiment weakened sharply. The market was driven downward by expectations flowing from the

East Asian crisis. While the RBI tried to reassure participants that the fundamentals of the economy remained strong, it also intervened in the foreign exchange market and sold $1590 million during November. However, we had not tried to stabilize the rupee at a particular level. In fact, I allowed the rupee to depreciate, given the fact that it was overvalued in real terms. The approach had been to reduce volatility and let the rupee depreciate or slide down smoothly. It must be noted that on occasions like these, there is always overshooting. The currency tends to depreciate more than what is warranted. Intervention seeks to moderate such a tendency.

In August 1997, the deputy governor of RBI, Y.V. Reddy, made a speech in Goa where he had remarked that there was a tendency for the rupee to be overvalued. Some had criticized this statement and the finance minister was also displeased. It must go on record that this speech was approved by me even though normally speeches of deputy governors did not require any prior permission. I take full responsibility for that statement and its timing. The REER had appreciated significantly and some signal was needed. The market volatility was not because of this statement. September 1997 did see volatility. But in October the situation remained normal and RBI made net purchases. The impact of the currency turmoil that engulfed East Asian countries could not but have an impact on India. The impact was well handled subsequently by my successor in December 1997 and January 1998 and stability returned to the market by January-end. As usual, intervention was supplemented by other strong measures to curtail demand and increase supply.

Guiding Policy

A committee that had a strong policy impact was the High Level Committee on Balance of Payments set up by the Government of India under my chairmanship in November 1991 to make medium-term projections of BOP and to suggest appropriate measures to bring the current account deficit to sustainable levels. This was the first committee to be appointed to look into the capital account of BOP. Most of the previous committees on the external sector were focused on exports and imports. The committee included as members secretaries who were directly involved with BOP. Y.V. Reddy, who was then Joint Secretary in charge of external commercial borrowings, was made Member Secretary. He contributed immensely to the writing of the report and for suggesting appropriate recommendations.

The report of the High Level Committee on Balance of Payments provided guidance to RBI and the government for the next five years on matters relating to management of the external sector. The recommendations of the committee were detailed and both RBI and the government went to the report when faced with new situations and when reforms were contemplated. The committee's recommendations regarding the exchange rate management have already been discussed earlier. Brief references to other recommendations are made here. The report is long and the analysis is as important as the final recommendations. In talking about the broad policy objective, the committee felt that an atmosphere of a liberal trade regime with a self-correcting exchange rate in a gradual movement towards international competitiveness would have to be the basic objective. The committee wanted a distinct shift in the policy framework in favour of equity as against debt in the matter of capital receipts from abroad. Specific recommendations relating to various areas are indicated below.

Foreign Currency Reserves

The committee wanted that a reserve target range should be fixed from time to time and that the foreign currency reserves should always be within this range and not allowed to fall below the floor. It has traditionally been the practice to view the level of desirable reserves as a percentage of the annual imports, e.g., reserves enough to meet three months' imports or four months' imports. However, this approach would be inadequate when a large number of transactions and payment liabilities, other than those relating to import of commodities, arise. Thus, liabilities may arise either for discharging short-term debt obligations or servicing of medium-term debt, both interest and principal. Hence, the committee recommended that while determining the target level of reserves, due attention should be paid to the payment obligations in addition to the level of imports.

External Assistance

Considering the vital role that can be played by timely utilization of external assistance in placing the country's balance of payments position on a sound footing, the committee recommended that immediate action be considered in the following areas:

i.   A review of existing projects with a view to identifying those where the progress is slow, those that need redefining of project scope or coverage and where cancellation would be better than continuing to pay commitment fees and keeping them in our books.

ii. As recommended by the National Development Council, 100 per cent of external assistance may be passed on to the states for all sectors.

Commercial Borrowings

The committee identified the major issues that have to be addressed in the context of external commercial borrowings. The committee recommended the following approach:

i.   Considering the maturity profiles and the fact that a large part of external commercial debt is through institutional sources, the amounts that can be subjected to refinance would be just about US$500 million per year for the next two years. As long as there is a possibility of raising commercial borrowings with longer maturity to sustain the overall balance, there is no advantage in giving signals of distortion for such small amounts by taking recourse to the debt refinance mechanism.

ii. There is a danger that recourse to debt–equity swaps would reinforce sentiments that would equate India with some of the countries that have defaulted in honouring their debt obligations. The committee, therefore, concluded that debt–equity conversion was not a desirable option for debt management in India.

iii. There is a need to keep the option of sovereign borrowing in external commercial markets open, but it should be exercised when the need and cost advantage are established.

NRI Deposits

The committee recommended that there was a need for a deliberate policy shift with regard to FCNR deposits with a view to reducing volatility and cost to make it attract the genuine savings of NRIs. To this end, the committee suggested that the NRI deposit scheme be modified on the following terms:

a.   FCNR deposits should have a minimum maturity of one year; and
b.   The differential between international interest rates and FCNR rates should be progressively reduced to ensure that the scheme benefits only the genuine savers.

Short-Term Debt

In light of past experience, the committee recommended that the policy of the government and RBI in regard to the management of short-term debt should be on the following lines:

i.   Short-term debt should be permitted only for trade-related purposes and under normal terms;
ii. Recourse to short-term debt should not be taken as an instrument for protecting the reserves;
iii. No rollover beyond six months should be resorted to in regard to any short-term facilities without careful consideration of the implications;
iv. Any short-term debt not governed by the above considerations should be specifically approved by RBI after satisfying itself that recourse to such debt was trade-related or on genuine cost considerations; and
v.   RBI should set up a monitoring system for short-term debt so that it is possible to ascertain with a reasonable amount of accuracy the extent of such debt that may be outstanding at any point of time.

Foreign Investment

The committee felt that the steps already taken would go a long way in promoting the confidence of foreign investors for investing in India.

Having recognized the concerns of foreign investors, the committee recommended that a National Investment Law be seriously considered, codifying the existing policy and practices in relation to dividend repatriation, disinvestment, non-discrimination subject to conditions that may be specified, employment of foreign nationals, non-expropriation, and sanction and servicing of external commercial borrowings. Such a law could also provide for policy procedures and an institutional framework for approval of investments under the non-automatic route, according pioneer status or domestic-investor status, new instruments of private commercial flows and applicability of local or international laws. Such an investment law need not, in any way, exclude consideration of bilateral investment treaties.

The committee noted with satisfaction the most recent liberalization measures in the Foreign Exchange Regulation Act (FERA) and recommended that an appropriate framework be evolved to promote Indian investment abroad in desired directions, countries and sectors in addition to liberalizing procedures.

Tarapore Committee

Another committee which addressed the important issue of capital account convertibility was the one set up under the chairmanship of S.S. Tarapore in February 1997. The committee, while agreeing that capital account convertibility might be a long-term goal, specified many conditions to be met before we could think of capital account convertibility. The conditions included modest fiscal deficit, price stability with low inflation, low current account deficit and improvement in the financial system. Since it would take time to meet these conditions, the committee made recommendations to relax controls in certain areas. Some of these recommendations are:

i.   Exporters/exchange earners may be allowed 100 per cent retention of earnings in Exchange Earners Foreign Currency (EEFC) accounts with complete flexibility in operation of these accounts including cheque writing facility in Phase 1.
ii. Individual residents may be allowed to invest in assets and financial markets abroad up to US$25,000 in Phase I.
iii. SEBI-registered Indian investors may be allowed to set up funds for investments abroad subject to certain overall limits.
iv. Banks may be allowed more liberal limits in regard to borrowing from abroad and deployment of funds outside India.

RBI in general followed the recommendations made by the Tarapore Committee. It was well recognized that a full implementation of capital account convertibility was not in the immediate reckoning. The conditions were not suitable for such a transition. In fact, the position on capital account convertibility was spelled out by me as early as 1994 in a speech. I had said:

> 'On capital account transactions, convertibility implies the movement of funds in and out of the country without restrictions. While such a regime may stimulate greater flow of investment, there are risks attached to it. The major risk is the possibility of capital flight. Another risk is the possibility of macroeconomic instability arising from the movement of short-term capital movements, very often described as "hot money". A free movement of funds will lead to integration of financial markets and, therefore, an efficient domestic financial system free from administrative restrictions is a prerequisite for the introduction of capital account convertibility.
>
> 'In relation to convertibility on capital account transactions, it must be noted that there already are some elements of the capital accounts transactions which enjoy that status. For instance, in the case of both direct and portfolio investments, foreign investors have the freedom to bring in funds and take them back. However, as far as resident Indians are concerned, they are subject to control as regards their external borrowings. It should be possible to introduce convertibility on capital transactions in stages, giving greater freedom regarding short-term and long-term borrowings.'

Conclusion

Some of the lessons learnt during the period are worth recalling. These relate to choice of exchange rate regime, exchange rate management in the context of large capital flows, adequacy of reserves and the role of real effective exchange rate.

Choice of Exchange Rate Regime

While IMF classifies the possible exchange rate regime into eight categories, there are, broadly speaking, three categories (1) fixed exchange rate, (2) floating rate, and (3) managed floating. The fixed exchange rate regime prohibits an independent domestic monetary policy. Thus, policymakers lose one policy instrument. Such a regime can also result in greater output volatility. The floating exchange rate regime provides greater flexibility on the other hand. But to live with a fully floating exchange rate regime, the economy has to be strong and the stability conditions such as low fiscal deficit and reasonable price stability have to be met more rigorously, particularly by emerging economies. That is why emerging economies prefer a managed floating rather than a freely floating system. What India adopted in 1993 was such a system. But 'management' must be guided by certain principles. The stated policy is that while the market will normally determine the exchange rate, RBI would intervene to maintain order in the market and prevent excessive volatility. The period of 1992–96 saw two extremes— surge in capital flows and sudden withdrawal of supply. The exchange rate regime that we had adopted in 1993 has stood the test of time even though the phenomena of surges and sudden withdrawals have continued.

Sterilization in the context of surges in capital flows has become an issue. When the inflows are large, the first course of action is to absorb them into reserves. Once they go beyond the level acceptable taking into account the impact on the money supply, liquidity has to be withdrawn. Two courses of action are possible. One is to raise the CRR and the second is to resort to OMOs, that is to sell government securities from RBI's portfolio. As reported earlier, the quantum of marketable government securities was limited. Later, when such a situation arose, the market stabilization bonds were floated. Sterilization has a cost as well.

In guiding the behaviour of the exchange rate, what should be the role of REER? In the case of surges in capital flows, the concern has been that the REER rises even when the nominal exchange rate remains the same. Exports, imports and invisible receipts are a function of the real exchange rate and not the nominal exchange rate. Thus, what is required is to ensure that over time, REER is kept stable. In the absence of capital flows, the exchange rate gets determined by the basic current account transactions of merchandise trade and services. But with capital flows becoming dominant, this is not true. In fact, whenever REER has been high, in times of stress, the rupee falls steeply. I had said in the R.N. Malhotra memorial lecture,

'The efforts to compute equilibrium exchange rates have remained inconclusive. For the exchange rate regime in India, continuous monitoring of the real exchange rate with an appropriate base is important. It provides valuable information to the authorities on the behaviour of the current account to which it is intrinsically linked. While it is not necessary to undertake continuous adjustments of the real exchange rate, trends in the real exchange rate need to be watched for any possible correction.'

The period between 1992 and 1997 saw significant changes in India's external sector. As we tried to move away from a policy of import substitution and get integrated with the rest of the world, there were equally significant changes in India's exchange rate regime as well as the capital account of BOP. Adoption of the dual exchange rate system in 1992 was only a transition measure. India adopted a market-determined exchange rate system in March 1993 with an explicit understanding that RBI reserved the right to intervene in the market. Adequate advance preparation and the willingness to intervene even in anticipation of changes made the changeover to the new exchange rate regime smooth. However, our own experience during this period and later had clearly shown that there could be occasions when the rupee was subject to pressure.

The capital account changes essentially meant the recognition of new sources of capital flows. FDI was made attractive. Investment in India's stock exchange by recognized foreign institutional investors became an important source of inflows. Portfolio investment had an inherent characteristic of volatility. Herd behaviour was common. Capital inflows that had started flowing in from 1992 became pronounced in 1993–94 and 1994–95 and as remarked earlier, this was the first time India was placed in such a situation. India until then had been hunting for funds. The problems that a surge in capital flows pose have been discussed. This experience would be repeated many more times later on. 1995–96 and the second half of 1997 would witness the attack on the rupee. In countries like India that experience strong capital inflows, sharp changes in sentiment can put pressure on the rupee. The response to such situations is not only to intervene and sell foreign currency but also take actions to reduce demand and increase supply. This was the strategy adopted in 1995–96 and repeated again many times later. Sharp attacks on the rupee originating from domestic causes are more difficult to handle than those emanating from external factors because in the former case, there is no alibi to offer. All in all, during this period, reserves rose. BOP was under control and lessons were learnt on how to handle the crisis.

8

Strengthening the Banking Sector

Years of Reform 1992–97

Even as reforms in the fiscal and external sectors were being implemented, it was recognized that real sector reforms must be supplemented by reforms in the financial sector. Real sector growth is closely related to the operation of a vibrant and sound financial system. The banking system, since the nationalization of major banks in 1969, had made tremendous progress in terms of extension of banking into rural areas and wider reach to agriculturists and small borrowers. However, this massive expansion led to low profitability and poor management of the loan portfolio. In the context of changes that were happening in the banking system in the rest of the world and the changes that were happening in the real sector in India, fundamental reforms in the banking sector became urgent. As early as August 1991, a high level committee under the chairmanship of M. Narasimham was set up 'to examine all aspects relating to the structure, organization functions and procedures by the financial system' so that the financial system may 'play its role in ushering in a more efficient and competitive economy'. It became obvious that the banking system had to become more competitive and efficient to play its larger role in the economy.

The Narasimham Committee recommendations covered a wide canvas. While most of the recommendations were accepted, there were differences on some, which were deferred to a later date. An important part of the reforms was the phasing of the measures. Another was acceptability. We had to carry the bankers, legislators and general public with us. Bankers were the ones immediately affected by the reforms. Some of them had to show losses as new prudential norms came into force. A certain amount of handholding of the banks was required. I had, on several occasions, to assure the public that the losses were not the consequence of events during the year but because of a correction of legacy problems. Section I of this chapter outlines the reform measures that were introduced. Section II deals with problems encountered while implementing the reforms. Section III discusses some of the questions that were raised about the reform package.

I) Banking Sector Reforms

The recommendations of the Narasimham Committee were the starting point of banking reforms and they were exhaustive. The key recommendations related to the reforms in the monetary sector, the introduction of prudential norms, reforms in the structure of the commercial banking system, and modification of the inspection and supervision system. Thus, it touched every aspect of the banking and the monetary system.

The banking sector reforms, in effect, fell into three broad categories: policy framework, improvement in financial health and institution building. The policy framework largely covered monetary policy issues that have been discussed in an earlier chapter. It is obvious that, without these monetary policy changes, banking sector reforms could not even be initiated. Take for example, deregulation of the interest rate. Without such a policy change, banks would not have been able to fix the interest rate on loans and deposits and in the absence of that freedom, profitability would not rise.

(A) Financial Health

We discuss in this chapter only reforms in relation to financial health and institution building. In improving the financial health of banks, the introduction of prudential reforms was a major step. These are indicated below under various heads:

(i) Capital Adequacy Norms

The need for strengthening the capital base of banks had become an acceptable proposition since Basel norms for capital adequacy came to be adopted by many countries after 1988. In tune with this trend, Indian banks with an international presence were required to achieve a capital to risk weighted assets ratio (CRAR) of 8 per cent by 31 March 1993 and all other Indian banks were advised to achieve a 4 per cent ratio by 31 March 1993 and 8 per cent by 31 March 1996. In 1994–95, banks were required to maintain Tier I capital of 5 per cent of the foreign exchange open position limit besides the existing capital adequacy requirements. Clarifications and modifications were announced from time to time. There were many nuances in the prescription of CRAR. Besides determining the risk weights for the various assets, there were issues associated with the composition of capital.

(ii) Recapitalization

The capital adequacy norms imposed a big burden on the government, as fresh funds had to be injected by it into public sector banks. Of course, the process of capitalization was facilitated by legislative changes, which enabled nationalized banks to tap the capital market as well. For the first time the government of India made a provision of Rs 5700 crore for recapitalization of nationalized banks in 1992–93. The recipient banks were required to invest the government's capital subscription in government bonds, which carried 10 per cent as the rate of interest. Thus, the immediate burden on the government was the interest they had to pay on the loans. Of course, in due time, the loans had to be repaid. These borrowings were not treated as part of the fiscal deficit. Every year since 1993–94, the government of India made provision for recapitalization.

(iii) Income Recognition

In order to get a true picture of the financial health of banks, prudential accounting norms, such as income recognition, assets classification and provisioning for bad and doubtful debts, were introduced in a phased manner over a three-year period beginning 1992–93. The term non-performing asset (NPA), which is commonly used now, was not in vogue until 1992–93. In that year, an NPA was defined as a credit in respect of which interest remained unpaid for a period of four quarters ending 31 March 1993, three quarters ending 31 March 1994, and two quarters ending 31 March 1995 and onwards. Banks were instructed not to charge and take to income account interest on NPAs. Banks were required to classify their advances into four broad groups: (a) standard assets, (b) sub-standard assets, (c) doubtful assets, and (d) loss assets. Provisioning norms stipulated the extent of provisioning to be provided and these norms varied according to the classification of assets. Provisioning norms kept changing as the circumstances warranted.

Regarding accounting standards for investments, banks were advised to bifurcate their investments in approved securities into 'permanent' and 'current' investments. Permanent investments were those which banks intended to hold till maturity while current investments were those which banks intended to deal in, i.e. buy and sell on a day-to-day basis. The ratio of 'permanent' and 'current' investment was fixed at 70:30 per cent for the year 1992–93. Depreciation in respect of permanent investments was not to be provided but for current investments, depreciation had to be fully provided.

(iv) Credit Delivery System

From 17 April 1995, a loan system for delivery of bank credit for working capital purposes was introduced to bring about greater discipline in credit flows in respect of borrowers with assessed Maximum Permissible Bank Finance (MPBF) of Rs 20 crore and above. The cash credit component was restricted to 75 per cent of MPBF while the loan component was fixed at 25 per cent. The loan component was steadily raised and by 1997–98, it had touched 80 per cent.

(B) Institution Building

The third set of measures covering institution building comprised steps taken not only to strengthen the internal structure of banks, but also institutions set up:

a. to improve competitiveness among banks
b. to better oversee the performance of banks in terms of regulation and supervision, and
c. to ensure speedier recovery of debts.

While prudential norms were aimed at improving the financial health of the banks, several steps were taken to improve the functioning of the banks as business institutions.

(i) Improving the Competitiveness among Banks

(a) Reducing the Share of Government in Nationalized Banks

An important step that was taken was to reduce the holding of the government in nationalized banks from 100 per cent to 51 per cent. The State Bank of India Act was amended in October 1993 to enhance the scope of the provision for partial private shareholding. The Nationalization Act was amended effective 15 July 1994 to permit nationalized banks to raise capital up to 49 per cent from the public. This measure was expected to have two types of effects. First, it could improve the manner in which the banks were run. With a significant private participation in the ownership, the banks could become more accountable as the shares were registered with the stock exchange and market prices would reflect the perceptions of investors. Second, it reduced the burden of the government regarding capitalization, as the banks expanded. While there may be some doubt about its impact on the management of banks, it certainly facilitated banks to go to the capital market and raise funds to meet the required capital as loans expanded.

(b) New Private Banks

In order to introduce greater competition in the banking system, RBI issued guidelines in January 1993 for the establishment of new banks in the private sector. It must be noted that this required no legislative change. The power existed in RBI; only it was kept in abeyance for two decades and more. The new banks were required to maintain a minimum paid capital of Rs 100 crore. They were to abide by all the regulations in force. Voting rights of an individual shareholder were limited to 1 per cent as stipulated by the Banking Regulation Act. This was subsequently modified and increased to 10 per cent in February 1994. In all, ten private banks were set up.

(c) Local Area Banks

In 1996–97, it was decided to permit the setting up of new private local area banks with jurisdiction over two or three contiguous districts. This was expected to take care of the needs of small borrowers. A minimum paid-up capital of Rs 5 crore was stipulated per bank. In January 1997, RBI granted 'in principle' approval for the establishment of three local area banks and they came into existence later. But this experience was short-lived. After these three banks, no licences were issued. The idea has taken a new incarnation in the form of small finance banks recently. In the case of these banks, the territorial restriction has been removed.

(d) Branch Licensing

Greater freedom was given to banks in relation to opening of branches. Banks that had attained the stipulated capital adequacy norms and followed the prudential accounting standards were permitted to set up new branch offices/upgrade the extension counters into full-fledged branches without the prior approval of RBI. Freedom was also given to close branches with restrictions. These measures were aimed at giving greater autonomy to banks.

(ii) Board for Financial Supervision

With the liberalization of the banking sector, the need for a strong regulatory and supervisory system became essential. Recognizing the lacuna in the existing system and to further strengthen the supervisory system, it was decided to set up the Board for Financial Supervision (BFS) in 1994 under the aegis of RBI. It comprised the governor, the four deputy governors and four members of the Central Board of RBI. The inclusion of four members of the board was intended to provide an outside look besides the insight of people from within RBI. The BFS exercised an integrated supervision in relation to commercial banks, all-India financial institutions and non-banking financial companies (NBFCs). Operational support to BFS was given from the newly created Department of Supervision.

The inspection system underwent a change as well. Besides on-site inspection, a scheme of off-site surveillance was introduced. The off-site surveillance essentially required banks to submit periodic returns on certain parameters so that the functioning of a bank could be continuously monitored. Banks were also evaluated under the widely adopted CAMELS model (Capital adequacy, Assets Quality Management, Earnings Liquidity and Internal Control Systems).

(iii) Debt Recovery Tribunals

With the introduction of new prudential norms and capital adequacy requirements, the pressure on banks to recover payment from the borrowers who defaulted had become urgent. Thus, to effect speedy recovery of loans, a new legislation was enacted in 1993 to set up debt recovery tribunals. Even as debt recovery tribunals were being set up in various state capitals, the Delhi High Court quashed the notification of the constitution of the tribunal for Delhi region. The Supreme Court put a stay on the order of the Delhi High Court. Subsequently in March 1996, the Supreme Court ruled that the notification of RBI was in order.

(iv) Banking Ombudsman

There was a grievance that customer complaints regarding the services provided by banks were not resolved expeditiously. To take care of this problem, the Banking Ombudsman Scheme was introduced in June 1995. In 1995–96 itself, ten ombudsmen were appointed. The scheme has undergone certain changes subsequently.

The above measures give a flavour of the reforms that were introduced to strengthen the banking system. In fact, the steps taken were much larger. The RBI publication *Trend and Progress of Banking in India* for 1997–98 provides a compendium of all the measures taken, which runs to forty-two pages. To understand the enormity of the task undertaken, one should go to this publication.

II) Difficulties in Implementation

The banking sector reforms need to be seen as part of the overall effort to improve the productivity and efficiency of the system. One thing must be noted at the outset. These measures were introduced at a time when the banking system was not facing an imminent crisis. Certainly the banking system was not in good shape. The profitability was low with the return on assets as low as negative in 1992–93. The safety and soundness of the system was a question mark. While the broad outlines of the reforms were clear, they had to be introduced with great circumspection so that the system did not collapse. Therefore the phasing was as important as the context of reforms.

The first shock that the implementation of the reforms faced was the scam that erupted in April 1992. This had nothing to do with reforms, as they were yet to be introduced in full measure. RBI used a more sober expression to describe the phenomenon that erupted as 'irregularities in securities transactions'. The basic problem was the use (or the ruse) of government securities to channel bank funds to stockbrokers. Actually, these transactions were posed as sell and buy back transactions. In this process, banks earned a higher rate of interest and brokers got the money they needed to transact in the stock market. As long as the stock market was buoyant, the transactions could continue indefinitely. Once the market crashed, everyone was in trouble. It was estimated that the siphoning of the funds amounted to Rs 5000 (Rs 4024 crore as per the Janakiraman report) crore. These types of transactions were prohibited by RBI guidelines. Bankers receipts (BR) and portfolio management schemes (PMS) were misused by banks and brokers. RBI set up the Janakiraman committee to investigate these transactions and provide suitable safeguards for the prevention of misuse of bank funds.

More or less at the same time, a joint parliamentary committee (JPC) was set up to go into the transactions. At this point in time, I was not in RBI. I was then a member of the Planning Commission. I did appear before the committee to explain the various nuances of the transactions that resulted in diversion of bank funds. The final report of the JPC was highly critical of the government, RBI and the banking system. After I took over as the governor, several months had to be spent to take care of the various recommendations of the JPC. In fact, in the context of these developments, a complete restructuring of the supervisory system became urgent and this was part of the reforms. One recommendation of the JPC was to ban 'repo' operations. I did not accept it. If that had been done, the emergence of the repo rate as a policy rate could not have happened. In one sense, the securities scam accelerated the process of reforms. However, an enormous amount of time was spent in answering the various queries raised by the JPC and in acting upon the recommendations. This put some brakes on the introduction of reforms.

Prudential Norms

The implementation of prudential norms had resulted in bringing down the profitability of banks. With the classification of assets according to the new norms and the need for additional provisioning, banks had to show lower profits. Some banks had to show losses. This was an agonizing period for several bankers. Bankers who were telling their borrowers to keep a strong balance sheet had themselves to show losses on their balance sheets. It was a case of 'Physician, heal thyself'. But people had to be assured that this was a passing phase and that the banks would emerge stronger after the period of suffering. In some sense, keeping this in mind, the process of reform, particularly in relation to prudential norms, was spread over three years. Some purists were critical of our stand in not implementing these at one go.

Burden on the Government

The introduction of capital adequacy norms came at a time when the government was wrestling with the problem of reducing the fiscal deficit. As the net worth of public sector banks had been eroded, the composition of capital adequacy norms required that the government come in with an injection of the required capital. This was certainly an inconvenient moment for the government. But the Central government accepted the need and explored different possibilities to meet the situation. As already reported, the banks were required to invest the additional capital brought in by the government in special bonds issued for the purpose. This avoided a cash flow problem for the government. Banks were able to satisfy the new requirements imposed by RBI. But the benefit was confined to interest income earned on the bonds. Some may think that this was a circumvention of the spirit if not the letter of the requirement. But such a management has been done in many developed countries as well. Many banks in these countries had resorted to cross holdings of ownership.

Amending the Acts

Reforms fall into two parts—those which required legislative changes and those which could be introduced without any legislative changes. Most of the reforms introduced fell in the second category. One measure that required legislative change was the induction of the private sector in the ownership of the State Bank of India and in the nationalized banks. A reference to this had already been made. The nationalization of banks in 1969 had a lot of emotional appeal to members of Parliament (MPs). Therefore, the amendment to the Banking Companies (Acquisition and Transfer of Undertakings) Act of 1970 had to be approached with great care. We had to reassure the MPs that the majority of ownership was still with the government and that the banks would be run in a manner in which social responsibility would always be kept in mind. A lot of background work had to be done to get the Act through. The setting up of debt recovery tribunals also required legislation.

Board for Financial Supervision

The need for a revamping of the supervisory and inspection system in RBI had become paramount for two reasons. One, the new set of regulations relating to prudential norms and capital adequacy demanded a continuous monitoring of the working of banks. Besides, banks were also given autonomy in terms of determination of interest rates, branch licencing, etc. Autonomy leads to accountability and this implies a watchful eye of the regulator. However, there were differences on how the monitoring structure should be. Second, the securities scam had also put pressure on restructuring the supervisory system. The Narasimham Committee had proposed a new structure of supervision and it said,

> 'While the Reserve Bank would normally be the appropriate agency for regulation, we however, propose that the supervisory function be separated from the more traditional central banking functions of the Reserve Bank and that a separate agency which could be a quasi-autonomous Banking Supervisory Board under the aegis of Reserve Bank be set up.'

The intention of the committee was clear. It wanted a separate body of supervision outside RBI but 'under the aegis of Reserve Bank'. We considered the recommendation and thought of a scheme that essentially captured the spirit of the recommendation but was somewhat different in structure. There is no uniform scheme of supervision across countries. There are countries in which the supervision function is totally separated from the central bank. At the other extreme are countries in which the supervisory function is totally part of the central bank. There were other countries in which the supervisory body is separate but the central bank is associated. The Board for Financial Supervision (BFS) that was set up was essentially a committee of the board of RBI. But the basic requirement of an integrated supervision was achieved. Unlike in the previous system, all the deputy governors were involved. A separate Department of Supervision was created. The four members of the board were so chosen that they had the required expertise. BFS has stood the test of time. It will now be twenty-five years since the board was set up.

Coordination with Other Regulators

The financial system has become increasingly overlapping. Each institution may perform more than one function and may be subject to supervision by different regulators. Sometimes, it may become necessary to take an overall view of the soundness of the institution and it is here the concept of a lead regulator comes into vogue.

Apart from banking reforms, the sector in which many reforms were introduced was the capital market. Initially, the regulation of the capital market was informal. At one time there was a feeling that the capital market regulation could also be with RBI. It was only in 1992 that the Securities and Exchange Board of India (SEBI) was set up under a separate statute. In order to bring about close coordination between the work of RBI and SEBI, a high level coordination committee comprising the governor, the chairman of SEBI and a representative of the government was set up. For example, there were sometimes difficulties in identifying the regulator under whom certain institutions should fall. Such issues could be resolved in the coordination committee. There was always the larger issue of coordinating the actions of different regulators over a market separated but interconnected. The committee used to meet regularly. Of course, with more regulators coming into operation subsequently, a different coordination mechanism was also thought of.

Asset Reconstruction Fund

Given the sharp rise in bad and doubtful debts in banks, an important question that arose was on how to deal with this issue. The Narasimham Committee advocated the setting up of an Assets Reconstruction Fund (ARF). The report said,

> 'It would be far more appropriate if these assets were taken off the balance sheets of banks and institutions, so that the funds realized through this process can be recycled into more productive assets. The committee

has looked at the mechanism employed under similar circumstances in certain other countries and recommends the setting up of, if necessary by special legislation, a separate Institution by the Government of India to be known as "Assets Reconstruction Fund" (ARF) with the express purpose of taking over such assets from banks and financial institutions and subsequently following up on the recovery of the dues owed to them from the primary borrowers. The share capital of this Fund could be subscribed to by the Government of India, the Reserve Bank of India, Public sector banks and financial institutions.'

Under the scheme, the fund could acquire from banks and financial institutions bad and doubtful assets at a discount. The implicit assumption is that the new fund could be more efficient in recovering the dues than the banks themselves. The scheme envisaged was a massive one. Apart from the funding problem, there was also doubt about the availability of enough experts experienced in debt recovery. In the section 'Assessment and Prospects', the annual report of RBI for 1991–92 said,

'While the Narasimham Committee has recommended the setting up of an Asset Reconstruction Fund (ARF) to take over bad and doubtful debts off the balance sheets of banks and financial institutions, there are certain issues which need attention and before implementing such a scheme, it would be necessary to be clear about the sources of funding. The impact of such a scheme on recovery climate would also need to be considered.'

Subsequently, the RBI was not averse to setting up asset reconstruction companies in the private sector. Some did come into existence. FDI in such companies was also encouraged.

Reorganization of the Banking Structure

Once the prudential norms and capital adequacy requirements were met by banks, an important question was how should the future of the banking system evolve. In this context, the Narasimham Committee reported,

'Consistent with this approach, the committee would like to put forward the broad pattern towards which the banking structure should evolve. In our view, this broad pattern should consist of

a.   3 or 4 large banks (including the State Bank of India) which could become International in character;

b.   8 to 10 national banks with a network of branches throughout the country engaged in general or universal banking;

c.   Local banks whose operations would be generally confined to a specific region; and

d.   Rural banks (including RRBs) whose operations would be confined to the rural areas and whose business would be predominantly engaged in financing of agriculture and allied activities.'

In the phase of financial sector reforms up to 1997, the concentration of the policymakers was to get the banks to conform to new regulations. That was in itself a tremendous task. Except for one merger, no step was taken in guiding banks in any direction. Since then, from time to time, there have been demands for the merger of banks. A study by me in the seventies submitted to the Banking Commission showed that there were economies of scale. But the scale economies withered away beyond a point. It is not always the case that the bigger the bank, the better it is. In any case the need for a merger must come from the banks and not be imposed from above.

Private Sector Banks

The licensing of new banks in the private sector was an integral part of the financial sector reforms. It was part of the effort to improve competitiveness in the banking industry. This required no legislative change. It was a power vested in the RBI. But for several decades, this power was not exercised. In fact, while discussing the performance of banks in the private sector, there is always a distinction made between private sector (old) banks and private sector (new) banks. The new private sector banks were set up with a reasonably high capital. They were expected to conform to the new guidelines on prudential norms from the very beginning. In all, up to 1997, ten banks were given approval. One advantage the new banks had was the induction of state-of-the-art technology. Strict conditions for diluting the share of the promoters were also laid down.

One big issue that confronted RBI was the selection of parties for licences. The large business corporates were keen to enter the banking field. Consistent with the principle that business and banking should be kept separate, we decided not to give licences to business corporates. The pecking order that we followed was first financial institutions, second, non-bank finance companies and third, professionals. The first set of licences went to financial institutions. Many of the leading private sector banks today were licenced at that time. It also shows that it takes two to three decades for banks to grow and provide a challenge. Several non-bank finance companies were given licences. But a mistake was made in giving a letter of intent (not a licence) to an NBFC that failed later. This was the beginning of reforms to regulate NBFCs. Earlier, only the deposit side of NBFCs was monitored, even though steps had been taken since 1992 to bring these institutions under strict control. In 1996 and 1997, a comprehensive attempt was made to regulate and monitor them. Of the private sector banks that were given licences, most of them are doing well. But some have been merged.

Over the next few decades after 1997, only a few licences have been given. Our decision to give licences today must depend on what our requirements will be a few decades later.

Non-Banking Finance Companies (NBFCs)

NBFCs are companies registered under the Companies Act and they offer a variety of financial services, including lending, hire-purchase financing, leasing, factoring, etc. The growth of these companies has been steady. Some categories of NBFCs are permitted to take deposits, though subject to limits set by RBI. The supervisory role of RBI until 1992 was essentially focused on the deposit side. Subsequently, several committees, particularly the A.C. Shah Committee and the P.R. Khanna Committee were appointed to bring the NBFCs under better regulatory and supervisory control. The JPC was also highly critical of the absence of a robust regulatory mechanism over NBFCs.

The A.C. Shah Committee, which was appointed in May 1992, submitted its report in September 1992 and RBI issued exhaustive guidelines in April 1993. Some of the new changes were: the duration of deposits of all NBFCs was uniformly stipulated; hire-purchase finance and equipment-leasing companies were required to maintain liquid assets at 10 per cent of deposits; loan and investment companies were required to maintain liquid assets to the extent of 5 per cent of their deposits. Half the liquid assets, i.e., 5 per cent of deposits in the case of equipment-leasing and hire-purchase finance companies, were required to be maintained in the form of government securities and/or government-guaranteed bonds. The Residuary Non-Banking Companies (RNBCs) were also required to maintain a minimum investment in government securities and/or government-guaranteed bonds to the extent of 10 per cent of their deposit liabilities, within the limit of 70 per cent investment in approved securities.

As mentioned earlier, since the mid-60s, legislative framework was structured mainly to regulate the deposit acceptance activities of NBFCs. However, in the changed scenario and in light of the recommendations of the Shah Working Group, as also the observations of the JPC, a comprehensive draft legislation was prepared in 1994. After extensive discussions which included RBI and the ministries of finance and law, an ordinance was promulgated by the government in January 1997, effecting comprehensive changes in the provisions of the RBI Act. The ordinance was later replaced by an Act in March 1997. The amended Act, among other things, provided for entry point norms of a minimum Net Owned Funds (NOF) of Rs 25 lakh, mandatory registration for new NBFCs for commencing business, maintenance of liquid assets ranging from 5 to 25 per cent of deposit liabilities, creation of a reserve fund by transferring not less than 20 per cent of the net profit every year, power to RBI to issue directions relating to prudential norms and capital adequacy, power to issue prohibitory orders and filing of winding-up petitions for non-compliance of directions. The Board for Financial Supervision assumed supervisory control over NBFCs.

The history of NBFCs is replete with many failures that had hit the depositors and the economy. The larger the size of the NBFC, the bigger the impact when it failed. During the period 1991–97, an attempt was made to put in place a strong regulatory and supervisory system in relation to NBFCs. The RBI Act was amended to give unambiguous legal backing to the new regulations. The number of NBFCs is large and their diversity is striking. In fact, over time the ability of NBFCs to raise deposits has been lowered. The supervisory authorities need to pay attention to systematically important NBFCs.

Financial Institutions

As prudential norms were being introduced to regulate the banking system, a question arose about the supervisory system relating to financial institutions. Financial institutions, such as the IDBI, Industrial Credit and Investment Corporation of India (ICICI) and Industrial Finance Corporation of India (IFCI), were basically long-term, leading institutions. They functioned by maintaining close touch with the government even though IDBI received funds from the Long-Term Operations Fund of RBI. However, after the introduction of prudential norms in banks, the next step was to introduce them in financial institutions. After some murmur and dissent, it was left to RBI to introduce these reforms.

It is interesting to note that in 1990, RBI actually rooted for a single regulatory authority over all financial markets. The then governor said in a letter to the government, 'More integrated markets would call for integrated supervision and avoidance of multiplicity of regulatory authority.' RBI made the claim that chapter III B Section 45 L of the RBI Act empowered it to exercise comprehensive oversight over the financial system. These observations were made in the context of the setting up of SEBI. The government, however, didn't accept the view. Separate regulatory authorities came into existence over a period of time. But as far as financial institutions were concerned, they were treated as part of the purview of RBI.

In March 1994, the financial institutions were required to implement prudential guidelines relating to capital adequacy, income recognition, assets classification and provisioning. All financial institutions achieved a capital adequacy ratio of 8 per cent by end of March 1996. The IDBI Act was also amended in 1994 to allow the institution to raise equity from the public. As in the case of banks, government holding in IDBI was not to go below 51 per cent of the issued equity capital.

When the programme of licensing new private sector banks was launched, and first preference was given to financial institutions, IDBI and ICICI decided to open banks. However, after some years, there was a reverse merger and the financial institutions merged into their respective banks. In retrospect, it is not clear whether the demise of financial institutions was good. Of course, it was expected that the corporate bond market would develop to take care of the long-term needs of corporates to some extent. But this did not happen. The universal banking system in which banks lend both short-term and long-term funds has the disadvantage that when banks come under stress, it affects both types of funding and pulls down the economic system. We have to ponder whether we should revive the system of separate long-term lending institutions.

III Critiques of Reforms

How does one assess the impact of the reforms on the performance of banks? Obviously, certain norms such as capital adequacy ratio were met because they were a fundamental requirement. The government played the ball with inducting sufficient capital into nationalized banks. At the end of March 1997, there were only two public sector banks that had not met the required capital adequacy ratio of 8 per cent. There were nearly sixteen banks which had a ratio exceeding 10 per cent. The net non-performing advances ratio of public sector banks came down to 10.07 per cent at the end of March 1997. Thus, while the net non-performing advances ratio came down, it still remained high. Gross profit as a percentage of total assets increased from 0.94 in 1992–93 to 1.60 in 1996–97. Thus, 1992 to 1997 constituted a period in which the sound base for an efficient banking system was laid.

The critics of the reforms in the banking sector fell into two categories. The first category included those who felt that the reforms were slow and patchy. The second category of critics had a fundamental difference with the reform approach. They faulted both the content and approach.

Going Slow

It took exactly six years to put through the reforms. It was this which helped the system to move smoothly to a new regulatory regime. The banking system had to work through a period in which changes were being made simultaneously in the monetary sector, exchange rate regime and in the regulatory and supervisory system. I do not think that the pace could have been accelerated without causing serious disruptions in the system. The real test of success, however, was how well the new institutions that were created could build the desired expertise and function effectively.

Fundamental Critics

These were critics who questioned the need for prudential norms and more particularly among them, capital adequacy norms. Their argument was that as the public sector banks were owned by the government, there was no possibility of the banks failing and therefore no need for a capital buffer. The trade unions took this view also. Does public ownership override the need for prudential regulations? It is a mistaken notion that nationalized institutions, particularly banks, need not be strong by themselves. In the absence of prudential norms, banks could reach a stage where they could be saved only at a high fiscal cost. Banks with international operations could lose credibility outside, if they did not conform to internationally accepted standards. Banks, whether owned by the government or private shareholders, have to follow uniform standards, which are considered important for ensuring the safety and soundness of banks.

The second criticism was on the approach to reforms. It has implications for the monetary policy as well. According to this school, the focus of banks must be on the allocation of credit, sector-wise and size-wise. It was an extension of the concept of directed credit. Of course, this is not a new approach. Even in the literature, there have been strong advocates of 'credit view'. While the credit view took an aggregative approach to credit, the critics of reforms took both an aggregative and sectoral view. The Narasimham Committee had expressed certain views on directed credit. As the reforms were being implemented, the policymakers took a different view. This will be explained in a later chapter. The core of the reforms was concerned with strengthening the financial muscle of banks and their ability to withstand shocks. The accounting norms were aimed at revealing the true health of banks. It was to prevent pushing weaknesses under the carpet.

Unfinished Agenda

A question that was raised but not adequately addressed in the early years of reforms was the roles of RBI and the government in relation to overseeing the banks, particularly public sector banks. At that point in time, the banking system was completely dominated by public sector banks. This issue was also related to the autonomy of banks. The general thrust of reforms was to give functional autonomy to banks subject to their fulfilment of prudential norms and accounting standards. Was this in anyway compromised by the ownership of the banks by the government? In a separate note, two members of the Narasimham Committee said:

> 'In line with the above and the concept of self-denial by the Government of its ownership rights, which the Committee has rightly advocated, we think that the Government should not appoint its officials on the boards of public sector banks and financial institutions. The Banking Division of the Ministry of Finance, as at present constituted, should consequently be abolished.
>
> 'We think that a decision by the Government not to have its representatives on the boards of public sector banks and financial institutions will serve as a strong message of autonomy to the system and will create a climate conducive to the successful implementation of the other recommendations of the committee.'

It was after the nationalization of banks that the issue of the role of RBI and the government regarding banks came up. Depending upon who was heading the banking department, the relationship with RBI was either smooth or rough. Apart from personality clashes, the question was how much control the government as owner should exercise over banks. It was very often argued by government representatives that, given the responsibility to be accountable to the Parliament, they could not abdicate the power to exercise control over banks. In some sense, it is part of a larger issue of the relationship between the government and public sector enterprises. It is a question of distance that the government should maintain from public sector units. This is all the more serious with respect to the finance sector institutions. When the chips are down, it is extremely important that political influence over lending should be avoided. Functional autonomy of banks is key to improving the efficiency of banks. The reforms, insofar as they introduced a new regulatory framework, were the first step. There were miles to go before achieving autonomy for banks.

Banking reforms had three major objectives. The first was to make the banks' accounts transparent and comparable. The accounting norms did this. The second objective was to strengthen the financial health of the banks through the introduction of prudential norms. The capital adequacy criterion led to the induction of more capital. And the third objective was to increase the competitiveness in the banking system by the licencing of new banks. The dilution of the government's share in the equity of nationalized banks also made nationalized banks accountable to a larger audience. It is important to note that the reduction in the share of the government was sought to be achieved by expanding the capital base and enabling the banks to approach the capital market. The reforms were carried through with conviction and commitment. Besides the introduction of prudential norms, there were other developments, such as computerization. After the foundation was laid against great odds in the late 1980s, more rapid progress was made. Credit growth picked up, except in 1997–98. Industrial growth touched new heights, though it slackened in 1997–98. In all, banking reforms created the necessary conditions for rapid and stable economic growth.

In conclusion, let me quote an observation that I had made in 1993 on banking reforms:

'Two questions arise in relation to financial sector reform. The first relates to the implications of recent revelations with respect to gross irregularities in the securities operations for financial sector reform. The second question is whether the scheme of financial sector reform as adumbrated by the Government lacks social content. Scams occur in various types of situations. The only way to avoid scams is really to see that when a scam occurs the guilty are found out quickly and punished adequately and the system appropriately improved. The irregularities that have surfaced have caused a great public concern and, the central regulatory authority, RBI has initiated several steps to fully comprehend the magnitude and dimension of the irregularities and follow up by taking several remedial actions to prevent the recurrence of similar lapses in the future. What has been revealed are gross violations of the guidelines issued by the Reserve Bank of India. Recent events have clearly underscored the need for a supervisory system that is efficient and prompt. But these events do not take away the need for banking sector reform aimed at improving the viability of the banks and at the same time ensuring their accountability. Banks should become both autonomous and accountable.

'As regards the social content, it is not the contention of anybody that the special needs of the various sectors of the economy should not be adequately taken care of by the financial institutions. Banks and term-lending institutions are legitimate instruments of social and economic change. In fact during the 80's priority sector credit as a proportion of total net bank credit increased even beyond the stipulated 40 per cent. What is stressed is only that social responsibility must be balanced with the needs to ensure the viability of the financial institutions.'

9

Social Responsibility of Banks

Developments in Rural Credit

Provision of credit to agriculture and rural areas has been one of the major concerns of RBI from its inception. To emphasize this, almost from the beginning, RBI had a separate agricultural credit department. Over the years, the emphasis and modalities over the expansion of rural credit had changed. New specialized institutions came into existence. Initially, the cooperative system was considered to be the most appropriate vehicle for providing credit to agriculture and allied activities. With the nationalization of banks, there was a strong emphasis on opening branches in rural areas. With the prescription that 40 per cent of net bank credit should go to the 'priority sector', it was felt that rural branches would make a big difference. Later, regional rural banks (RRBs) were set up as specialized institutions to provide rural credit. In addition, credit to agriculture was provided at rates of interest that were concessional. Special refinancing facilities were made available to institutions providing rural credit. Thus, a three-pronged strategy was adopted for expanding rural credit and it included:

1. Expansion of the institutional structure
2. Directed lending, and
3. Concessional or subsidized credit supplemented by funding

After liberalization, how did this three-pronged strategy change? What were the modifications that were made in each of these elements? The Narasimhan Committee that went into this issue wanted a real break from the system of directed credit. It said,

> 'The Committee, therefore, suggests that the system of directed credit programmes should be gradually phased out. This process of phasing out would also recognize the need that for some time it would be necessary for some special credit support through direction to be in operation and that some sectors may continue to need such credit support. The Committee, therefore, proposes that directed credit programmes should cover a redefined priority sector, consisting of the small and marginal farmer, tiny sector of industry, small business and transport operators, village and cottage industries, rural artisans and other weaker sections. The committee proposes that the credit target for this redefined priority sector henceforth be fixed at 10 per cent of aggregate bank credit which, the committee has observed, would be broadly in line with the credit flows to these sectors at present.'

On the institutional infrastructure for rural credit, it said,

> 'The Committee believes that it would be advantageous for the sponsor banks to segregate the operations of their rural branches through the formation of one or more subsidiaries, depending on the size, administrative convenience and business assessment of each sponsor bank. Each subsidiary should have a compact area of operations. This would be particularly desirable from the point of view of recruitment and deployment of manpower apart from providing the needed thrust to business operations and effective improvements in the control, supervision and formation systems.'

Priority Sector Credit

While the Narasimhan Committee strongly dissented from the concept of directed credit, it still recommended a smaller percentage of credit to be extended to the extremely vulnerable sections. However, an assessment at that time showed that this percentage of 10 per cent was inadequate to cover the needs of these designated sectors and actually these sections received a higher percentage of net bank credit at that time. After much debate, the view that was taken by the government and RBI was to let the priority sector scheme continue with 40 per cent of net bank credit allocated for this purpose. But there was one important deviation and it was that the interest rate charged would be the same as in the rest of the system.

As already reported, the administered structure of interest rates was steadily deregulated and by 1997, banks had full freedom to determine interest rates on all credit above Rs 2 lakh. Concessional credit was thus limited to small loans below Rs 2 lakh. Another change that was made was to widen the scope of priority sector lending. This applied to rural credit as well. Thus, while priority sector lending was retained, its burden, because of concessionality of interest rates, was reduced.

With the sharp reduction in reserve requirements, the retention of 40 per cent of net bank credit as priority sector credit essentially meant a much larger flow of credit in absolute amounts. A simple arithmetic will show this. With pre-emption at 60 per cent of bank deposits, an addition of Rs 100 deposits will mean priority sector credit will be Rs 16, that is 40 per cent of deposits available for lending. With the pre-emption of 35 per cent of deposits, the flow of credit for the priority sector will be Rs 26. Actually, the flow of credit expanded strongly between 1991 and 1997 not only in nominal terms but also in real terms. In nominal terms, priority sector credit increased by 81 per cent and in real terms by 20 per cent.

Developments in the 1980s

The 1980s saw a strong commitment to use the banking system to help agriculture and related activities. This resulted in quantitative targets being fixed for the provision of credit to agriculture and other activities. In fact, quantitative targets have the inherent demerit of ignoring quality. This particularly has a serious consequence in the case of provision of credit. The Integrated Rural Development Programme (IRDP) was one key programme of the government to help small farmers and others in rural areas. This was financed to a significant extent by bank credit while the government also provided capital subsidy. To enable banks to fulfil the various credit targets, several new schemes were adopted such as the Special Area Approach (SAA). The earlier schemes such as the

Lead Bank Scheme were pursued vigorously. Against the background of declining efficiency indicators, it was hoped that these programmes would help to improve the quality of the delivery system in rural lending. For example, the recovery under IRDP was below 30 per cent. Apart from this, there were many other deficiencies that several studies had noted. One important decision taken in the early 1980s was the setting up of NABARD in 1982. It took away many of the functions RBI was earlier performing. It became the central point for facilitating the flow of credit to rural areas. NABARD received financial assistance from RBI. To smoothen the coordination between NABARD and RBI, the first chairman of NABARD was also a deputy governor of RBI. But this practice was later given up.

In 1989, the Agriculture Credit Review Committee chaired by A.M. Khusro drew attention to many shortfalls in the credit delivery system. It pointed out that low interest rates on agricultural advances and loans under IRDP, relatively poor deposit mobilization in rural branches and lower staff productivity contributed to the declining profitability of rural business. It recommended a scheme of two interest rates, one a concessional rate for small and marginal farmers and two, a general rate for others. After liberalization, this was in effect implemented as the rate of interest after 1990 was linked to the size of the loan.

Institutional Changes since 1990

On the creation of new institutions, there were several suggestions that came up, such as the setting up of a national cooperative bank and a national rural bank by merging all RRBs. RBI was not in favour of either of the suggestions as the viability of such institutions was in serious doubt. Out of 196 RRBs, 152 banks had registered losses and merging them could be of little benefit. What was needed was a view on the functions of RRBs and steps needed to make them viable. After liberalization, these banks were allowed to lend to categories other than those prescribed originally so that there could be some element of cross-subsidization. Investment avenues were also widened. One of the recommendations of the Narasimhan Committee was that each public sector bank should amalgamate its rural branches into one or more subsidiaries. The government and RBI did not act on this recommendation as they did not see any particular advantage over the existing system.

Another step in expanding the institutional framework was the introduction of local area banks, which were mentioned in an earlier chapter. Local area banks were privately owned and were similar in concept to RRBs. RRBs were government-owned either directly or indirectly. The thinking behind the concept of local area banks was that it would be possible for privately owned small banks to help small borrowers and remain viable at the same time. But this idea was not pursued after 1997. It has been revived with some modifications recently.

Loan Waiver

One issue that has come up frequently is the attitude towards general loan waivers. This issue came up in 1990 when V.P. Singh took over as prime minister. The finance minister in his Budget speech of 1990–91 said:

> 'In order to relieve our farmers from the burden of debt, an assurance was given in the National Front's manifesto that relief will be provided to farmers with loans up to Rs 10,000 as on October 2, 1989. I am glad to inform the House that we are now ready with the scheme of implementation of debt relief to fulfil the promise, and redeem the pledge given to the kisans and artisans. It is proposed to introduce a scheme for providing debt relief which will have the following features. The relief will be available to borrowers who have taken loans up to Rs 10,000 from public sector banks and Regional Rural Banks. The relief will cover all overdue as on 2nd October 1989 including short-term as well as term loans. There will be no limit on the size of the borrower's land holdings. However, wilful defaulters, who in the past did not repay loans despite their capacity to do so, will be excluded. The Central Government will compensate the public sector banks and regional rural banks suitably for the debts which are thus written off.'

The scheme of debt relief became effective from 15 May 1990. The Central government made a provision of Rs 1000 crore to implement the scheme. The RBI had always been somewhat uncomfortable with general loan waivers because of the adverse impact it might have on the repayment ethic. The government had always taken the view that financial institutions should not have any problem as they were being fully compensated by the government. 'Loan waiver' was treated as part of the government's policy to help farmers. It is easy to see that periodic loan waivers can only make those who repay them 'innocent fools'. If the farmers are in difficulties, the first step should be rescheduling and if that doesn't work, a more drastic thing like waiver can be thought of. A case by case approach is preferable to the 'general' waiver.

RBI and NABARD

As mentioned earlier, NABARD was set up in 1982 and it started performing many of the functions that were being performed by RBI. NABARD became the primary refinancing agency for institutions that provided short-term and long-term credit. The major source of funding for NABARD came from RBI. Under Section 46 of the RBI Act, the bank was required to contribute every year such sums of money as it might consider necessary and feasible to the NRC (LTO) fund and NRC (stabilization) fund, which were maintained by NABARD. This was strictly followed by RBI and during the years 1989–90, 1990–91 and 1991–92, RBI contributed Rs 340 crore, Rs 385 crore and Rs 420 crore respectively to these funds. In 1992–93, the government desired that a larger share of the profits of RBI be transferred to the Central government. As a consequence, RBI did not make any contribution to the statutory funds from 1992–93. This obviously put NABARD in a difficult situation, as the funds from RBI were made available free of cost. It had to tap new sources, which would result in the cost of funds rising. Interestingly, the statutory auditors as well as the legal department of RBI opined that section 46 imposed an obligation on the part of RBI to make a contribution and therefore it would be unlawful for RBI not to make such contributions. To avoid the legal problem, RBI made a token contribution of Rs 1 crore to each of the funds. However, an amendment was made in 1994 to section 46 of the Reserve Bank Act to make such contributions 'enabling' rather than 'mandatory'. Besides the provision of long-term funds, RBI also provided a general line of credit (GLC) to support refinancing short-term credit by NABARD. This continued and kept increasing. For example, during 1995–96, RBI enhanced its GLC for NABARD by Rs 300 crore to Rs 5250 core and further to Rs 5500 crore in 1996–97. The discontinuation of the contribution to NRC funds did disturb RBI very much. It therefore decided to steadily raise the capital of NABARD. NABARD's capital in 1992–93 stood at Rs 100 crore. It was raised to Rs 120 crore during 1993–94. This process was continued. During 1995–96, the share capital was raised by Rs 170 crore to Rs 500 crore with equal contribution from RBI and the government. A plan was drawn up to raise the capital of Rs 500 crore to Rs 2000 crore in the next five years. During 1996–97, the share of capital of NABARD was doubled from Rs 500 crore to Rs 1000 crore comprising a contribution of Rs 400 crore from RBI and Rs 100 crore from the government. Thus, in a sense what was taken away by one hand was given back through the other hand. In the account books of RBI, contribution from the profits was treated differently from investment in share capital. The latter formed part of the investment portfolio of RBI.

Rural Infrastructure Development Fund (RIDF)

In his Budget speech for 1995–96, the finance minister said:

'To encourage quicker completion of projects in rural infrastructure, I propose to establish a new Rural Infrastructural Development Fund within the National Bank for Agriculture and Rural Development (NABARD) from April 1995. The Fund will provide loans to State Governments and State owned Corporations for completing ongoing projects relating to medium and minor irrigation, soil conservation, watershed management and other forms of rural infrastructure. The loans will be on a project-specific basis with repayment and interest guaranteed by the concerned State Government. Priority will be assigned to projects which can be completed within the least time period. Resources for the Fund will come from commercial banks which will be required by Reserve Bank of India (RBI) to contribute an amount equivalent to a bank's shortfall in achieving the priority sector target for agricultural lending, subject to a maximum of 1.5 per cent of the bank's net credit. This is expected to create a corpus of about Rs 2000 crore for completion of rural infrastructure projects.'

The creation of RIDF was to take care of two problems. It was found that commercial banks were not fulfilling the sub targets fixed for agriculture under the priority sector. Despite several communications, the position continued to remain the same. Therefore, we had to think of some mechanism that would bite banks. Even though the finance minister started with the need for rural infrastructure investment and the method for financing, the actual discussions that I had with him were inverted, that is to say they started from the angle of making the banks that were defaulting learn a lesson, and investment in rural infrastructure was thought of as a way to solve the problem. It was also important to note that the financing of projects was meant to provide loans mainly to complete projects. It was thus a 'last-mile' funding. Care was also taken to see that this did not become an easy route for banks not to fulfil the sub targets fixed. The rate of interest paid by NABARD was made a floating rate equal to one half of one percentage point above the maximum permissible rate on term deposits. Thus, investment in such bonds would not be too attractive to banks. Of course, unlike loans, there was no risk attached. By 1998, four tranches of RIDF were issued and the total corpus came to Rs 10,000 crore. One criticism of RIDF was that while it facilitated completion of rural infrastructure projects, it did not help farmers as direct lending would have done.

SHG-Bank Credit Linkages

An important development in the 1990s in rural credit was the growth of Self Help Groups (SHGs) and their links with the banking system. SHGs are groups of persons of the size of ten to twenty who come together to undertake various activities. They encourage savings and come together to borrow from banks. In a sense, this movement was inspired by the Grameen banks of Prof. Muhammad Yunus. But these groups are not banks. They are first, associations of people with a similar background coming together to borrow and take on productive activities. They are not NGOs. NGOs may help them and put them in touch with banks. They have also played a key role in organizing new SHGs.

The big question that arose was the nature of the link between SHGs and banks. SHGs needed credit to pursue productive activities as well as for consumption. To take a view on this, a pilot project was launched in 1991. By the middle of 1997, it was clear that the credit link with SHGs was proving to be effective. However, one question that was nagging regulators was that SHGs were informal groups but not registered societies under any Act. These loans would have to be treated as joint loans. SHGs were largely women's associations and encouraging these institutions would also be a case of empowerment of women. The most impressive aspect of the functioning of SHGs was the excellent repayment record. The peer pressure was a key factor in achieving this. In 1994, RBI set up a Committee to study the problems relating to the SHG–bank credit linkage scheme. Finally, RBI recognized the importance of this linkage and issued a circular in April 1996, which said:

'As the efficacy of the SHGs as an effective mode for rural savings mobilization and credit delivery to the poor has been demonstrated in the pilot phase and since the linkage of targeted 500 SHGs has already been achieved, it has been decided to extend the SHGs linkage programme beyond the pilot phase as a normal business activity of banks to improve the coverage of the rural poor by the banking sector. Accordingly, the banks may consider lending to SHGs as part of their mainstream credit operations both at policy and implementation level.'

In a lecture I delivered in April 1996, I dealt with several problems in relation to the SHG–bank linkage scheme. Some of the observations are reproduced here.

'Self-help groups (SHGs) have been found to help inculcate among their members sound habits of thrift, saving and banking. What is perhaps most relevant in the case of SHGs is the peer pressure they are able to exert in order to ensure that credit is utilized for the purpose for which it has been taken and is repaid according to schedule.

'Normally, the SHG gets established as a response to a perceived need besides being centred around specific productive activities. The main advantage to the banks of their link with the SHGs and VOs is the externalization of a part of the work items of the credit cycle, viz., assessment of credit needs, appraisal, disbursal, supervision and repayment, reduction in the formal paper work involved and a consequent reduction in the transaction cost. Improvement in recoveries will lead to wider coverage of the target group.

'In this regard the role of VOs is somewhat distinct from SHGs. VOs have a role in organizing the rural poor into SHGs and in ensuring their proper functioning. So far, in the Indian context, most of the VOs have concentrated their activities in the areas of education and health, and to some extent, with other general development activities. Their role in providing an effective link between organized credit-disbursing agencies and those which have the need and are eligible to obtain credit from such institutions has been minimal. Today, we have a fairly large number of programmes aimed at providing credit to the poor. Effective utilization of credit by eligible borrowers can be enhanced if VOs can forge links with the formal credit agencies on one side and the poor on the other. Their mediatory role can go beyond facilitating the obtainment of credit to include its effective use and recovery.'

The SHG movement has taken deep roots. But the growth has also created in its wake several problems. The repayment culture has also suffered. Certainly, the promotion of SHGs can be one mechanism for the extension of credit to small borrowers. But it must be remembered, the total credit extended to SHGs is still a small part of overall credit. The attempt to politicize the SHG movement must be avoided. Otherwise it will meet the same fate of cooperatives.

Alongside the growth of SHGs, another important development was the beginning of microfinance institutions providing credit to small borrowers. These institutions were registered as Non-Bank Finance Companies (NBFCs). In the early 1990s, they had just begun. Subsequently, they have grown into an important segment, and their regulation assumed importance. These issues have been dealt with by several committees including the one on financial inclusion chaired by me in 2008.

Provision of rural credit at affordable rates of interest has been one of the major planks of RBI's policy. The government and RBI adopted a multiagency approach to make credit available. Though cooperatives were initially considered the most appropriate vehicle, the drawbacks of the cooperative movement coupled with new thinking on additional institutions resulted in a multiagency approach. The needs of rural credit were so large, it was hoped that each type of institution would find its own niche. Bank credit was also linked to government programmes aimed at promoting different types of rural activities. Liberalization basically accepted this approach. As already mentioned, while the priority sector mandate continued, the financial burden on banks was reduced as rates of interest were linked to the size of the loan. The various aspects of rural credit programmes were studied by different committees and action was taken on the recommendations. For example, after the Mehta Committee Report, the subsidy provided by the government in IRDP was back-ended than front-loaded. RBI continued its role as provider of funds to the system through NABARD. New vehicles for providing credit to the poor were experimented with. A good example was the SHG–bank credit linkage scheme. This was the beginning of financial inclusion. The rural credit system required continual assessment and evaluation. The organized financial system has yet to reach out to the majority of rural households. The National Sample Service Organization (NSSO) Survey of 2003 found that 51.4 per cent of the total farmer households did not access credit either from institutional or non-institutional sources. Only 27 per cent of the total farmer households were indebted to formal sources and of this, one-third also borrowed from informal sources. The committee I chaired, a reference to which was made earlier, suggested a mission made for extension of financial inclusion. Given the enormity of the task, the provision of credit is important. But is equally necessary to provide other financial services like savings, payments and micro insurance. Aadhar-enabled payments system has facilitated the delivery of savings and payment services. Direct Benefit Transfer (DBT), which enables the crediting of the benefits of the various programmes such as the Mahatma Gandhi National Rural Employment Guarantee Act (MGNREGA) directly to the accounts of the beneficiaries, has been an important development. It helps to avoid leakages. These are some of the recent developments. The one lesson from our experience is that unless steps are taken on the demand side, that is in the 'real sectors', mere supply side solutions from the financial sector will not work. Credit is necessary for this, but not sufficient. Credit has to be an integral part of an overall programme aimed at improving the productivity and income of small farmers and other poor households. Putting in place an appropriate credit delivery system to meet the needs of marginal and sub-marginal farmers must go hand in hand with efforts to improve the productivity of such farm households.

10

Widening the Knowledge Base

Developments in Research and Computerization

Right from the beginning, RBI had a research department focusing on economics and statistics. In fact, for almost three decades from 1950, RBI had a galaxy of distinguished economists and statisticians who contributed immensely to the discussions on various models of economic growth and planning. Apart from the economists at the university and a few research institutions, the leading economists were in either the Planning Commission or RBI. There were good economists in the finance ministry but their numbers were limited. When I moved to RBI in 1982 and was in charge of research departments, I felt that, while at the top and the middle there were good economists and statisticians, at the lower level, there was a need to improve quality. This I found out was due to the discontinuance of the recruitment of young, promising economists and statisticians at the entry level as Grade B officers. I took steps to bring back into operation the recruitment of talented young economists and statisticians as Grade B officers. RBI was taken to court by the union on the grounds that, under the agreement with the RBI, only entry level officers could be directly recruited and that the entry level was grade A and not grade B. We had to argue that, as far as the research departments were concerned, the entry level was grade B and not grade A. We overcame the problem and I am happy to note that the economists who are at the top today in RBI are those who were recruited as Grade B officers after the resumption of such a practice in the early 1980s.

One other issue in training good economists and statisticians in the bank was that while they were very good at the time of their recruitment, they needed further development, particularly by acquiring a PhD degree. Therefore, we decided to facilitate such young officers to acquire a PhD. They were provided necessary leave. In addition, some arrangements were worked out with institutions such as IIT Mumbai, which enabled officers to work for their PhD while continuing to work at RBI. Much later, after the Indira Gandhi Institute of Development Research (IGIDR) became a deemed-to-be university, it was easier to work out an arrangement between IGIDR and RBI.

The publications of RBI provide an indication of the research activity being carried on at the bank. The major publications were the annual reports, the *Report on Currency and Finance*, the report on *Trend and Progress of Banking in India* and the monthly *RBI Bulletin*. Some of these publications were statutory requirements. The annual reports during the 1980s and later became more informative. The section 'Assessment and Prospects' became a window for letting readers know RBI's views on various issues confronting the Indian economy. On the three related areas of monetary policy, fiscal policy and exchange rate management, RBI became more and more explicit in its views. Thus, the annual report became a channel for some forthright articulation of RBI's views. The annual reports in the 1990s also became more informative with the discussion of specific issues in boxes. The *Report on Currency and Finance* was a treasure house of data and RBI's systematic presentation of data on a comparable basis on all aspects of the economy year after year was most helpful to students, researchers and analysts. The *Occasional Papers* was an important publication of the research departments. This publication offered an opportunity to the officers to publish their research work. The high quality of this publication speaks of the seriousness with which research was and is being pursued in RBI. The *RBI Bulletin*, which was a monthly publication, published speeches of senior executives of RBI, more particularly of the governor and deputy governors. Besides being analytical, these speeches were also a mine of information. In short, the high quality of the publications during this period reflected the seriousness with which research was viewed by RBI.

1985 marked the completion of fifty years of RBI. Discussions started as early as 1983 as to how to celebrate this event. It was felt that apart from the celebration of the day with a meeting where the prime minister and finance minister would be present, there must be some steps which would have a lasting impact. Manmohan Singh as governor in 1983 started consultations with many people not only from within but outside RBI. One idea that came up was to set up an institute of high quality research. On this issue itself, there were two opinions. One view was that the focus of the institute must be on problems and issues with which RBI was closely associated. This could mean an emphasis on monetary and financial issues. The other view was a much broader one, which could mean a wide range of issues, such as development and planning besides money and finance. The latter view prevailed as the very name of the institute (Indira Gandhi Institute of Development and Research) incorporates the terms Development and Research. However, there was no difference of opinion that the faculty selected should be of the highest quality. Malhotra and I took a deep interest in developing this institute. I initially managed the institution until Kirit Parikh was appointed as the first director. Incidentally, the original name chosen for the institute was Jawaharlal Nehru Institute of Development Research. But by the time the institute could be established, Indira Gandhi had died and the government, particularly, found it appropriate to name it after Indira Gandhi, and the necessary permission was obtained. There is no doubt that IGIDR has grown into an outstanding institution of research in economics. Later, it also became a teaching institution. Credit is due to Kirit Parikh, his colleagues and the successive directors and their colleagues. The quality of research output coming out of IGIDR is truly world-class. It must also be pointed out that RBI behaved in an exemplary manner, giving the fullest freedom to IGIDR to run its programmes. IGIDR literally operated without a 'budget constraint'. In fact, this caused some resentment within the bank.

Golden Jubilee Scholarships

One important decision to commemorate the golden jubilee of RBI was to institute a scheme of golden jubilee scholarships. Under the scheme, select officers would be sent abroad each year to undertake further studies. The period was limited to one year. We expected that, over the years, such a scheme would result in a core of officers well trained in areas crucial to RBI. I chaired the committee to select the officers to be sent abroad for studies. This scheme was welcomed by the officers and it turned out to be a big success. Very few officers sent abroad decided to stay away. Almost all of them returned back to the bank, and both the officers and bank gained.

Process of Computerization

Far-reaching changes in computer and communication technologies have completely revolutionized the way banking is conducted the world over. But in India, the introduction of computers in the banking industry met with stiff resistance in the mid-1980s. A brief reference to this is important to understand how the process of modernization of banking was interrupted because of the needless opposition to computerization.

In this context, we at RBI in the mid-1980s had to deal with two sets of problems: bringing about changes in one, RBI and two, in the commercial banking industry. Of course, the latter was more challenging. The reports of the two committees that I chaired laid the foundation for the computerization of the banking industry. Given the attitude of the unions, these two reports were cautious. They touched on three aspects of computerization. The first was to computerize back office transactions so that the entries are posted into the ledgers and respective accounts speedily. Reconciliation of accounts had become a big problem in the early 1980s. The second aspect of computerization was to computerize the front office operations so that customers who came to banks benefited. The third aspect of computerization related to the transfer of funds and data across banks and within banks. The third aspect was dealt with more extensively in the early 1990s. In the 1980s, only the first two aspects were taken up. It is interesting to note that the first committee appointed in 1983 was called the 'Committee on Mechanization'. Even the use of the word 'computerization' was an anathema. The objective of front-office computerization was to enable customers to go to any counter and carry out whatever transaction they wanted to put through. Previously, each counter dealt with only one type of banking transaction. In fact, the machines installed were also not described as computers and they were called Advanced Ledger Posting Machines (ALPMs). The memory of these machines was crippled to ensure that only a prefixed number of transactions could be put through! It must also be noted that *every* employee in the banking industry was given one increment so that they would agree to the programme of computerization. I must also record here that the hostility to computerization was so high that when I, as deputy governor of RBI, went to attend the board meeting of State Bank of India in the SBI office in Delhi, I was surrounded by the bank employees and my coat was torn. I preserved it as a memento for a long time. It must, however, be recorded that by the early 1990s, there was a big change and the process of computerization in the banking industry moved forward at a rapid pace. Today, we are in a fairly advanced stage of computerization. It was sad that we had to go through an initial phase of misguided resistance.

The introduction of computers in RBI was no less difficult. Interestingly, RBI installed its first set of computers not within the bank but at the premises of the Bhabha Atomic Research Centre in 1967. However, later it was moved into one of the RBI buildings. Basically, this computer system (Honeywell) was utilized to tabulate the enormous amount of data being supplied by the banks to RBI. By 1982, it became clear that there were four areas in which computerization had become urgent. First was in relation to the operations of the clearing house. The second was in relation to the activities of various departments. The third was to keep pace and be in sync with computerization in the banking industry and the fourth was in terms of the flow of funds and, in general, the payments system. The first major step in computerization was in relation to the clearing house operations. The number of cheques passing through the clearing house, for example, in Mumbai had increased enormously. The sorting work could no longer be done manually. A decision was therefore taken to set up a high-speed reader/sorter system linked to mainframe computers in Mumbai, which could help in clearing up to a million cheques overnight. But this required the issue of a new type of cheques using Magnetic Ink Character Recognition (MICR) technology. In order that the cheques were acceptable and could be read by the machines, RBI had to standardize the thickness and quality of paper, quality of ink, etc. We seemed to be in an entirely new business! The National Clearing Centre (NCC) was set up in Mumbai in 1983. Later, it was extended to Chennai, New Delhi and Kolkata. The attempt was to ensure that any cheque deposited by a customer and drawn on the bank branches in any one of these cities got cleared and deposited within four days. The introduction of the high-speed reader/sorter system was also not without difficulties. Some officers claimed that lifting of the trays loaded with cheques and putting them into the reader/sorter amounted to manual labour and therefore they could not be expected to do that. We were forced to search for the proper definition of manual labour. Finally, we even converted steel trays into plastic trays!

The installation of computers in the various departments of RBI took their own time. However, the process continued with an assurance to the employees that there would be no reduction in labour. RBI took special interest in speeding up the payment system. By 1997, the process of computerization in RBI had reached an advanced stage and there was a clear acceptance by the unions on the necessity and inevitability of computerization. In March 1996, the Institute for Development and Research in Banking Technology (IDRBT) was established by RBI at Hyderabad as an autonomous centre for development and research in banking technology.

Talking on the development of banking technology in 1996, I said:

'The process of computerization in the banking industry in India has just begun. We have truly miles to go. Customers have become more demanding. They are no longer willing to accept or condone delays in the collection of cheques or encashing of instruments. Borrowers want quick decisions. The banking industry must rise to the occasion. The world over banks face stiff competition not only among themselves but also from a host of other institutions ranging from finance companies to departmental stores. Far-reaching changes in communication technology have brought about such a situation. In the banking industry in India, there is now a greater awareness and a willingness to accept the induction of high technology. We need to take advantage of this. Managements must take all steps to demystify computers. Obviously, the role and the extent of computerization must take into account the special features of our country. Nevertheless, it is clear that in widening and improving customer service and ensuring higher productivity, a technology orientation has become a necessity. Only sustained increase in output and productivity can result in enlarged employment opportunities in the banking industry and elsewhere. Computers and telecommunications are not the only answers to the banking industry's problems. A lot needs to be done in many other areas. However, in creating a viable and efficient banking system which can respond adequately to the needs of a growing economy, technology has a key role to play. The issue in Indian banking is no longer whether technology is needed or not. The real issue is how much, what type and how quickly.'

Over the last two decades, banks have realized the importance of computerization over the entire gamut of their operations. Deploying emerging technologies, they have innovated new products and new business models to deliver better customer service. Mobile phones and apps have emerged as new and powerful channels to deliver products and services in real time. Mention must be made of the rapid strides made by India in faster adoption and spread of digital payments and their clearing. RBI deserves credit for having established the National Payment Corporation of India (NPCI) in 2009. Incidentally, it was a committee headed by me which suggested in 2009 that IDRBT transfer its payment services to the NPCI platform, the new umbrella unit for payments.

11

Emerging Contours of Monetary Policy

The preceding chapters have dealt with the evolution of monetary policy between 1982 and 1997. A question that may arise in the minds of the readers is how relevant this narration is in today's context. This is a general question that is always asked of history. Does history repeat itself? How do we draw lessons from history? However, the period dealt with in this book is not far into the past. It is only three decades ago. What may strike one is that the issues discussed then are not very different from what one is discussing today. The conflict and trade-off among objectives of monetary policy, autonomy of the central bank, ability of the central bank to maintain prices and output stability, the link between financial stability and exchange rate stability with traditional objectives of monetary policy—these are some of the issues discussed then and also now. However, the context has changed and may require slightly modified answers. The chapter provides a review of the key issues in monetary policy.

Evolution of Monetary Policy

Monetary policy has emerged as an important tool of economic policy both in developed and developing economies. It is clear that the challenges for monetary policy have been changing over time, even though some basic issues have remained of perennial concern. As the institutional environment faces both domestic and global changes, the tasks of monetary policy also undergo a change. The monetary and financial system is far more complex today than it has been in the past. Financial intermediation has reached a high level of sophistication, which has itself become a source of concern in recent days. The menu of financial products available has expanded enormously. Derivative products, which were unknown till a few decades ago, have become common. All these changes have an important role to play in relation to the transmission mechanism. The impact of monetary policy action can be felt through a variety of channels, some of which, though recognized in the past, have become more important. The speed at which funds can move across borders has raised issues regarding coordination of monetary policies among countries. While the traditional issues such as the objectives of monetary policy and the possible trade-off among them remain relevant, they need to be related to the far-reaching changes in the institutional environment at home and abroad.

Monetary policy has had its ups and downs in the post-Second World War period. In industrially advanced countries, after decades of eclipse, monetary policy re-emerged as a potent instrument of economic policy in the fight against inflation in the 1980s. Issues relating to the conduct of monetary policy came to the forefront of policy debates at that time. The relative importance of growth and price stability as the objective as well as the appropriate intermediate target of monetary policy became the focus of attention. The recent churning of the financial system has raised several new questions not only with respect to objectives but also to the overall conduct of monetary policy itself.

A similar trend regarding monetary policy is discernible in developing economies as well. Much of the early literature on development economics focused on real factors such as savings, investment and technology as mainsprings of growth. Very little attention was paid to the financial system as a contributory factor to economic growth even though attention was paid to develop financial institutions that provide short-term and long-term credit. In fact, many writers felt that inflation was endemic in the process of economic growth and it was accordingly treated more as a consequence of structural imbalance than as a monetary phenomenon. However, with accumulated evidence, it became clear that any process of economic growth in which monetary expansion was disregarded, led to inflationary pressures with a consequent impact on economic growth. Accordingly, the importance of price stability and, therefore, the need to use monetary policy for that purpose also assumed importance in developing economies. Nonetheless, the debate on the extent to which price stability should be deemed to be the overriding objective of monetary policy in such economies continues. The increasing integration of these economies with the rest of the world has also raised the relationship between monetary policy and exchange rate management. The impossible trinity is a reality and countries have to make the relevant choice.

Trends in India's Monetary Policy

The evolution of India's monetary policy reflects the changing concerns over the last seven decades. In the first three decades after Independence, the primary concern of the government was to get the plans implemented. Fulfilment of plan targets was the dominant objective and all policy instruments, including monetary policy, were tuned towards that goal. RBI played a major role in widening the financial infrastructure by creating new institutions. Allocation of credit consistent with plan priorities also became a major concern. In terms of monetary policy, planners talked of non-inflationary deficit financing. For example, the First Plan document said, 'Judicious credit creation somewhat in anticipation of the increase in production and availability of genuine savings has also a part to play' (Planning Commission, 1952). Jawaharlal Nehru's letter to Governor Rama Rau while accepting his resignation was clear. It indicated that the government was the dominant partner and that the role of RBI was to abide by the larger concerns of the government. As long as inflation was moderate, this approach did not matter. But in the seventies, inflation touched unacceptable levels and the growth of the money supply had to be reined in.

The 1980s saw a continuous 'battle' between RBI and the Ministry of Finance on the control of inflation and the need to contain the fiscal deficit and more particularly its monetization. Though this period recorded an average annual growth rate of little over 5 per cent, the growth path was uneven. The average inflation rate was close to 7 per cent. The annual M_3 growth rate was 17 per cent. The Chakravarty Committee, which submitted its report in 1985, emphasized the need for regulation of the money supply and wanted the money supply growth to be consistent with real growth and acceptable levels of inflation (RBI, 1985). It also emphasized the need for close coordination between monetary policy and fiscal policy because money supply growth was driven by reserve money and the most important factor determining the creation of reserve money was RBI credit to government. Thus, the committee envisaged a scheme of what came to be described as flexible monetary targeting. Even though the government accepted in principle the recommendations, the latter part of the 1980s still saw a higher fiscal deficit and higher money supply growth. All these landed us in the crisis of 1991. The early 1990s saw, as a part of the liberalization programme, far-reaching changes in the way the central bank was functioning. By doing away with the issue of ad hoc treasury bills, the automatic monetization of the fiscal deficit came to an end. By moving to a market-determined rate of interest, government securities became marketable and it has enabled the emergence of OMOs as an instrument of credit control. The dismantling of the administered structure of interest rates enabled the rate of interest to emerge as a policy variable. RBI was deeply concerned with price stability as a dominant objective of monetary policy and therefore regarded regulation of the money supply as a key factor in monetary policy. Post-1997, RBI adopted the approach of multiple indicators. But the issues connected with multiple objectives remained. In the years before and after the 2008 crisis, RBI focused on financial stability and, in fact, acted well in anticipation of the international crisis. In 2016, RBI moved to a new monetary policy framework which may be described as one of flexible inflation targeting. The interest rate (repo rate) became the operating target. Moving to the new policy framework clarified the objective of monetary policy. But RBI still has to contend with many other issues with respect to monetary policy. The question of when to raise or lower the interest rate will always be a contentious issue. Discussions on monetary policy after the new framework are not dissimilar from the issues discussed earlier.

Enunciation of Objectives

In any monetary policy framework, a key ingredient is the enunciation of its objectives as its actions are guided foremost by the objectives. A recurring question in this context is whether monetary policy should be concerned with all the goals of economic policy. The issue of 'objective' has become important because of the need to provide clear guidance to monetary policymakers. Indeed, this aspect has assumed added significance in the context of the increasing stress on the autonomy of central banks. Autonomy goes with accountability and accountability, in turn, requires a clear enunciation of the goals. Thus, an accountable central bank is one with clearly articulated and publicly stated objectives.

The various enactments setting up the central banks normally specify the goals of central banks. The Federal Reserve Act in the US requires the central bank to conduct monetary policy 'so as to promote effectively the goals of maximum employment, stable prices and moderate long term interest rate' (Federal Reserve System, 2016). Even though the Act lists three distinct goals, the authorities have always treated the mandate as the 'dual mandate', as the third mandate on interest rates was treated as implicit in the first two mandates. The European Central Bank is most categorical about price stability as the primary objective. The relevant article specifies, 'the primary objective of the ESCB shall be to maintain price stability. Without prejudice to that objective, it shall support the general economic policies in the Union in order to contribute to the achievement of the latter's objectives' (European Central Bank, 2013). The Reserve Bank of India Act in its original preamble requires RBI to conduct its operations 'with a view to securing monetary stability in India and generally to operate the currency and credit system of the country to its advantage' (RBI, 1934). This was subsequently expanded in 2016 by an amendment. Most central bank legislations are not helpful in clearly charting out the path that a central bank should pursue, as a multiplicity of objectives mentioned in the legislation tends to obfuscate the issue. In the last few decades, most central banks in the industrially advanced countries have accepted price stability as the most important objective of monetary policy (Fischer, 1996). According to Eldie George, former governor of the Bank of England, 'It is true that most central banks at least would traditionally have regarded controlling inflation as a core responsibility. In some cases—most famously in the case of Bundesbank—the duty of preserving the value of the currency has long been written into the central bank's statutes. But what is remarkable today is the extent of the international consensus on effective price stability—in the sense of eliminating inflation as a factor in economic decisions—as the immediate aim of monetary policy; and this is increasingly reflected in more or less explicit targets for low rates of inflation against which monetary policy performance can be measured' (George, 1996). This is clearly built into the mandate of the European Central Bank. After the 2008 financial crisis, central banks in industrially advanced countries are groping their way to integrate the objective of financial stability with other objectives.

In talking of the objectives of monetary policy in India, I had said on an earlier occasion (Rangarajan, 1998a),

> 'In a broad sense the objectives of monetary policy can be no different from the overall objectives of economic policy. The broad objectives of monetary policy in India have been: (1) to maintain a reasonable degree of price stability and (2) to help accelerate the rate of economic growth. The emphasis as between the two objectives has changed from year to year, depending upon the conditions prevailing in that year and in the previous year.'

In fact, what I had said was a version of the Taylor rule in its most discretionary form.

The choice of a dominant objective arises essentially because of the multiplicity of objectives and the inherent conflict among such objectives. Faced with multiple objectives that are equally relevant and desirable, there is always the problem of assigning to each instrument the most appropriate objective. This 'assignment rule' favours monetary policy as the most appropriate instrument to achieve the objective of price stability. The fundamental reason to adopt price stability as the dominant objective is that inflation is economically and socially costly. While attempts have been made to estimate the economic costs, the social costs are difficult to estimate. Quite clearly, inflation hits the poor harder than the rich. Of course, policymakers also need to take into account the cost of output loss flowing from a disinflationary policy.

Trade-off between Growth and Price Stability

A crucial issue that is being debated in India as elsewhere is whether the pursuit of the objective of price stability by monetary authorities undermines the ability of the economy to attain and sustain high growth. A considerable part of the relevant research effort has been devoted to the trade-off between economic growth and price stability. Empirical evidence on the relationship between growth and inflation in a cross-country framework is somewhat inconclusive because such studies include countries with an inflation rate as low as 1 to 2 per cent to those with inflation rates going beyond 200 to 300 per cent. These studies, however, clearly establish that growth rates become increasingly adverse at higher rates of inflation (Sarel, 1996; RBI, 2002).

The trade-off between price stability and economic growth has also been discussed in the framework of labour and output markets. The well-known Phillips curve postulated an inverse relationship between unemployment and wage rate. Several economists have challenged the basic microeconomic underpinning of the wage and price mechanism that leads to the possibility of a trade-off between inflation and growth. Several studies have established that in the long run there is no trade-off between the two (Friedman, 1975). The Phillips curve becomes purely vertical, if the role of expectations is explicitly included. An environment of reasonable price stability is more conducive to economic growth; price stability is thus a necessary condition for long-run growth. However, there is a possible trade-off in the short run. It is, nevertheless, important not to overuse this opportunity as it can undermine the long-term imperative. The long-run implications of short-run actions need to be kept in view. There is also an argument that is going on in the developed economies whether the short-run Phillips curve has become flatter. A flatter Phillips curve will enable a central bank to support employment aggressively during downturns.

In resolving the short-run trade-off between price stability and output growth in the industrial countries, a solution is sought through the adoption of Taylor's rule, which prescribes that the signal interest rate be fixed taking into account the deviations of inflation rate from the target and actual output from its potential (Taylor, 1995). The rule is specified as follows:

$$r = p + .5y + .5(p - 2) + 2$$

where

r is the federal funds rate

p is the rate of inflation over the previous four quarters

y is the per cent deviation of real GDP from a target.

The last term 2 is the 'equilibrium' real rate.

The rule requires the federal fund's rate to be raised, if inflation increases above the target or if real GDP rises above trend GDP. In the original version, the weights of deviation from target inflation and potential output were assumed to be the same at 0.5. While the rule is intuitively appealing, there are serious problems in determining the values of the coefficients. There is also a lot of judgement involved in determining the potential output and target inflation rate. However, the rule offers a convenient way of determining when the central bank should act. The dilemma of central banks, however, arises if the inflation rate is above its target and the actual output is below potential. The first situation would require the central bank to raise the policy rate while the latter phenomenon would require it to lower the rate. In this context, the value of the parameters matters very much.

Threshold Level of Inflation

Another way of reconciling the conflicting objectives of price stability and economic growth in the short run is through estimating the 'threshold level of inflation', a level beyond which costs of inflation begin to rise steeply and affect growth. It is this inflation threshold that will provide some guidance to the policymakers. Below and around this threshold level of inflation, there is greater manoeuvrability for the policymakers to take into account other considerations. Interestingly, the Chakravarty Committee regarded the acceptable rise in prices as 4 per cent (RBI, 1985). This, according to the committee, will reflect changes in relative prices necessary to attract resources to growth sectors. I had estimated that in the Indian context, inflation rate should not exceed 6 per cent, if we had to avoid adverse consequences (Rangarajan, 1998b). There is some amount of judgement involved in this, as econometric models are not in a position to capture all the costs of inflation. This approach provides some guidance as to when the policy has to become tight or to be loosened. Possibly we need to re-estimate the equations from time to time to see if the same relationship holds. It is also necessary for the policymakers to note that this order of inflation is higher (around 6 per cent) than what the industrial countries are aiming at. This will have some implications for the exchange rate of the currency. While the open economy helps to overcome domestic supply shocks, it also imposes the burden to keep the inflation rate in alignment with other countries.

Inflation Targeting

The concept of a threshold level of inflation leads to another critical issue that is being debated in many countries—whether countries should adopt inflation targeting as a goal of monetary policy. Inflation targets give in a sense greater precision to the concept of price stability. This framework would require that the monetary authorities should keep inflation within the target level. Since 1990, when it was first adopted by the Reserve Bank of New Zealand, there has been a widespread adoption of inflation targets by several central banks. Some twenty-eight central banks since then have adopted inflation targeting. Many regarded such a system to be quite durable, until the 2008 international financial crisis. Writing before the crisis, Marvin Goodfriend (Goodfriend, 2007) had titled his essay 'How the World Achieved Consensus on Monetary Policy'. In fact, he wrote, 'The spread of explicit or implicit inflation targeting has demonstrated its virtues. The new working consensus on monetary policy has helped to reduce the volatility of both inflation and output.' With respect to price stabilization, a question that is sometimes raised is whether the target of stabilization is the inflation rate or price level. Obviously, price level targeting and inflation targeting have very different implications for the time path of the variance of prices. In inflation targeting, bygones are bygones. It does not require overshoots or undershoots to be fully made up. It is easier to operate inflation targeting than targeting a price level.

The adoption of inflation targeting by India has given rise to many doubts and concerns. The new monetary policy framework requires RBI to maintain consumer price inflation at 4 per cent with a margin of + or − 2 per cent. Thus, in a sense, it is flexible targeting. The amendment to RBI Act also provides for the setting of a Monetary Policy Committee that will determine the policy interest rate in order to abide by the inflation mandates.

Conflict with Other Objectives

Does the focus on inflation targeting by monetary authorities mean a neglect of other objectives such as growth and financial stability? Hardly so. What inflation targeting demands is that when inflation goes beyond the comfort zone, the exclusive concern of monetary policy must be to bring it back to the target level. When inflation is within the comfort zone, authorities can comfortably look to other objectives. This at least is my interpretation of inflation targeting. It is sometimes said that the crisis of 2008 has sounded the 'death knell' of inflation targeting. It is not so. Many monetary authorities in the West failed to grasp the true meaning of inflation targeting. The rise in asset prices, which happened prior to 2008, should have alerted monetary authorities and they should have taken action to raise the interest rate even though consumer prices were low. It is a different question whether a rise in the interest rate in those circumstances would have worked. As I said earlier, control of inflation becomes the exclusive concern only when inflation goes beyond the limits set.

It is also important to observe that the objective of control of inflation is not independent of the objective of growth. For example, the Amendment Act of 2016 relating to RBI says, 'whereas the primary objective of monetary policy is to maintain price stability while keeping in mind the objective of growth' (RBI, 2016). This is more or less the statement in almost all countries which had adopted inflation targeting. It is interesting to see the minutes of RBI's Monetary Policy Committee. Before taking a decision on price rates, discussions have centred on output gap, extent of liquidity, likely trends in GDP and possible supply shocks on prices. Without taking away the importance of price stability as the prime objective, there is no exclusion of considerations of growth.

Ability to Control Inflation

Can RBI, or for that matter any central bank, effectively implement an inflation mandate? Do they have enough instruments to achieve the goal? The ability of the central banks to control inflation when such inflation stems from excess demand is normally conceded. It is when inflation is triggered by supply shocks that some doubts are raised. Such supply shocks are most common in countries like India where agricultural production is subject to the vagaries of nature. Even when inflation is triggered by food inflation, monetary policy and fiscal policy have a role to play. If food inflation lasts long, it gets generalized. Wages rise, leading to general cost-push inflation. If the headline inflation exceeds the acceptable level, monetary policy must act at least to ensure that the return on financial assets is positive in real terms. In a situation of supply shocks, it may take longer for monetary policy to bring inflation down. Our experience with inflation post 2009–10 is a good example of this. That is why the inflation mandate as already mentioned must provide for a range and a time frame for adjustment, which should not be too short. Nevertheless, monetary policy must act irrespective of what triggered inflation, particularly when inflation goes beyond the comfort zone. Obviously, supply-side management is needed in situations of supply shock and that should be the responsibility of the government.

There is, however, an asymmetry in the way monetary policy functions. Monetary policy is able to better handle a rise in inflation than deflation. There is the famous observation of Tarshis, which says that the central banking system is equipped with efficient brakes but the accelerator is uncertain (Tarshis & Furniss, 1947). It is basically a case of the old saying, 'You can take the horse to the pond but cannot compel it to drink.' Most developed countries today are concerned more with the role of monetary policy in reviving the economy. There is a general belief that inflation continues to remain low despite expansionary policies to stimulate the economy—a slope in the shape of the Phillips curve.

The neutral interest rate is also deemed to have fallen. As the vice chairman of the Federal Reserve System said recently, 'All else being equal, a fall in neutral rates increases the likelihood that a central bank's policy rate will reach its effective lower bound (ELB) in future economic downturns. That development, in turn, could make it more difficult during downturns for monetary policy to support spending and employment, and keep inflation from falling too low' (Clarida, 2019).

The possibility of inflation rising to unacceptable levels is not ruled out in developing economies. Obviously, a generally low inflation globally has its complications. Central banks in developing economies still have to be vigilant on the inflation front.

Transmission Mechanism

The transmission mechanism plays a critical role in the conduct of monetary policy. There are two components in this mechanism. The first is how far the signals sent out by the central bank are picked up by the commercial banks and the second is how far the signals sent out by the banking system influence the real sector. The former is called the 'inside leg' and the latter the 'outside leg'. In advanced economies, the banks' reaction to the signals sent out by central banks is immediate. In fact, the financial structure is so well knit that even changes in the short end of the market spread quickly to the long end. Banks in India normally react quickly to RBI's signals. But it does happen, as it is happening now, that for a variety of reasons, including balance sheet problems, the banks may be unlikely to act according to the signals of RBI. The burden of NPAs is not giving enough space to banks to lower interest rates, even when the signal from the central bank is to lower it. The impact of banks' actions on the real sector is a much larger question. The speed and extent of change depends on a variety of factors. Recently, in the Indian context, questions have been raised whether a change in interest rates will have the expected effect on prices or output. Many studies have been done in India and elsewhere to understand the impact of interest rates on investment demand and consumption demand. It is normally found that the interest rate affects those sectors like housing, where repayments cover a long period. In studying the impact on prices, most econometric models use the money supply or an equivalent liquidity measure to understand the impact of monetary policy. Until recently, such liquidity measures in the Indian context have been found to be good explanatory variables. Post 2008, when the interest rate fell close to zero, 'quantitative' easing became the prime instrument. Even when monetary authorities signal changes through adjustments in the policy rate, steps will have to be taken by them to act on liquidity. Central banks cannot act like King Canute. They cannot order interest rates. They must act on liquidity such that the proposed changes in the policy rate stick. Thus, 'availability' and 'price' are interrelated. RBI must choose an appropriate measure of liquidity to monitor. In steering monetary policy, the two—liquidity and price (interest rate)—must be taken together.

Very often, liquidity is being talked about in terms of funds placed by banks with RBI or borrowed from RBI. These are for very short periods and can be treated as temporary liquidity. But the focus must also be on 'durable liquidity'. The older term for durable liquidity was money supply. To bring about significant changes in the system, RBI must pay attention to durable liquidity (Rangarajan & Samantaraya,

2017). Some measure of durable liquidity is much needed. The best choice is reserve money.

In the evolution of monetary policy in India, in the 1970s and 1980s, monetary authorities tried to influence the level of credit to achieve the objectives in mind. In fact, the attempt was to ensure that the government had enough access to credit to meet its plan efforts. That was how SLR was raised from time to time. Also, bank credit was pre-empted for certain sectors, which came to be described as the priority sector. There were, however, periodic bouts of inflation and they had to be dealt with. The interest rates were directly regulated. An attempt was made in the latter half of the 1980s to regulate the money supply in order to keep inflation under control. The early 1990s saw a big change in the institutional framework in which monetary policy operated. With the dismantling of the administered structure of interest rates, interest rate emerged as a policy variable. Money supply targeting served a useful purpose not only in India but also elsewhere as long as there was stability in the demand function for money. As Bernanke and Mishkin point out, 'Using an intermediate target such as money growth is acceptable in an optimal control framework only if the intermediate target contains all information relevant to forecasting the goal variable; in this extreme case, using the intermediate target is equivalent to targeting the forecast of the goal variable' (Bernanke & Mishkin, 1997).

The choice of policy variable, whether it is the quantity or price, depends on a number of factors. As John Taylor mentioned, 'While quantities are no less important than prices in models of financial markets—as in the most basic supply and demand model of any market— it turns out that measurement problems have forced econometric modelers away from the quantity of credit and foreign exchange toward the prices of these items' (Taylor, 1993).

Even with respect to price variables, it is not clear whether the relevant interest rate is short term or long term. This was the old controversy between Hawtrey and Keynes, the former arguing that monetary policy works through changes in inventories and the latter arguing it acts through changes in investment. As mentioned earlier, changing the policy rate will be an empty gesture unless action is taken to affect quantity.

Exchange Rate Stability

While traditionally the trade-off among the objectives has been discussed in relation to price stability and growth, of late, exchange rate stability and financial stability have also emerged as competing objectives. Monetary authorities in the developed world have generally let the market determine exchange rates. However, there have been several exceptions. There have been occasions when central banks in the developed countries have intervened, sometimes in a concerted way when exchange markets have become volatile. However, in general, exchange rate considerations have not been important in the formulation of monetary policy in these countries. The general argument is that flexible exchange rates give autonomy to central banks in the formulation of monetary policy.

In the Indian experience, with the market-determined exchange rate system introduced in 1993, there have been several occasions when RBI had intervened strongly to prevent volatility. While the stated policy of RBI has been to intervene in the market only to prevent volatility, interventions have assumed a new dimension with the influx of large capital inflows. These interventions in the foreign exchange market were aimed at preventing the appreciation of the rupee. The consequent accumulation of reserves has a monetary impact. The money supply expands with the accumulation of reserves unless offset by sterilization, which has to take the form of either normal OMOs or through the issue of special sterilization bonds. The extent of accumulation of reserves and the degree of sterilization influence the growth of the money supply. The monetary authority has to take a view on the permissible expansion of the money supply in the context of large capital inflows. If there are limits to sterilization, the accumulation of reserves would have to be limited.

As objectives of monetary policy, exchange rate stability and price stability play complementary roles in a regime where the exchange rate is by and large determined by the current account of the BOP. The Purchasing Power Parity theory essentially enunciates that the external value of the currency is determined by the internal value. Under these circumstances, monetary policy geared to domestic price stability helps to avoid disruptive adjustments in the exchange rate. Stabilizing the real exchange rate under these circumstances essentially means that price stability and exchange rate stability are two sides of the same coin. However, the condition where the exchange rate is largely determined by the current account is no longer true even in developing economies. Capital inflows have come to dominate BOP and the exchange rate may begin to appreciate, even if there is a significant current account deficit because of large capital flows. Obviously, no monetary authority can afford to ignore prolonged volatility or misalignment in the foreign exchange market. The need for intervention in those circumstances becomes obvious. However, the framework evolved must be such that large interventions to stabilize the exchange rate have to be an exception than the rule. Price stability considerations must be kept in view while intervening in a big way.

Financial Stability

Increasingly, macroeconomic stability as an objective of central banking is closely linked to financial stability. It is easy to see how the two are interlinked. Financial stability broadly implies the stability of the important institutions and markets forming the financial system. Key institutions need to be stable, that is, there should be a high degree of confidence about meeting the contractual obligations without interruption or outside assistance. While the complementarity between the objectives of macro stability or price stability and financial stability is easily recognized, one must also be conscious of the potential cases of conflict between the two objectives. Normally, price stability is favourable to the development of financial products and markets.

Prior to the 2008 financial crisis, the link between financial stability and monetary policy was not clearly perceived. Most central banks treated financial stability as an extension of the regulatory responsibilities, even as monetary policy primarily focused on inflation control. Financial stability considerations did not generally play a major role in the formulation and implementation of monetary policies. There was only an imperfect understanding of the fact that financial stability is necessary for effective transmission of monetary policy. Disturbances in the market can make the standard interest rate policies much less effective. We need to know more on how to incorporate financial factors in the standard model of the transmission mechanism.

There is a raging debate going on as to whether the 2008 financial crisis in the West was precipitated by monetary policy failure or regulatory failure. It has been argued that lax monetary policy led to low interest rates, which caused many distortions in the system culminating in the crisis. The macro conditions preceding the crisis included low real interest rates due to the Great Moderation with a long period of very stable growth and stable low inflation. This led to systematic underestimation of risks and very low risks premia in financial markets. Those who argue that the crisis was triggered by regulatory failure point to lax regulation and supervision that led to increased leverage, regulatory arbitrage and less due diligence in loan origination. Those who argue that monetary policy was not responsible for the crisis only concede that a low interest rate regime could have at best facilitated an environment of high risk-taking. They also doubt whether a different monetary policy could have prevented the crisis. The key issue, however, is the role of monetary authorities in the context of rising asset prices. Should they intervene, and, if so, in what manner? The policy of clean up after the bubble burst rather than taking preventive action was a choice that cost the economies heavily. When the bubble explodes, it becomes the responsibility of the central banks to restore confidence in the market. There is no doubt that asset prices should be considered as important inputs in monetary policy formulation. Obviously, price stability alone is not enough to achieve financial stability. It was fortunate that in the post-crisis period, sharp reductions in interest rates were facilitated by declining inflation. It was a comfortable coincidence. A rising inflation in that context would have made the task very difficult. Even as monetary policy encompasses financial stability as part of its mandate, the major responsibility with respect to financial stability still rests with regulation and supervision. It is ironic that a serious regulatory failure should have happened at a time when extensive discussions were being held at Basel and elsewhere to put in place a strong regulatory framework. Many central banks were preparing financial stability reports, even as the Financial Stability Forum (FSF) was set up. There were many shortcomings in the financial system of the industrially advanced countries. The 'soft touch' approach left many segments of the financial markets go without adequate supervision. The distorted incentives for commercial and investment banks to increase the leverage had to be plugged. The 2008 crisis in the US and other advanced countries is a reflection of both monetary policy and regulatory failures. While regulatory failure bore the primary responsibility, monetary policy played a facilitating role. We need to draw appropriate lessons from the crisis. The regulatory framework needs to incorporate both micro and macro prudential indicators. Distortions in the financial markets not only affect the effective functioning of the transmission mechanism of monetary policy but also have a direct impact on the real sector as the 2008 crisis showed.

Rules and Discretion

To get back to monetary policy, yet another issue is whether the authorities should be guided by rules. The issue of 'rules versus discretion' has been discussed extensively in the literature (Pierce & Tysome, 1985). In fact, the issue applies not only to monetary policy but also to other policy instruments. As early as 1936, Henry Simons took a fundamental position in favour of rules. He considered it as part of 'liberal faith'. He wrote, 'The liberal creed demands the organization of our economic life largely through individual participation in a game *with definite rules*. It calls upon the state to provide a stable framework of rules within which enterprise and competition may effectively control and direct the production and distribution of goods . . . It is this danger of substituting authorities for rules which especially deserves attention among students of money' (Simons, 1936). Not many will agree with the issue of 'rules versus discretion' being identified with the basics of a liberal system. Institutional discretion is not inconsistent with liberalism.

Rules can be rigid as well as flexible. The gold standard was not only an international monetary arrangement in which the value of each currency was expressed in terms of quantity of gold but also had well-laid-out rules to be followed by countries. The golden rules of the gold standard as they came to be known were rigid and the system finally collapsed. Milton Friedman proposed the rule of a fixed rate of growth in the money supply and there were no takers (Friedman, 1975). On the other hand, the Chakravarty Committee recommended a flexible monetary targeting system (RBI, 1985). The target itself was based on several variables and its operation was not rigid.

There is considerable amount of debate on what constitutes a rule. Some regard even the principle of raising the interest rate when inflation is above a level and lowering it when it is below a level as a rule, even though there may be discretion on the extent of change. Rules do not fall from the sky. They evolve out of experience and theory. Taylor's formula was not originally meant to be a rule. It was a derivation of actual experience. Later, it came to take the form of a rule. Bernanke and Mishkin argue that inflation targeting is not a rule but a framework (Bernanke & Mishkin, 1997). The flexibility in terms of the range in which inflation can fluctuate as well as the freedom given in terms of time to bring inflation back to normal give a lot of discretion to the authorities. This is a case of 'constrained discretion'. Of course, there can be bad rules. That is why policymakers need to make a choice after full discussion. Rules must recognize that there are far too many imponderables in the economy. Rules cannot be too rigid. Some flexibility must be built into the rules. On the other hand, absolute discretion throws accountability out of the window. It can even lead to suboptimal decisions (Kydland & Prescott, 1977). In the final analysis, we need both rules and discretion.

Autonomy of Central Banks

A perennial question with respect to central banking is how much independence should a central bank enjoy. In the history of central banks, almost all of them until recently were treated, in the final analysis, as subject to the control of the government. Central banks did enjoy the freedom to state their views. Most governments respected their views because of the credibility enjoyed by the heads of central banks. Particularly in the parliamentary form of government, the finance minister who was responsible for economic policy claimed that the last word on major decisions was his or hers. In fact, in 1982, the Democratic floor leader in the US Senate burst out and said, 'It is time for Congress to wrest control of monetary policy from the hands of a tiny band of monetary ideologues in the White House, the Administration and the Federal Reserve. It is time for basic economic policy once more to be set by elected officials who must bear the final responsibility.'

The argument in favour of independent central banks rests on the premise that monetary stability, which is essential for the efficient functioning of the modern economic system, can be best achieved only if the task is entrusted to professional central bankers who can take a long-term view of the monetary policy stance. Too much concern with the short term can result in 'stop-go' policies. Implicit in this kind of reasoning is the assumption that the political leadership normally tends to take too short term a view and such an approach is not conducive to ensuring stability. This is what is referred to as the problem of 'dynamic inconsistency'.

In India too, the dominance of the government over the central bank was implicit all through. Jawaharlal Nehru in his letter to Governor Rama Rau at the time of his resignation said, 'You have laid stress on the autonomy of the Reserve Bank. Certainly it is autonomous, but is also subject to the Central Government's directions . . . Monetary policies must necessarily depend upon the larger policies which a government pursues. It is in the ambit of those larger policies that the Reserve Bank can advise' (RBI, 1998).

In fact, Nehru's letter was harsh in its tone. The then finance minister sounded even more aggressive. Unfortunately, this exchange of letters sealed the relationship between the government and RBI for several decades.

In India, persons who were appointed as governors were men of erudition, scholarship and rich administrative experience. Governments listened to them. However, when the chips were down, the government had its way. It was not just a matter of 'fiscal dominance'. The government wanted RBI to consult it before any decision was taken. If the government differed, it had its way.

Section 7 of the RBI Act says, 'The Central Government may from time to time give such directions to the Bank as it may, after consultation with the Governor of the Bank, consider necessary in the public interest' (RBI, 1934). The Government of India has never used this section. Also, it always acted through other channels.

Monetary policy is part of overall economic policy. Monetary policy and fiscal policy running in different directions can impose a burden on the economy. There has to be close dialogue and coordination between RBI and the government. At the same time, there is an advantage in specifying the areas in which RBI has a clear mandate. The system of the issue of ad hoc treasury bills to replenish the cash balances of the Central government implicitly amounted to automatic monetization of the fiscal deficit. It certainly weakened the role of RBI. It was good that this system was abolished in the early 1990s. The then government and finance minister saw the rationale for the abolition of the practice and were willing to go along with RBI. This was an act of great statesmanship on the part of the finance minister. The Fiscal Responsibility and Budget Management (FRBM) Act later took it forward by preventing the entry of RBI in the primary market in government securities. In fact, the new monetary policy framework is a major step forward in enhancing the autonomy of RBI. It not only establishes the primacy of price stability as the objective of monetary policy but also gives the power to set the interest rate exclusively to the Monetary Policy Committee. As of now, the finance minister gets to know of the decision on the interest rate along with others.

Central banks like RBI perform multiple functions. They are not only monetary authorities but also regulators of the banking system. This in some ways complicates the autonomy question. As a regulator, they have only the freedom other regulators enjoy.

In determining the mandate to RBI, the government has complete authority. Once the mandate is given, RBI must be given the freedom to take such actions as it deems fit. This is sometimes called 'instrument independence' as distinguished from 'goal independence'. It is important to make the distinction between 'autonomy' and 'independence'. It is in the best interests of the government itself to cede certain areas to the central bank and let RBI act in those areas according to its best judgement.

As the developments in 2018 and 2019 have shown, the pressure of the government on RBI can come on issues unrelated to monetary policy or even regulation. The attempt to put pressure on the governor through the board was also an unwise development. It is not unreasonable to expect the government and RBI to have on occasion differing stances on monetary policy or regulation. But what is required is to demarcate in advance the areas in which each will have the final say. The new monetary policy framework is a good example. The mandate is fixed by the government after discussion and the management of the mandate is left to RBI. When all is said and done, a spirit of dialogue and accommodation must prevail.

Conclusion

Central banks, particularly in developing economies, have a special responsibility in helping to create appropriate financial institutions and widen and deepen the financial infrastructure. 'Financial inclusion' has assumed critical importance in recent years because of the failure of the system to reach out to small borrowers and vulnerable groups. RBI has played a key role in discharging this responsibility and this must continue.

Monetary policy as an instrument of policy has the chief merit of responding quickly to changes. Monetary policy influences the economy through changes in the availability and price of credit and money. There are, however, occasions when the impact is minimal. In the depression of the 1930s, because of the 'liquidity trap', monetary policy had very little influence. Post 2008, when the interest rate in advanced economies touched zero, monetary policy again was found to be weak in influencing the economy. Even unorthodox measures, such as 'quantitative easing', had only minimal effect. Monetary policy is most effective when inflation rules high because of an increase in aggregate nominal demand. Monetary controls work best in these circumstances. While monetary policy can have multiple objectives, it needs to steer in a clear direction and prioritization of objectives becomes essential. It has to create a hierarchy of objectives. The mandate of the central bank has become wider. In that sense, the contours of monetary policy are changing. This is inevitable with the increasing complexity of the system in which central banks operate. However, to deal with other objectives, such as financial stability, standard instruments of monetary policy will not be adequate. Regulation and supervision combined with an appropriate monetary stance will be necessary to maintain financial stability. Total discretion with respect to objectives will make monetary policy indeterminate. Central banks need to be transparent and explicit with respect to objectives. What is needed is a good combination of rules and discretion. Among the various objectives, such as price stability, growth and financial stability, the dominant objective for central banks, particularly in developing economies, must be price stability. Having an inflation target helps in this regard. In such a situation, inflation expectations get truly anchored. In ordinary circumstances, by maintaining price stability, a central bank can pave the way for the fulfilment of other objectives as well over the medium term. However, extraordinary circumstances will warrant extraordinary responses. It is sometimes said that central banking is neither a science nor an art but a craft. This is at best a half-truth. Central banking is no longer the application of well-known tools to well-known problems. The issues that surface are complex. We need to continually enlarge our knowledge and understanding of how the economy functions and how the different participants of the economy react to policy changes. Successful central banks are those which respond to problems with speed, tact and intelligence.

The monetary policy framework adopted by India and many other countries is correctly described as 'flexible inflation targeting'. Most of these countries set not only an inflation target but also provide a range within which it can fluctuate. This flexibility is extremely important because it emphasizes the uncertainties against which central banks have to operate. The range implies two things. First, there can be sudden and unexpected supply shocks. This has special implication for developing economies like India where agriculture is still a significant part of the economy. Advanced countries think mostly in terms of 'oil' when they talk about supply shocks. In fact, some countries, to avoid the impact of supply shocks, look at 'core' inflation, which excludes oil or any other item that may be subject to supply shocks. But supply shocks do have an effect not only on items directly affected but also other components in the retail price index. This is particularly true in the case of food inflation in countries like India. On the whole, it is better to deal with headline inflation with a range rather than excluding certain items. The range also underlies the fact that there is always a lag between monetary policy decisions and the impact on inflation. The range thus provides flexibility in terms of the time required to bring inflation back to the desired level when it deviates. It is best for economies like those of India to have a flexible inflation targeting approach. It satisfies both the objectives of price stability and growth in a coordinated way.

12

Men (and Women) and Matters

It was sometime in the middle of 1981 that I received a call in the early morning from I.G. Patel. He asked me whether I would like to be considered for the position of deputy governor of RBI. At that time, I was a professor at the Indian Institute of Management Ahmedabad (IIMA). It took a few minutes to digest the message, as I had not thought of moving out of academia. However, the offer seemed attractive and I said 'yes' after some time. After that, I heard nothing either from the government or RBI for several months. I then decided to meet IG during one of my visits to Bombay. At that meeting, IG was non-committal. I came to the conclusion that that chapter was closed. I was also in correspondence, at that time, with some foreign universities regarding a visiting position. But then suddenly in January 1982, an announcement came appointing me as deputy governor. If I remember right, I saw it first in the newspapers. Then came the call from IG saying, 'Welcome aboard.' At that time, I was teaching a course and I had to wind it up before taking the new position. The director (V.S. Vyas) gave me a year's leave and I was to decide within a year whether I would resign. The earliest I could go was in early February and I joined RBI on 12 February 1982. Thus began a new phase in my life.

The first few months at RBI were far from happy. I was looking forward to being in a position to influence monetary policy. I thought, given my background, I would be given the portfolio of the department that was in charge of monetary policy. This was not to be. I was given the two research departments of economic analysis and statistics besides the training institutions. I had known I.G. Patel for a long time, almost since 1965. In fact, I had known Mrs Patel first as both of us were at the Indian Statistical Institute (ISI), Delhi. Though many issues were discussed at the weekly meetings of top executives of RBI, ultimately the deputy governor in charge played a key role. There was one instance when a monetary policy decision was announced even without informing me, let alone consulting me. I did hint to IG my concerns. I felt that if that position continued, there was no point in my being in RBI. I had contemplated going back to IIMA. The only person in whom I confided my unhappiness was Tarapore. That is why he wrote in an article in 2011, 'It is not known that Rangarajan had seriously considered resigning from the post of Deputy Governor.' I somehow stayed on. Dr Patel was succeeded by Manmohan Singh, whom I had known from 1966, when he was working in the UN and I was teaching at New York University. Steadily, things started changing. Monetary policy, exchange rate management, management of public debt and associated functions came under my charge. I felt more comfortable. Right from the beginning, I wanted RBI to look at the broad problem of inflation from the angle of money supply and growth of the economy. Credit policy and credit allocation must be consistent with the acceptable rate of growth of the money supply. The money supply in turn was related to the increase in reserve money, which in the Indian context, was largely determined by RBI credit to government. It took some time to make RBI think along these lines. The approach was not inconsistent with credit allocation but only made the desired credit expansion fit within a monetary framework. Manmohan Singh is an outstanding economist. He is a trade specialist and is largely interested in real sector problems. Of course, he is credited with the successful handling of the inflation spiral in 1972. Manmohan Singh brought to bear on monetary policy his twin concerns with growth and inflation. Largely speaking, he held three important positions in macroeconomics. First, he was a firm believer in keeping inflation under control. Inflation control, he said at one time, was an important anti-poverty programme. Second, he did not want an overvalued rupee. He felt that the value of the rupee in terms of intervention currency must be adjusted to offset inflation differentials. And third, he was in favour of cross-subsidization of interest rates so that small borrowers paid a lower interest rate as compared to large borrowers. We worked closely because of the congruence of our views. Manmohan Singh's tenure as governor turned out to be short. At RBI he thought about long-term issues and that is why he appointed the committee to review the working of the monetary system under the chairmanship of Sukhamoy Chakravarty. He left before the report could be submitted. There were other important committees such as those on urban cooperative banks and computerization of the banking industry. Thus, Manmohan Singh had big ideas on reshaping RBI. He also took a firm position on RBI's powers on issuing licenses for foreign banks to operate in India. On this matter, I was not directly involved. But he left after two years and three months to become deputy chairman of the Planning Commission.

There was some interregnum between Manmohan Singh's departure and Malhotra's arrival. This period was filled in by my then colleague Amitav Ghosh. Both Amitav and I were appointed on the same day. But he took charge a fortnight earlier and that made the difference in making the choice!

Malhotra, when he was appointed governor, was India's executive director at IMF. Unlike his two immediate predecessors, he was not an economist by training. But he had abundant experience in dealing with economic problems. As executive director at IMF, he also had an opportunity to look at how other countries, both developed and developing, handled the various economic problems faced by them. To him, the solution to economic problems lay in applying strong common sense to the problems on hand. In his case, the application of common sense was supplemented by a long and rich experience in dealing with economic problems. Our views were similar on most of the issues relating to monetary policy and exchange rate management. As mentioned previously, the Chakravarty Committee report was handed over to him by me as Sukhamoy was abroad at that time. Malhotra went along fully with the recommendations of that committee. He was as much concerned as I was on the expansionary impact of high fiscal deficits. He repeatedly urged the government to limit its borrowings and avoid monetizing the deficit. He had a good rapport with the finance minister, more particularly with V.P. Singh. Despite this, the 1980s was characterized by an excessive flow of RBI credit to government. The simplification of the interest rate structure also had his full backing. The spate of new money market instruments that were introduced had his blessings. To reiterate what has been said before, the approach was to contain money supply growth with a view to moderate inflation without disturbing the need for credit allocation for priority sectors and a cross-subsidization of interest rates. On the exchange rate management side, the period since 1983 saw a sharp depreciation of the rupee to prevent a real appreciation of the rupee. This policy was vigorously followed as Malhotra strongly advocated such a policy. The intellectual scaffolding for these approaches both in relation to monetary policy and exchange rate management was provided by the various lectures given by Malhotra and me. Malhotra spent a long time with the deputy governors and decisions were made after a long discussion. Many of the changes made in the realm of monetary policy and monetary markets needed the consent of various departments and I must acknowledge the support given by the various deputy governors and more particularly Amitav Ghosh. Even though some new instruments were opposed initially, they finally came around to support them. Tarapore, who was then executive director working with me, was a source of strong support. He had clear ideas on monetary policy and the direction in which we should move.

In the days leading to the crisis of 1990, we worked hard to get the government to move fast. Initially, the government was in denial mode. The August 1990 letter specifically requested the government to approach international institutions. In fact, by the time we went to IMF, the damage had been done. We were in deep trouble. That had an impact on the negotiations.

It was the Chandra Shekhar government that gave permission for the negotiations with IMF. In fact, in one meeting, Chandra Shekhar asked 'what option you had left me'. Even as I was in Washington taking part in the negotiations, news came of the possible departure of Malhotra. When I returned to Bombay, I met him and, of course, talked about the news of his departure. I was told that the ostensible reason was that government wanted someone else to be at the helm to handle the crisis. Malhotra was offered a position as chairman of the Expenditure Commission, which he rejected.

Venkitaramanan took over as governor in December 1990. He played a key role in mobilizing resources to tide over the crisis. He was energetic and tapped all known friends. His dynamism was evident to everyone. We travelled together to Europe and the US to get the required support. Of course, on monetary policy, he did express certain concerns but largely continued on the same path. A restrictive monetary policy became inevitable given the circumstances. In August 1991, I left RBI to become a member of the Planning Commission. When I left RBI, I thought I was permanently leaving the institution. Venkitaramanan was doing so well that I thought he would continue for a full term of five years, even though he was appointed initially for two years. He and I kept in close touch when I was in the Planning Commission.

In a sense, for every academic, membership of the Planning Commission was an aspirational goal. That way, I was happy to move to the Planning Commission. It was a challenge to refashion the planning mechanism to be in tune with the change in policy direction and philosophy. I worked closely with the deputy chairman, Pranab Mukherjee. At no time in many of my conversations with him had he expressed any dissent from the new approach. The plan document was largely my creation since I was appointed as chairman of the Drafting Committee. Prof. Hashim also played an important role. However, Mukherjee, like many of the old-time stalwarts, would still heap praise on the past. He wouldn't want to admit that we had gone wrong. We can't fault the policymakers in the fifties and sixties for the stand they took. At that time, there was no clear model for ushering in faster growth in underdeveloped countries. The Soviet Union was the only example that stood before them. But the real mistake was the failure to reverse the policies in the seventies. Reforms were delayed by two decades. That was a big loss that was detrimental to the country's progress. Writing of the plan document took most of my time. The mathematical appendix and other relevant materials were released after I left. But they had been the basis of our plan document. An interesting aspect of the work at the Planning Commission was the discussion with the state governments at the time of determining the annual plan. What most chief ministers focused on was the size of the state plan. It depended very much on the grants from the Planning Commission and the size of the market borrowings as determined by the Planning Commission after discussion. The formal meetings of the Planning Commission with the chief minister and other representatives of the state government were preceded by meetings of the chief minister with the deputy chairman of the Planning Commission. I sat in on those meetings. Once the size of the state plan was determined, the formal meeting became a routine. While other issues were taken up in the formal meetings, these were not taken that seriously. In fact, even the National Development Council meetings to approve the plan documents were not exciting. Prepared speeches by chief ministers were read out. Occasionally, there were some dissenting issues that were raised. Sometimes at the end, there were announcements of certain committees being set up. Despite differences, the plan document was always approved. When all is said and done, the planning process essentially led to the dominance of the Centre. In fact, at a later date, I once suggested the inclusion of some state chief ministers in the Planning Commission. If Central ministers could be members of the Planning Commission, why not some chief ministers? But that suggestion did not find favour with the Centre.

My tenure at the Planning Commission was short. In early December 1992, Manmohan Singh asked me whether I could take on the role of governor, RBI. He mentioned that the government had decided not to extend Venkitaramanan's tenure. The government was apparently uncomfortable after the setting up of the JPC to inquire into the irregularities in securities transactions. It came as a bit of a surprise as Venkitaramanan had done exemplary work in dealing with the BOP crisis. I understood later that he was offered some other positions but he rejected them. I finally returned to RBI in December 1992. My mood at that time was very subdued.

The events that took place between 1992 and 1997 have already been reported. I was happy to be part of the team that had initiated and carried through the reforms. In the initial part, one had to contend with restoring the economy to normality. There were many things to be done to stabilize the economy. That part was done by the end of 1992. Tightening of monetary policy, devaluation of the rupee and shipping of gold were some of the actions to be taken from the monetary side to maintain stability. 1992 saw the introduction of banking sector reforms. But the reform agenda was long. It had to include changes in the institutional framework of central banking, development of markets, phased dismantling of the administered structure of interest rates, fundamental changes in the exchange rate mechanism, changes in capital flows and a lot of modifications in relation to the banking system and its regulation. While all of these have been dealt with in earlier chapters, in this chapter, I shall deal with only some aspects of the relationship between RBI and other agencies such as the government, the Parliament, banks and the public.

For any central bank, the relationship with the government is crucial. It depends on two things: one, the structure of the central bank as defined by the statute which established them and two, the personalities involved—the governor, the minister and the relevant Secretaries to the government. Quite often, the clash between RBI and the government is only a clash of personalities.

The period between 1991 and 1997 was a special period in many aspects. The country faced an acute economic crisis initially. The possibility of India defaulting on payment of external obligations loomed large. The crisis had to be fought on a war footing. Then came the reforms. All parts of the administration had to work together. When I came on as governor, Manmohan Singh, who had earlier been governor, was finance minister. We thus had a finance minister who fully understood the sensitivities of RBI. Dr Singh is an economist with a good understanding of India's economic problems. He had dealt with them effectively over three decades. In 1991, he broke away from the old mindset and moved on to usher in a new framework of liberalization that could unleash the energies of the country much better. That was indeed brave of him. As he mentioned in his first Budget, it was an idea whose time had come and he was ready to steer the economy in the new direction. RBI, as a central bank, has its own identity. Setting up such an institution away from the government is to maintain a certain distance from the government and to be able to act independently. In a parliamentary form of democracy, one also has to accept the fact that the finance minister ultimately is responsible to the Parliament on the management of the economy. It is in this context, as mentioned in an earlier chapter, the 'instrument independence' becomes relevant and it must rest with the central bank.

The special situation prevailing in the early 1990s brought together RBI and the government in taking care of the crisis and initiating reforms. In short, the conditions did not permit the 'luxury' of the governor and the finance minister fighting with each other! This apart, there was a continuous dialogue between RBI and the government at all levels. It was not just confined to the top levels. On the relationship between RBI and the finance minister, a question was put to Manmohan Singh in 2016 and he said,

'There have always been differences between the finance minister and the RBI governor. But in our time, the relationship was smooth. Rangarajan was a superb technocrat and I had known him for twenty to twenty-five years. During our time, when I was the finance minister, we entered into a historic agreement with the RBI on doing away with automatic monetization of the deficit. Rangarajan wanted it and I endorsed it. It was one way to ensure that financial policy was supportive of what we wanted to do. When I was the finance minister, I got on well with the RBI governor.'

Manmohan Singh was succeeded by Chidambaram. Between June 1996 and November 1997, I worked with him as governor. My relationship with Chidambaram was cordial. When he was commerce minister earlier, there was some misunderstanding about one action that I had taken to curb the dollar outflow. Chidambaram as finance minister was extremely systematic. His opinions when he agreed and disagreed were spelt out clearly. We met often; we spoke to each other often, almost daily. Thus, the exchange of views was exhaustive. On exchange rate management, he sounded a bit more on the side of a strong rupee. But I had always held the view that the rupee must settle down at a level consistent with inflation differentials.

The point to make is that there were differences between RBI and the government but these were settled through mutual discussions. The Ministry of Finance had at that time a team of outstanding officials, starting from Montek Singh Ahluwalia to Shankar Acharya, Geetha Krishnan, Ashok Desai, M.R. Sivaraman, N.K. Singh and Y.V. Reddy, who were intellectually alert and personally cooperative, and most things went through smoothly. Dialogues were based on mutual understanding and respect. RBI is an independent institution and must hold on to its views despite good personal equations.

However, the congruence of views on larger issues helped to tide over smaller differences. For example, while welcoming capital inflows, there were differences on the extent and conditions under which certain flows might be permitted. But that was sorted out. In the case of monetary policy and exchange rate management, RBI had a direct or primary responsibility. In relation to banking, there is a mixed responsibility. While RBI once again had direct responsibility for regulation, on banking development the government had a say. This was further complicated with the government owning the bulk of the banks. The situation would have been different if the government did not own the leading banks. Thus, in areas where RBI has primary responsibility, it should stand up and act consistently with the broad mandate it has. The division of labour between RBI and the government is most desirable. Of course, if there are fundamental differences on the mandate itself, the governor has to move away.

RBI's relationship with commercial banks was not only that of 'friend, philosopher and guide' but also a regulator. The first role was relevant in the context of the reforms we were initiating. The second role of regulator is a statutory obligation.

My own policy was to meet with the chairpersons of banks as often as I could. We always met them before any monetary policy meeting. That meeting was focused on one issue of monetary and credit developments. Apart from that, there were several meetings to understand the problems of banks. Banks at that point in time also needed a certain amount of hand-holding as the introduction of prudential norms did affect the balance sheets of banks adversely. We were also embarking simultaneously on reforms over a wide canvas. We had interactions with the banks on all these issues. The phasing of the reforms was largely an outcome of these discussions. The regulatory mechanism underwent a change. Details were spelt out in an earlier chapter. The introduction of offsite supervision in a systematic manner was a major step forward. The need for close interaction between banks and RBI is a necessity for smooth functioning of the system.

The effectiveness of RBI as an institution depends on the support it receives from the people who work in the institution. I did undertake a certain amount of reorganization of the institution. The annual conferences with the senior executives were extremely useful.

As mentioned elsewhere, the banking development and regulation and supervision departments underwent a change, consequent upon the establishment of the Board for Financial Supervision (BFS). I must acknowledge the support that I received from the entire staff and officers. We maintained a cordial relationship with the union, even though there were one or two strikes. The introduction of computerization did run into problems. But after the first few years, there was greater acceptance. Tarapore, who was deputy governor, worked closely with me and provided solid support and assistance to the measures taken. He was a true central banker, conscious of the role a central bank could play in moulding the economy. His commitment to inflation control was absolute. He chaired the Committee on Capital Account Convertibility and produced a report that became a standing reference on this subject. D.R. Mehta, who came from the Government of India, served as deputy governor for two years looking after banking development and supervision. He went on to become chairman of SEBI, which was a recognition of his talents and integrity. S.P. Talwar looked after these departments after D.R. Mehta left and was a great help in setting up BFS and in reorganizing departments of supervision and regulation. My association with the department of economic analysis and policy (as it was then called) and also the statistics department was close and it spanned nearly fifteen years. I must also record the support I received from V.B. Kadam, N.A. Mazumdar, A. Vasudevan, S.L. Shetty and many others. Not all of them had similar views on various problems. Some of them could even be too sharp and acerbic in expressing their opinions. Vimala Viswanathan in the early stages and later Shyamala Gopinath and Usha Thorat rendered exemplary service. Y.V. Reddy joined as deputy governor and was with me only for a year and a half. He came with rich experience in administration. He had handled the difficult BOP position in 1990 and 1991 and had worked closely with me. He was truly a pillar of strength and support to me. His subsequent elevation as governor was richly deserved and he proved himself to be one of the ablest governors of RBI.

Communication with the public has also become important. There was a time when it was the practice that governors were neither seen nor heard. Only their actions stood. Letting the stakeholders know the thinking of the central bank has become essential. There has always been a debate whether central banks, to be effective, should surprise markets. On occasion, it may be necessary. But that cannot be a general rule. Markets and other participants should have a good understanding of the central bank's approach to many problems. After every announcement of monetary policy, efforts should be made to convey to everyone the thinking behind the measures and the purpose of the measures. For example, when the decision to devalue the rupee was done in two steps in 1990, it became necessary to go out to assure all that there would be no further devaluation. If exporters felt that there could be further devaluation, there could be a tendency to postpone the bringing of earnings. Sometimes, even governors' speeches can become a source of pressure. To cite one example, while RBI had been writing about the need to dispense with monetization of the fiscal deficit, I took the opportunity to come out openly on the subject by speaking extensively on this in the Kutty Memorial Lecture in Kolkata on 17 September 1993. Apart from markets and financial institutions, there is also the need for the general public, including legislators and sometimes even judges, to understand the policies of the central bank. Of course, RBI must also be sensitive to the reactions to its own policy. With multiple news channels and other electronic communication media, the task has become increasingly harder. But there is no escape.

The relationship between RBI and the Parliament is one step removed. The nodal ministry as far as the parliamentary committees are concerned is the Ministry of Finance. However, parliamentary committees do visit RBI. The governor and other officials appear before parliamentary committees. Interaction with parliament members is necessary for both RBI and the Parliament to understand each other. The spirit of the meetings must be one of understanding. In fact, the world over, governors of central banks appear before their respective parliaments. On issues of monetary policy, the interactions are usually smooth. It is with respect to banking issues that some dissonance arises. However, it is important for parliament members to recognize the special nature of RBI. It is not a department of the government.

With the surfacing of irregularities (scams) in the securities transactions that amounted to siphoning off about Rs 5000 crore from the banking system through a nexus between stockbrokers and officials of banks, the appointment of a parliamentary committee to inquire into this became inevitable. Most of these actions violated the guidelines issued by RBI. In the guise of portfolio management, they undertook operations that were contrary to the letter and spirit of the RBI instructions. Ready forward transactions were put through without the support of underlying securities. Banks thought of this as a means of earning additional income. There was no monitoring of the end use of funds. Essentially, the funds were diverted to the stock markets, resulting in unprecedented increases in stock prices. This could not be sustained beyond a period. The JPC inquiry went on for about two years. While RBI had independently examined the problems by setting up the committee under the chairmanship of Deputy Governor Janakiraman, the proceedings of the JPC attracted much attention. When the JPC was set up, I was in the Planning Commission and I appeared before the JPC to explain the nature and nuances of the various transactions. Later, of course, when I was governor, many queries raised by the JPC had to be answered. In fact, it was necessary for the governor to have two executive assistants instead of one to take care of the additional load!

The JPC report was highly critical of RBI, the government and nationalized banks. Some of the observations were almost strictures. The period after the JPC report was published saw RBI introducing a host of measures. A good summary of these measures is given in *History* on p. 844. RBI imposed heavy fines on banks that were found to have violated the rules prescribed by RBI. The list of banks included not only nationalized banks but also a number of foreign banks. While some foreign banks appealed several times, we stood by our decision. The regulatory system, which was undergoing a change anyway, incorporated several shortcomings thrown up by the securities scam. A reference to the JPC is being made here to indicate that parliamentary intervention in banking issues is unavoidable. A pure monetary authority does not face such a problem.

What is the relationship between the management of RBI and the Central Board of Directors? Before we discuss the legal position, it is best to look back at the actual experience. The directors of the board are appointed by the Central government. There is no mention in the statute of the Central government having to consult the governor before appointing the directors. But in actual practice, such consultations do happen. Very often, the governor does send a list of names for consideration. But ultimately, it is the choice of the Central government. The statute does make a distinction between voting and non-voting members. The statute lays down certain conditions relating to the appointment of directors, their tenure and their termination. There is no mention in the statute of who should be appointed. Generally, the government tries to see that the appointment of directors represents different interests in the economy. Usually, there is a fair representation of captains of industry, academics, persons with interest in rural problems, professionals like lawyers and chartered accountants, and so on. Generally speaking, people who are appointed to the board are people of high calibre and talent. Pure party men are avoided but there have been exceptions. The quality of discussions in the board is normally good and free from acrimony. While there are some actions that need the board's approval, by and large, the importance of the board meetings lies in the expression of opinions by the various members, which acts as guidance for the management. Even though the term of a director is only four years, some directors have continued for a longer time because they can continue as members until someone is appointed to replace them. In fact, several directors appointed in 1983 continued up to 1991. The reconstitution of the board in 1994 happened when I was governor. While I was consulted, the final list was entirely that of the government. There was also one person who was a member of the Congress Party. I must, however, admit that he provided good support to the board and did not allow party interests to influence his advice. There were a few directors, mostly academics, who felt (or regretted) the board was not really a decision-making body. One was hurt that even though the board had met only a few days before the policy announcement, it was not fully taken into confidence. I found the board helpful in enabling the governor to reach decisions.

For understanding the relationship between the government and the board, we have to go to Clause 2 of Section 7 of the RBI Act. It says that 'the affairs and business of the Bank shall be entrusted to a Central Board of Directors which may exercise all powers and do all acts and things which may be exercised or done by the Bank'. However, Clause 3 says, 'Save as otherwise provided in regulations made by the Central Board, the Governor shall also have powers of general superintendence and directions of the affairs and business of the Bank and may exercise all powers and do all acts and things which may be exercised or done by the Bank.' It is argued by some that Clause 3 of Section 7 abridges the powers of the board. To me, the right way of interpretation is that both the board and the governor have concurrent powers in almost all matters. The board has members nominated by the Central government from various walks of life, including industry. It does create a problem. This can result in a conflict of interest because the actions taken by RBI could directly affect their interest. Therefore, the tradition that had evolved is that the board has largely functioned as an adviser. Two things need to be clarified in this context. First, it is not as if the board has not passed resolutions on matters that are operational and policy-oriented. The changes in the bank rate in the past had the prior approval of the board. In fact, in the weekly meetings of the Committee of the RBI board, the first resolution used to be on the bank rate. But with the governor's concurrent powers, in the past on occasion, the bank rate had been changed without going to the board. Second, strictly speaking, the board has powers to discuss and even pass resolutions and it has done so. But given the nature of the board and the interests of the members, it becomes difficult to let the board take binding decisions. It is, however, true that in the case of the Federal Reserve System in the US, the board does take decisions with voting if necessary. But then the nature of the board is very different. To summarize, Section 7 of the RBI Act is a mix of things. First, it gives powers to the board and second, it gives powers to the governor as well. But the way the relationship between the board and the governor has evolved over time in India is a good one. The board by and large has played an advisory role. Against this background, while the governor can act on his own, he must listen to what the members feel and the sense of the board must be fully reflected in his actions. The crux of the problem is that RBI, the board and the government must understand the limits to which they can push. A spirit of accommodation must prevail.

PART III

Beyond RBI

13

The Days at Raj Bhavan

As my term as governor of RBI was drawing to a close, I was planning to go back to academia for some time. That would be a fitting way of ending a career which started in academia. However, the closing months were also a difficult period. The impact of the East Asian crisis had to be dealt with. The Indian rupee was under pressure. My attention was focused on that. At that time, I.K. Gujral was prime minister. I had met him a few times to apprise him of the developments in the financial sector. A few months before my term was to come to an end, the then chief minister of Andhra Pradesh had inquired from Y.V. Reddy whether I would be available and willing to come to Andhra Pradesh as governor since he wanted a non-politician as governor. Krishna Kant was governor then and he was to be elected vice president. When Krishna Kant was elected, Chandrababu Naidu moved to get a replacement. In fact, I had not met Naidu until I was chosen as governor. The position of governor of Andhra Pradesh was left vacant for some time; some other governor was looking after it. The process of selecting a successor to me in RBI began only after it was decided that I would go to Andhra Pradesh. The finance minister did discuss with me the various possibilities. In dealing with the East Asian crisis, two factors had to be kept in mind. First, we had not allowed capital account convertibility in any big way. The Tarapore

Committee had made a number of recommendations. We were implementing them one by one depending on the conditions. We had taken the view that capital account convertibility was contingent on certain milestones being achieved. This cautious approach to capital account convertibility was a help. Second, even before I left RBI, I had let the value of the rupee fall. We wanted to make it clear that we were not wedded to a particular rate. This, I believe, enabled my successor to act without any commitment on the value of the rupee. Bimal Jalan was chosen as my successor. He came with long experience in handling economic matters. He was well grounded in theory and action and had handled many problems with consummate skill and efficiency. I had known him from the days I was deputy governor and enjoyed a cordial relationship with him.

I took the oath as governor of Andhra Pradesh on 24 November 1997. It was a bit of a spectacle. Horses and limousines jostled together. I spent some time drafting a speech that was broadcast that evening. Chandrababu Naidu was then a powerful political personality. He had a big role in shaping the government at the Centre. I had decided that my actions as governor would be strictly according to the constitutional provisions. At the time I took over as governor, Naidu was in a strong position in Andhra Pradesh also. He had a clear majority even though the route he chose to become chief minister was controversial. Without doubt, Naidu was a reformer. He was completely in sync with the liberal road chosen by Rao–Singh. He desired very much to push these ideas at the state level. He wanted to make the state industrially strong. He wanted Andhra Pradesh to be the investment destination of domestic and foreign capital. In a good measure, he succeeded. More importantly, he had a special fascination for information technology. He wanted to make Hyderabad a second Bangalore. The seed that he had sown at that time had grown and the tree is flourishing. In pursuing liberal policies and promoting information technology, I offered my help because of my background. One of his ambitions was to make Hyderabad a financial centre. Because of his influence at the Centre, he was able to get Insurance Regulatory and Development Authority (IRDA) to be located at Hyderabad. I insisted on his meeting me at least once a month and briefing me, which he did willingly. His party won a comfortable majority in the election held in 1999 and he became chief minister again. My term as governor ended in 2002, and he wanted me to continue. But I had made up my mind not to have a second term and move on to a position where I could do something on my own. In fact, it is desirable that in such constitutional positions, people are appointed for only one term.

After I took over as governor, there was the nuclear explosion experiment. At that time, the World Bank almost put a freeze on projects sanctioned to India. Andhra Pradesh also had one such project, which was already sanctioned by the World Bank. But an exception was made and the project came through. I also had some role to play in this. Thus, largely speaking, there was a willingness to listen to my advice. I have, however, some general observations to make on the role of a governor which I shall share at the end of the chapter.

The five-year period was also marked by the involvement of my wife and me in the intellectual, social and cultural life of Andhra Pradesh. My weekly schedule contained a minimum of two appearances. I spoke at various conferences. I took the initiative to speak seriously and I had prepared lectures for every occasion, which I usually wrote myself. I went to all prominent colleges in the state. There were many requests for me to speak outside the state. These were basically professional conferences in my field of economics and finance. During this period, I brought out three books. I mention all of these only to indicate that the governor as a nominal head of state can play a role in activating the intellectual environment of the state.

In influencing the cultural life of Hyderabad and Andhra Pradesh, my wife (Haripriya) played a role along with me. In Raj Bhavan at Hyderabad we had a monthly programme of classical music or dance. We extended the invitation to a wide cross section of people. We had a mix of Carnatic and North Indian classical music. Dance performances belonging to different schools—Bharatanatyam, Kuchipudi and Odissi—were held. We encouraged local artistes. As one commentator said, Raj Bhavan was converted into Raag Bhavan.

The social life of Andhra Pradesh was enriched by the deep involvement of my wife and me in the Red Cross movement. The governor of the state was always the head of the Red Cross and his wife (usually called 'lady governor', an expression I learnt only after becoming governor) was the executive head. My wife put her heart and soul into the Red Cross. The Red Cross was at the front whenever any tragedy or mishap happened. Cyclones are common in coastal Andhra Pradesh. Besides, the focus was on setting up blood banks. Blood banks are essential not only for providing blood for people undergoing surgery but also for patients suffering from thalassaemia. My wife decided on a programme of setting up a blood bank in each district. The first step was to set up one in Hyderabad and the one there bears her name. During the period of our stay, several blood banks were set up in various district headquarters. Blood donation camps were organized systematically. She was out every Saturday and Sunday to be at one blood donation camp or the other. The annual meetings of the Red Cross were organized at Raj Bhavan and on that day, the place was full of volunteers from all parts of Andhra Pradesh.

At the time of the earthquake in Gujarat, Red Cross volunteers went all the way to Bhuj and helped the local Red Cross. Out of the donations collected, two primary schools were built in Bhuj. Thus, our lives were full with a mix of activities.

During my time in Andhra Pradesh, I was also asked by the Government of India to chair a commission to study the Indian statistical system and make recommendations. When I was first asked, I was not sure whether it was consistent with my holding the position of governor. I talked to the home minister (L.K. Advani) and he felt that there was no inconsistency as the task that I was asked to perform was non-political. Since I felt the same way too, I accepted it. It was a truly gigantic task as we had to recommend the proper methodology for the collection of a vast set of data touching various aspects of the Indian economy. The two-volume report that was submitted ran to nearly 1000 pages. The commission felt that the statistical system must satisfy the three criteria of timeliness, credibility and adequacy. The members and I undertook a long and painstaking effort to produce a document that could provide clear guidance to the statistics departments at the Centre and in states on how to collect data on various variables. The commission broke new ground to provide guidance on the collection of data in the service sector.

Our commission also recommended the setting up of a national statistical commission as an apex institution to maintain the credibility of the Indian statistical system. Such a commission has been functioning through executive orders since 2005.

It so happened that during my tenure in Andhra Pradesh, I had acted as governor for varying periods in the neighbouring states of Odisha, Tamil Nadu and Kerala. Whenever a governor goes on leave, the governor of a neighbouring state is asked to act as governor of that state. I went to Kerala twice or thrice each time for a month or less. Thiruvananthapuram was a place I knew. On the first occasion, it was E.K. Nayanar who was the chief minister. On the second occasion when I went, A.K. Antony was the chief minister and at that time, there was a strike by the government servants. But the chief minister stood firm and I provided him much-needed support. I spent most of that month in Kerala rather than in Hyderabad.

I acted as governor of Odisha for more than a year. At that time, the well-known trade union leader Gopala Ramanujam was governor of Odisha. He fell sick and his condition became critical. The government did not want him to resign as he could then lose all the medical benefits he would be entitled to as governor. In fact, he had come to Chennai from Bhubaneswar. Fortunately, there were good air connections between Bhubaneswar and Hyderabad. I spent roughly one-third of the time in Bhubaneswar. There were a lot of problems in being governor of two states. The governor is the chancellor of state universities and presides over the convocations. With two states, the number of universities became very large. So I had to miss several of the convocations. Convocations provided an opportunity for a governor to interact with the faculty and deans at various universities. While addressing the Legislatures could be managed, the real problems arose with Republic Day proceedings. Normally in states while the national flag is hoisted by the chief minister on Independence Day, it is hoisted by the governor on Republic Day. This becomes impossible when one is in charge of two states. The same problem arises for the 'At Home' given in the evening. However, when I was acting as governor of Tamil Nadu, I could hold the 'At Home' both in Hyderabad and Chennai because the two places were much nearer. In any case, understanding the problems of two states became difficult without adequate physical presence.

When I was acting as governor of Odisha, the famous (perhaps the better word is notorious) cyclone of 1999 happened. When the cyclone hit, I was in Hyderabad, and it took me a few days to get to Bhubaneswar. Raj Bhavan was also damaged and the bedroom in which I normally slept was hit. I did my best to assist the state government. I really understood at that time how difficult it was to be governor of two states.

Initially, when I went to Bhubaneswar, J.B. Patnaik was chief minister. Later, Giridhar Gamang became chief minister. They had a good majority in the Legislature and the Central government gave them no problems. Gamang was a believer in astrology and numerology. He told me one day, 'I shall call on you on at 11.13 a.m.!' I was puzzled at the timing. He explained to me that was the auspicious time according to numerology!

During my tenure at Odisha, I was told by my secretary that I should visit Puri on the occasion of the Rath Festival. He told me all governors did. I was hesitant and had doubts in my mind whether a governor in a secular democracy should be present at a religious festival. Noting my hesitancy, my secretary said, 'Sir, you may not go. But if it happens that the monsoon fails this year, people will blame you and put it on your absence from the Rath festival.' That clinched it and I went.

My additional charge as governor of Tamil Nadu came under an odd set of circumstances. This was in July 2001. At that time, the governor of Tamil Nadu was the distinguished retired judge of the Supreme Court, Fathima Beevi. Jayalalitha was chief minister. She had arrested Karunanidhi late in the night and it became a controversial action. Fathima Beevi was asked to send a report by the Centre. Then, DMK was part of the Central government. Apparently the Centre was not happy with the report (this is at best a guess) and Fathima Beevi was asked to resign. It was under these circumstances I was given additional charge of Tamil Nadu. After I took over as governor, when we were discussing the events of the day, she (Jayalalitha) mentioned to me in a hurtful tone that those who criticized her had overlooked the fact that Karunanidhi, when he was chief minister, had arrested her, put her in a cell and made her climb steps when her knees were in bad shape. I was keen that normality was restored soon. Karunanidhi was released on bail. I had expected a new person to be appointed as governor soon. But that was not to be. I had mentioned to the home minister that I hailed from Tamil Nadu and it was not normal practice to appoint as governor of a state someone hailing from that state. It was, however, easy to visit Chennai from Hyderabad. I spent roughly two days a week in Chennai. The Chief Secretary used to meet me and briefed me on the developments. But very soon, there was another twist. Jayalalitha had been convicted on a corruption case. She went on appeal and she was granted bail. She was sworn in as chief minister when she was on bail. This was contested and the case was pending in the Supreme Court. The Supreme Court ruled that her appointment as chief minister was invalid. I had planned to be in Chennai on the day the judgment was to be delivered. As the judgment was delivered, I had a problem on hand. By virtue of the judgment which took immediate effect, Jayalalitha ceased to be chief minister. She came to meet me within a few hours of the delivery of the judgment. She was in a subdued mood. But she accepted the reality. I told her that her legislative party must elect a leader by the evening. The party had a clear majority in the Legislature. She demurred a bit but I explained to her the constitutional position. O. Panneerselvam was elected as leader and he was sworn in along with his Cabinet members at around 11 p.m. Everyone who took office that day did so crying. A new governor was appointed in January 2002 and it was a little more than six months after I took over.

The five-year period in Andhra Pradesh was peaceful. There was one incident of communal violence. At that time, the President of India sent a message to be watchful. I found the chief minister strongly committed to maintaining communal harmony. I visited the old city where the violence had broken out and spoke to the chief of police to maintain law and order at any cost.

While I accepted the invitation from various organizations to address them, I was careful not to visit purely religious abodes such as temples. In fact, I had visited various temples only once. One of my predecessors used to visit the Tirupati temple regularly. I had gone only two or three times in my five-year tenure. The message went around that I was a 'non-believer' and I let it go as this was partially correct. I recall here an incident. After attending a certain function in which Prime Minister Vajpayee participated, we were returning to Hyderabad. From Hyderabad, the prime minister was going to Puttaparthi to meet Sathya Sai Baba. At Hyderabad, I requested the prime minister to excuse me as I wanted to stay back. The prime minister was gracious enough to say 'yes' and he had a broad smile on his face.

While the focus of the Naidu government was on industrialization and development of information technology, it was not as if he neglected other areas. For example, the self-help group movement gathered momentum in Andhra Pradesh during this period. I had a soft corner for this movement. In fact, it was during my tenure as governor of RBI that this movement got a fillip because I allowed banks to lend to such groups as part of normal banking activity. The self-help groups initially used the banks' credit only to provide consumer loans. Later, they began to use credit to produce small consumer goods such as papads and eatables. Then, they moved on to make other goods, such as sanitary napkins. My wife and I kept a close watch on the growth of these groups. The Naidu government did provide adequate help to nurture these groups. One good thing at that point in time was they remained apolitical. Subsequently, the situation changed all over India. However, the image of Naidu as urban-oriented remained. That perhaps affected his political future. In fact, in my Republic Day addresses, I had continued to emphasize the importance of taking care of all sectors of the state economy, including agriculture.

My stay at Hyderabad would not be complete without a report of an accident. In 2011, one night when we were sleeping, a part of the ceiling above the bed fell on my wife and me. I was not affected that much but my wife was. She was bleeding heavily below the knee. The staff had heard the sound and rushed in. It was early morning and we had to rush my wife to the hospital (NIMS). We were completely shaken up. Naidu got the message and he was at the hospital by the time we reached there. The surgery took more than an hour to get the calf muscle cleaned, stitch the wound and put on a bandage. From the hospital we went to the guest house of Raj Bhavan and that was where we stayed till the end of the term. The accident attracted a great deal of attention. It also showed the love and respect with which we were held by the people of Andhra Pradesh. We later found out that the accident had happened because some cement plaster that was put on the mortar had fallen. The Raj Bhavan building had been constructed in 1936 and it was all mortar. To cover a crack in the ceiling of the bedroom, some engineer had put cement on it. I was told that cement and mortar were not friends. They did not stick together. That was the mistake and my wife paid the price. Later, the building was fixed using mortar, which, in fact, became difficult to get. The days of using mortar have receded into the past.

Finally, I must refer to the Padma Vibhushan award. When I was leaving RBI in 1997, P. Chidambaram was finance minister and he wrote to the home minister strongly recommending me for the Padma Vibhushan award. I understood later that Shankar (Acharya) had a hand in writing the note. At that time, Indrajit Gupta was the home minister. He raised an objection questioning whether the governor of a state could be given a Padma award. With due respect to the late Indrajit Gupta, I do not know whether this was the real reason or whether he had a fundamental objection to giving the award to a 'liberalizer'. Anyway, it did not go through. This issue was raised every year. In 2001, perhaps the then Cabinet Secretary and the Secretary to the President took a strong stand and it went through. Like many other things in life, this is also a game of chance. Sometimes deserving people don't get the award and sometimes non-deserving people get it. For example, in economics, P.R. Brahmanand deserved the Padma Vibhushan very much. He had a remarkable career, standing alone at times to advocate a line of thought. He was proved correct later in his views on the strategy of planning. Despite my writing more than once to give him an award, I did not succeed. Personally, the award to me was a matter of satisfaction. I felt that there was some recognition of the work I had done.

Powers of the Governor

As I was about to take over the governorship of Andhra Pradesh, I went through the constitutional provisions relating to the office of the governor. Later, as governor, I went through some of the judgments bearing on the role and functions of a governor. There were also occasions when I talked to the law officers in the Andhra Pradesh government.

We have a written Constitution unlike the UK. It helps. It is also a disadvantage if it is not comprehensive. Articles 152–162 of the Constitution deal with the various aspects of the office of the governor. Besides these, there are other articles which also deal with the functions of the governor.

One of the major decisions taken at the time of drafting the Constitution was to make the office of the governor a post of 'nomination' rather than 'election'. This has a fundamental bearing on the office of the governor. If he or she is elected, that would make the office of governor powerful. As the chief minister is also elected, such a situation would create a lot of tension. Two centres of authority can only lead to conflict. This has happened in several countries where the President and prime minister are elected. The governor of a state under the Indian Constitution is a nominal head of government. The administration is run in his name but in a parliamentary form of government, the real power is vested in the chief minister and the Council of Ministers. The governor is normally expected to act on the advice of the Council of Ministers.

The powers that a governor can exercise have been classified into four categories: (a) executive powers, (b) legislative powers, (c) financial powers, and (d) discretionary powers. Except with respect to the last category, the governor is expected to act on the advice of the Council of Ministers while exercising his powers. These powers include the power to summon the Legislature and also prorogue it, and to issue ordinances. The governor also has the power to appoint various officials, on the advice of the Council of Ministers.

Article 163 says:

'Council of Ministers to aid and advise the Governor

1. There shall be a Council of Ministers with the Chief Minister at the head to aid and advise the Governor in the exercise of his functions, except in so far as he is by or under this Constitution required to exercise his functions or any of them in his discretion.

2. If any question arises whether any matter is or is not a matter as respects which the Governor is by or under this Constitution required to act in his discretion, the decision of the Governor in his discretion shall be final, and the validity of anything done by the Governor shall not be called in question on the ground that he ought or ought not to have acted in his discretion.

3. The question whether any, and if so what, advice was tendered by Ministers to the Governor shall not be inquired into any court.'

Two comments are relevant in relation to Article 163. One, the article itself does not list what the discretionary powers of the governor are. In fact, clause (2) of the article makes it even more confusing. However, over the years, some conventions have developed. Just because the governor takes the oath to 'preserve, protect and defend the Constitution', it does not give the governor wide powers. Chief Justice A.N. Ray in his judgment in *Shamsher Singh and Another vs State of Punjab* said, 'Under the Cabinet system of Government as embodied in our Constitution, the Governor is the constitutional or formal head of the State and he exercises all his powers and functions conferred on him by or under the Constitution on the aid and advice of his Council of Ministers save in spheres where the Governor is required by or under the Constitution to exercise his functions in his discretion.' Justice Krishna Iyer in the same case went further and mentioned the areas of discretions. He wrote,

'We declare the law of this branch of our Constitution to be that the President and Governor, custodians of all executive and other powers under various Articles, shall, by virtue of these provisions, exercise their formal constitutional powers only upon and in accordance with the advice of their Ministers save in a few well known exceptional situations. Without being dogmatic or exhaustive, these situations relate to

a.   the choice of Prime Minister (Chief Minister) restricted though his choice is by the paramount consideration that he should command majority in the House;

b.   the dismissal of a Government which has lost its majority in the House but refuses to quit office;

c.   the dissolution of the House where an appeal to the country is necessitous, although in this area the Head of State should avoid getting involved in politics and must be advised by his Prime Minister (Chief Minister) who will eventually take the responsibility for the step.'

The Constitution, of course, gives to governors of North-eastern states specific powers to act in certain areas. These are explicit. In areas where they have discretion, governors' actions cannot be questioned by the judiciary. However, the court can look into whether relevant materials have been examined and if the action was mala fide. In *S.R. Bommai vs Union of India*, the Supreme Court held that the material used to come to the decision to impose President's Rule could be questioned to ensure that there was no mala fide use of power. As said by Justice Sawant, 'The validity of the Proclamation issued by the President under Article 356(1) is judicially reviewable to the extent of examining whether it was issued on the basis of any material at all or whether the material was relevant or whether the Proclamation was issued in the mala fide exercise of the power.'

Despite clarifications by the Supreme Court, decisions of certain governors regarding the choice of the chief minister or recommendations to the President to impose President's Rule have been a source of controversy. One other area where there is continued confusion is the governor's powers to delay giving assent to a bill passed by the Legislature. There seems to be no specific limit set on how long a governor can delay!

Governors have to understand not only the powers they have but also their limitations. Purely political appointees have a problem in dealing with chief ministers who do not belong to their party. There is a tendency to administer pinpricks. The idea that the governor is an 'agent of the Central Government' is also repugnant. Quite clearly, two centres of power in the state were not contemplated in the Constitution. Furthermore, individuals who are appointed as governor have often held responsible positions in the past. They were 'hands-on' administrators and were used to exercising power. The 'itch' to act is evident sometimes. This is what they must learn to control.

The Constitution implies a continuous dialogue between the governor and the chief minister. The Constitution specifically states that all relevant information asked for by the governor must be given to him. But I also know some chief ministers are reluctant to seek advice or even have a conversation with the governor on state matters. This attitude is also wrong.

A public spat between a governor and a chief minister is undesirable. Whoever starts it makes a serious mistake. If the governor disagrees with what the chief minister is doing, he or she can discuss it with the chief minister or even write about it in their letter to the President. Beyond that, he or she cannot make a public display of disagreement.

When all is said and done, despite all the limitations, the governor has an important role to play in the state. He or she is the 'nominal head' and not a 'figurehead'. The governor can play a constructive role by virtue of his or her own abilities. Governors should position themselves in such a way that the chief ministers are able to learn from them.

We have inherited the parliamentary form of government from Britain. It is not necessary to follow all their practices blindly. One such practice is the address of the governor (or President) at the beginning of each new year. We are too fixated on the notion of 'my Government'. The government is really run by the prime minister at the Centre and the chief minister in each state. There is no point in putting in the mouth of the governor the words of the chief minister. I took over as governor of Andhra Pradesh in late November 1997 and my first address was in January 1998. That session ended in pandemonium. The Congress Party, which was in the opposition, led the charge. The speech was torn and I had to end the address abruptly and leave. This was meant to be a rebuke of the government as I had personally been in Andhra Pradesh less than two months. More recently, the governor of a state, before reading a paragraph of the address, said, 'I am going to read this para (paragraph 18) because the Honourable Chief Minister wants me to read this, although I hold the view that this does not come under the definition of the policy or programme.' There was also a case where the governor of a state had to read a speech in which almost every alternate paragraph mentioned the chief minister by name and praised the work of the chief minister. These are avoidable. In the case of the Centre, the President's address is followed by the Budget where within a month one hears a repetition of the government's achievements. If the government really wants to present what it proposes to do a year ahead, it would be appropriate for the prime minister at the Centre and the chief minister at the state to give an address that can be debated. There is no need for the governor to speak in the chief minister's voice.

The governor of a state is the chancellor of all the state government universities. This is according to the statute, and it also creates a difficult situation. After all, higher education is a part of the domain of the state government. In that sense, it is no different from other areas of public administration. The chancellor has certain powers in appointing the vice chancellor. As in many states, in undivided Andhra Pradesh as well, the procedure was that the government, on the basis of the recommendations of a search committee, would present to the governor a panel of three names from which he or she would select one. At the time when N.T. Rama Rao was chief minister, there was a difference of opinion between him and the governor on the choice of the vice chancellor for a university. Since the Act provided for the governor to ultimately choose one name from the panel, the governor had her way. As a consequence, N.T. Rama Rao, who had a commanding majority in the Legislature, amended the Act to permit the government to recommend only one name to the governor. It is true that governors can play an effective role in improving the quality of higher education. But too active a role can lead to conflict.

President Venkataraman in his memoirs, *My Presidential Years*, compared the President of India to an emergency light. It comes into operation only if the normal power fails. That is a pretty good analogy.

P.S.: This chapter was written almost three years ago. Since that time, there have been several explosive interactions between the governor and chief minister in several states. Some of these can be avoided by suitable clarification provided by the Supreme Court or by constitutional amendment. For example, on the time taken in giving consent to a statute passed by the Legislature, a limit can be set. It is my view that the two power centres situation is not the intention of the Constitution.

14

Fiscal Federalism: At the Finance Commission

As my term as governor of Andhra Pradesh was drawing to a close, I had planned to go back to Chennai and perhaps get involved with some academic activities. I had decided against a second term in Andhra Pradesh, even if it was offered. But then it so happened that it was also the time when the government was constituting the Twelfth Finance Commission and was looking for a chairman. The previous practice was largely to look for a seasoned politician with experience in finance to be chosen as chairman. Of course, there were exceptions. Even for the Eleventh Finance Commission, the then government chose Prof. Khusro, a well-known economist as chairman. The government in 2001 also decided to follow this practice and approached me. I accepted the offer. However, my departure was delayed until the government decided on my successor as governor of Andhra Pradesh. Once that decision was made, I left Hyderabad for Delhi. In fact, even though a Finance Commission is appointed every five years, the Government of India is ill-prepared every time for accommodation of the office and chairman and members. This is indeed a pity. A lot of time and energy is spent by every commission to find accommodation and get the commission going. I had my own quota of problems. A suitable

247

house was not available. I had to stay more than a month at the AP guest house in Delhi. I had to accept whatever house was available. All these are avoidable.

Finance commissions have a long history. Our commission was preceded by eleven such commissions. During the time of our commission, we celebrated the diamond jubilee. The then President of India, A.P.J. Abdul Kalam, inaugurated the function. We had convened, at that time, a meeting of eminent economists and experts in public finance. We also had a meeting of past chairmen and members of the commission. The concern always is on determining how much of the tax revenues of the Centre should be shared with states and how that amount should be distributed among states. Though put this way, the issues may look simple. But that is not the case. Complex issues of fiscal federalism are involved. There is, however, no mathematical model that can derive the numbers. A lot of subjectivity is involved in choosing the criteria and giving them weight. Before going into the issues that the Twelfth Finance Commission had to address, an outline of the broad picture about fiscal federalism and fiscal transfers may be in order.

Federalism, as a Form of Government

Federalism is an old concept. Its origin is mainly political. It is well known that the efficiency of government depends, among other factors, on the structure of government. Federalism as a form of government has, therefore, been concerned with functions and instruments that are best centralized and those that are best placed in the sphere of decentralized levels of government. Particularly in large countries, it has been felt that sub-national governments are required and that only a federal structure can efficiently meet the requirements of people from different regions. Underlying this proposition is the premise that preferences vary from region to region. Thus, the rationale of federalism lies in promoting welfare through decentralization and sub-national autonomy in combination with the benefits of a large market.

In our own country during the Independence struggle, provincial autonomy was regarded as an integral part of the freedom movement. However, after Independence, several compulsions, including defence and internal security, led to a scheme of federalism in which the Centre assumed greater importance. Also in the immediate post-Independence period when the Centre and all states were ruled by the same party and when many of the powerful provincial leaders migrated to the Centre, the process of centralization gathered further momentum. Economic planning at a nation-wide level and the allocation of resources by a central authority also helped this centralizing process.

Fiscal Federalism

Fiscal federalism is the economic counterpart to political federalism. Fiscal federalism is concerned, on the one hand, with the assignment of functions to different levels of government and on the other, with appropriate fiscal instruments carrying out these functions. It is generally believed that the Central government must provide national public goods that render services to the entire population of the country. A typical example cited is defence. Local governments are expected to provide goods and services whose consumption is limited to their own jurisdictions. The argument here is that the output of such goods and services can be tailored to meet the preferences and circumstances of the people in that jurisdiction. Such a process of decentralization enhances the economic welfare above that which could result from the more uniform levels of such services that are likely under a centralized regime. Apart from the provision of national public goods, the Central government is to be vested with the responsibilities for economic stabilization and for income redistribution. While income redistribution to some extent is possible even within sub-national government jurisdictions, a true redistribution effort is possible only at the national level. An equally important question in fiscal federalism is the determination of the specific fiscal instruments that would enable the different levels of government to carry out their functions. This is the 'tax-assignment problem' which is discussed extensively in the literature. In determining the taxes that are best suited for use at different levels of government, one basic assumption that is made is in relation to the mobility of economic agents, goods and resources. Very often it is assumed that while there is no mobility across national barriers, there is much greater mobility at decentralized levels. This proposition holds good only partly in an era of globalization. Once again, it is generally argued that the decentralized levels of government should avoid non-benefit taxes on mobile units. This has the implication that the Central government should have the responsibility to levy non-benefit taxes and taxes on mobile units or resources. Building these principles into an actual scheme of assignment of taxes to different levels of government in a Constitution is indeed very difficult. Different Constitutions interpret differently what is mobile and what is purely a benefit tax. For example, in the US and Canada, both federal and state governments have concurrent powers to levy income tax. On the contrary, in India, income tax is levied only by the Central government though shared with the states. It is interesting to note that the revenues collected by the federal or Central government vary very sharply among different countries. For example, the federal government collects 69 per cent of the total revenue in Australia, 65 per cent in India and 48 per cent in Canada. Thus, the traditional issues in fiscal federalism have been how to determine the assignment of taxes and responsibilities to different levels of government. Recognizing the possibility of imbalance between resources and responsibilities, many countries have a system of intergovernmental transfers. In fact, intergovernmental transfers constitute a distinctive economic policy instrument in fiscal federalism. For example, intergovernmental transfers as a percentage of provincial or state revenues have been 41 per cent in Australia, 40 per cent in India and 20 per cent in Canada in recent years. Correcting vertical and horizontal imbalances has been a major concern with which fiscal federalism has wrestled. While actual designs of fiscal transfer systems differ across federations, these constitute experiments in search of satisfying the twin objectives of equity and efficiency in a multi-tiered system of government. Conceptually, the emphasis has been on providing enough resources at the sub-national level to ensure the provision of a set of services at comparable or minimum acceptable levels in all jurisdictions.

Fiscal Transfers

The roots of fiscal federalism in India go back to the Government of India Acts of 1919 and 1935. While the Act of 1919 provided for a separation of revenue heads between the Centre and the provinces, the 1935 Act allowed for the sharing of the Centre's revenues and for the provision of grants-in-aid to provinces. The Indian Constitution carried these provisions a step forward by providing for a Finance Commission to determine the distribution between the Union and the states of the net proceeds of taxes and the grants-in-aid to be provided to the states that are in need of assistance. While the constitutional provisions relating to the functions of the Finance Commissions have remained unchanged, one notable change in the framework of federal fiscal arrangements was brought out by the Eightieth Amendment, which broadened the ambit of the shareable Central taxes. The enlargement of the shareable pool to cover all Central taxes, except those listed in Articles 268 and 269 and earmarked cesses and surcharges, has enabled states to share in the overall buoyancy of taxes. It has also provided greater stability to resource transfers as fluctuations in individual taxes are evened out. With the 73rd and 74th Amendments to the Constitution, which have provided constitutional support to the process of decentralization, the Finance Commissions are also required to suggest measures to augment the resources for the panchayats and municipalities.

The Indian Constitution lays down the functions and taxing powers of the Centre and states. It is against this background that the issues relating to the correction of vertical and horizontal imbalances have been addressed by every Finance Commission, taking into account the prevailing set of circumstances. Central transfers to states are not, however, confined to the recommendations of the Finance Commissions. There are other channels, such as those through the Planning Commission until recently, as well the discretionary grants of the Central government.

Fiscal transfers require to be guided by certain definitive principles. Most analysts agree that a good transfer system should serve the objectives of equity and efficiency and should be characterized by predictability and stability. Equity can be conceptualized and understood in a number of ways both with respect to its vertical and horizontal dimensions. The considerations that should go into determining the distribution of transferred resources among states have been examined in great detail by the various Finance Commissions. Equity issues have dominated such discussions as they should. The effort has been to identify variables that reflect the equity concerns. Equity factors have had a maximum weight in resource transfer formulae. In designing a suitable scheme of fiscal transfers, three considerations seem relevant: needs, cost disability and fiscal efficiency. Needs refer to expenditures required to be made but not met by the local government's own resources. Cost disabilities refer to such characteristics of a state that necessitate more than average per capita cost in service provision due to factors that are largely beyond its control, such as large areas with low density of population, hilly terrains, poor infrastructure and proneness to floods and droughts. Fiscal efficiency encompasses parameters like maintaining revenue account balance, robust revenue effort, economies of expenditure linked to efficient provision of services and the quality of governance. Equity considerations must aim for ensuring the provision of selected services at minimum acceptable standards across the country. It is seen that on average, the low-income states spend only half of the average per person expenditure of high-income states in social services. In a competitive environment, states that are able to access the market better are likely to grow faster than others. The growth experience of the 1990s shows that developed states with a broad industrial base and developed market institutions and infrastructure have performed much better than those without them. The transfer system has also to take this factor into account. At the same time, 'efficiency' in the use of resources should be ensured and promoted. States that perform more efficiently in the delivery of services or raise more revenues relative to their tax bases should not be penalized. The task of formulating a sound transfer system has to establish a fine balance between equity and efficiency, a system where fiscal disadvantage is taken care of but fiscal imprudence is discouraged.

Issues before the Twelfth Finance Commission

Article 280 (3) stipulates the duties of the Finance Commission. These are:

i.   The distribution between the Union and the States of the net proceeds of taxes which are to be, or may be, divided between them under Chapter I Part XII of the Constitution;

ii. allocation between the States of the respective shares of such proceeds;

iii. the principles which should govern the grants-in-aid of the revenues of the States out of the Consolidated Fund of India and the sums to be paid to the States by way of grants-in-aid of their revenues under Article 275 of the Constitution for purposes other than those specified in clause (1) of that article;

iv. measures needed to augment the Consolidated Fund of a State to supplement the resources of the panchayats and municipalities in the State on the basis of the recommendations made by the Finance Commission of the State; and

v. any other matter referred to the commission by the President in the interests of sound finance.

The terms of reference of the Twelfth Finance Commission, besides stipulating the responsibilities enshrined in the Constitution, also required the commission to review the state of the finances of the Union and the states and suggest a plan for restructuring public finances with a view to restoring budgetary balance, maintaining macroeconomic stability and bringing about debt reduction along with equitable growth. This is somewhat similar to what the Eleventh Finance Commission was asked to do.

The balancing of resources against responsibilities is qualitatively different, when governments at all levels are nursing large and rising revenue deficits than when the Centre and some of the states have a surplus. There were days when some of the states had a pre-devolution surplus. In 1988–89, the combined revenue deficit of the Centre and states was 2.9 per cent of GDP at current market prices. This rose to 3.6 per cent in 1994–95; 6.3 per cent in 1999–2000 and 7 per cent in 2001–02. There has been some reduction subsequently. The approach and recommendations of the Twelfth Finance Commission can be briefly summarized under five heads.

Vertical Transfers

In the scheme of fiscal transfers, the correction of vertical imbalance is, to some extent, based on judgement. An assessment has to be made of the gap between resources and responsibilities at the two levels of government. Sometimes, it is not recognized that the share of states in the combined revenue receipts undergoes a radical change after tax devolution. For example, during the Twelfth Finance Commission's period (2005–10), the share of states, which was 36.10 per cent before transfers, became 61.55 per cent after transfers. Correspondingly, the share of the Centre came down from 63.81 per cent to 38.45 per cent. There has been considerable stability in those ratios over a period of time. It is important to note that during this period, the shares of the Centre and states in the total revenue expenditure were 47.59 per cent and 52.41 per cent respectively. D.K. Srivastava and I have shown that if the stability in the ratio of revenues going to the Centre and states after transfers is to be maintained, there is need for an upward adjustment of the share of central revenues going to states if the buoyancy of central taxes is higher than that of the buoyancy of states' taxes. It is relevant to note here that the transfer of resources from the Centre to the states happens through channels other than the Finance Commission. Until 2014, another important channel was the Planning Commission. There has been a debate whether the Constitution recognizes any channel other than the Finance Commission for transfer of sources. There is one strong legal opinion that the Constitution recognizes only one channel and that is the Finance Commission. The Twelfth Finance Commission also looked at these opinions but decided to stay with the existing arrangements, which included a Planning Commission channel. Even post-liberalization, planning continued to play a role and we decided not to interfere with it. Taking into account a variety of factors including the historical trends, the commission recommended an increase in the share of states in the divisible pool of taxes to 30.5 per cent from the previous level of 29.5 per cent. This increase was also found to be necessary to provide some cushion to states whose share in the total tax devolution might go down as a result of any modifications in the formula of horizontal distribution. The commission felt that this increase could be accommodated by the Central government by pruning their activities that fall in the domain of the states. The commission had raised the indicative limit of overall transfers out of the gross revenue receipts of the Centre from 37.5 per cent to 38 per cent.

Horizontal Transfers

In the context of horizontal imbalance, the Twelfth Finance Commission felt that the equalization approach to transfers was appropriate as it was consistent with both equity and efficiency. Horizontal transfers in general are expected to achieve two types of equalization, one of fiscal capacities and the other of correcting cost differentials. Transfers for equalizing fiscal capacities are meant to ensure that all state governments have 'sufficient revenues to provide reasonably comparable levels of public services at reasonably comparable levels of taxation'. Equalization of cost differentials is required to particularly compensate states with serious disadvantages because of terrain and certain other factors. A system of equalization transfers is considered desirable as it is consistent with equity and efficiency. It puts an end to inefficient migration. It has not, however, been possible to implement this approach fully in India, as the extent of disparities in the per capita fiscal capacities of the states is too large and some of the better-off states are also in serious fiscal imbalance. In the allocation scheme recommended, the commission has endeavoured to strike a balance among different criteria reflecting deficiency in fiscal capacities, cost disabilities and fiscal efficiency. While the commission had retained, by and large, the indicators used by the Eleventh Finance Commission for determining the horizontal transfers, it altered the weights to some extent. The distance criterion combined with the criterion of population, representing together the deficiency in fiscal capacity and needs had a combined weight of 75 per cent. The cost disabilities got a weight of 10 per cent through the area criterion. The fiscal performance got a weight of 15 per cent.

Role of Grants

The Twelfth Finance Commission took a slightly different view on grants from the previous commissions. In Canada, all transfers are only through grants. In the case of Australia, even though the total quantum of transfer is determined by what is collected through value added tax, the transfer of resources is through grants. The Australian system carries the equalization principle far beyond Canada.

The Twelfth Finance Commission increased the proportion of grants to tax devolution in the scheme of transfers. Grants constituted around 19 per cent of total transfers compared to around 13 per cent in the Eleventh Finance Commission. Grants achieve certain purposes that cannot be fulfilled by tax devolution. First, they provide greater stability to revenues of states, which has become an important issue in the recent period. Second, they enable the application of the equalization principle. The Twelfth Finance Commission made an effort in this direction by focusing on education and health, which were two critical merit services. The attempt was to help states that had lower per capita expenditure on education and health than the national average. An elaborate scheme was worked out to help states that were willing to maintain a higher level of per capita expenditure. Third, special purpose and conditional grants can be given, which promote specific objectives. It is therefore necessary that, in judging the transfer to states, tax devolution and grants should be taken together into account. The coefficient of correlation between comparable Gross State Domestic Product (GSDP) per capita (average of 1999–2000 to 2001–02) and the recommended per capita transfers, comprising tax devolution and all the grants, among the general category states excluding Goa, is estimated at -0.89, which emphasizes the redistributive character of the transfers.

Debt Restructuring

The commission had recognized that the debt burden of the states was heavy. It therefore recommended a scheme of debt relief, which was in two parts. First, there was the relief that came from consolidating the past debt and rescheduling it, along with interest rate reduction. The second part consisted of a debt write-off, which was linked to the reduction in the absolute levels of revenue deficits. Both reliefs were available, only if states enacted appropriate legislations to bring down the revenue deficit to zero by 2008–09 and commit to reducing the fiscal deficit in a phased manner. With the relief that had been recommended, it should be possible for states to pursue their developmental goals with fiscal prudence. The condition imposed also mitigated the moral hazard problem. The impact of the relief was summarized by the commission as follows:

> 'In terms of our debt write-off package, if a state achieves, through a consistent performance, a zero revenue deficit by 2008–09, it will have the facilities of having all the repayments due from 2005–10 on central loans contracted up to 31.3.04 and consolidated by us written-off. The total amount which would be written-off if all states achieve revenue balance by 2008–09 is approximately Rs 32,200 crore in a period of five years.'

Institutional Changes

There were several institutional changes that were recommended, which included accounting procedures, etc. At this distance of time, I would like to refer to only two recommendations. Both relate to the broad issue of borrowing. The first one was to discard the Central government borrowing and then on lending to states. It is best to quote from the report:

'In the context of the debt burden of states, the direction in which future lending policy of the centre should move was considered by us. While there might have been some justification for the centre to act as a banker to states when market rates of interest were high and in the process of on-lending to states, an indirect subsidy was granted to states by way of concessional interest, this is no longer valid in a low-interest rates regime. In some ways, central lending to states, which is done at much higher rates of interest than the marginal cost of borrowing, results in a reverse subsidy from the states to the centre. In most federal countries, the federal government's loan intermediation role has been discontinued over the years, subjecting the states to market discipline. Such a dispensation allows the constituent units to borrow on terms that reflect their credit risk. While fiscally prudent states manage to borrow at rates lower than those offered by the federal government, the fiscally imprudent states would find their access to loan finance curtailed. We feel that it would be appropriate for states to take advantage of the market rates and avoid the spread charged by the centre. We, therefore, recommend that, in future, the central government should not act as an intermediary and allow the states to approach the market directly. If, however, some fiscally weak states are unable to raise funds from the market, the centre could resort to lending, but the interest rates should remain aligned to the marginal cost of borrowing for the centre.'

Under the Constitution, the state governments need the permission of the Centre to borrow only as long as they are indebted to the Centre. This is under Article 293. It was my hope that with the recommendation we had made, many of the states might come out of compulsion to seek the Centre's permission.

The second suggestion was the setting up of a loan council comprising representatives from the Ministry of Finance, Planning Commission, RBI and the state governments. The council should, at the beginning of each year, announce borrowing limits for each state, taking into account the sustainability considerations. Such a council could have a salutary effect both on the Centre and the states.

Some Key Issues

Controversies over the issues relating to vertical and horizontal imbalances continue. Since the Twelfth Finance Commission, three more commissions had studied these problems.

The Fourteenth Finance Commission made a big change in the allocation of resources. One of the major recommendations of the commission has been to increase the share of tax devolution to 42 per cent of the divisible pool. This is a substantial increase by almost ten percentage points. The Fourteenth Finance Commission has argued that this does not necessarily affect the overall transfers but only enhances the share of unconditional transfers. The chairman writes, 'The balance in fiscal space thus remains broadly the same in quantitative terms but tilts in favour of states in qualitative terms through a compositional shift in favour of devolution and hence fiscal autonomy.'

It must be noted that the recommendation of the Fourteenth Finance Commission sailed through smoothly because of one important institutional change and that was the abolition of the Planning Commission as it existed before. What the Planning Commission was previously allocating became part of the tax devolution. The critical question to ask is what will happen if a future government revives the Planning Commission with financial powers. There can be questions asked whether a Planning Commission with financial powers is necessary. Niti Aayog, which is the successor to the Planning Commission, is essentially a think tank with no power to allocate resources. Will this model be continued under a different regime? It must also be pointed out that the erstwhile Planning Commission also allocated resources among states based on a formula very similar to the Finance Commission's.

In correcting vertical imbalance, there is need for a rethink on the roles of the Centre and states on expenditures. It is argued that centrally sponsored schemes have ballooned over time and they have 'encroached' on the territory of states. But it is also a fact that the performance of the Central government is also judged not only on the basis of actions taken which fall strictly in its jurisdiction but also on the initiatives taken in the areas which fall in the concurrent list and the state list. Centralized planning, which held sway for several decades, has something to do with it. At the time of the election, the Central government is held responsible for the state of the economy. Thus, there is a big difference between what the Constitution says and what the perception of the people is. This is an aspect which Finance Commissions cannot ignore.

In deciding on the horizontal distribution among states, equity considerations have dominated. While this is legitimate, two factors need to be borne in mind. First, in the present scheme of tax assignment, some of the taxes have been listed in the Centre purely from the angle of administrative convenience and prevention of leakage. Some part of tax revenue legitimately belongs to states. In the days when income tax was the primary tax shared, states' 'collection' was also a criterion in determining the share that goes to the states. States that contribute more to the central pool should not be ignored. Second, the above-mentioned consideration applies even more strongly when the tax devolution share touches such a high level as 42 per cent. With the reduction of the number of states to twenty-eight recently, the Fifteenth Finance Commission, in its first report for 2020–21 itself, reduced it to 41 per cent. Therefore, consideration must be given to assigning some weight to 'contribution', even though one must accept that there are problems in conceptualizing a variable to measure it.

The terms of reference to the Fifteenth Finance Commission led to a big controversy on the issue of population as a criterion in horizontal distribution. The fear of the southern states was that their share would go down if 2011 population was used instead of 1971 population as all previous commissions had done. Whatever the justification for using 1971 population, quite plainly, using 1971 population data implies consciously using information that would be fifty years out of date. (Both the Fourteenth and Fifteenth Commissions found a way to take care of the concerns of states that had contained the population growth by adding an extra variable on population.)

In fact, the major reason for the southern and some other states getting a 'lower' share is the use of 'income distance criterion'. Under this criterion, the share of the state increases as the distance from the highest income state increases. Its weight in the horizontal distribution was as high as 61.5 per cent at one time. In the more recent period, it has been 50 per cent. Technically speaking, the highest income state should get no allocation under this criterion. Of course, all commissions have modified the formula slightly to enable even the highest income state to get some allocation. It is the application of the income distance criterion that plays a critical role in the allocation of funds. The states that raised a big hue and cry over population should have turned their attention to this criterion. But then it is difficult to argue against this criterion. This criterion is rooted in the principle of equalization. This also brings into stark reality the difficulties in the application of the principle of equalization in a country where even the 'richest' states need help. A balancing of criteria thus becomes a compulsion.

In fact, a way out is to look more carefully at the financial (taxation) powers of the state. The gap between powers and responsibilities can be bridged by increasing the powers. GST is a good tax reform. States did get additional powers to tax services. Unfortunately, the implementation of the reform has been unsatisfactory. Some states bemoan the loss of sovereignty. This is inevitable. The Centre also loses sovereignty. It is the GST Council that has the ultimate power. That is why this was called a 'grand bargain'.

In increasing the taxation powers of states, two ideas stand out. One is to allow states to levy income tax and the second is to allow states to charge an additional levy on selected special goods or goods of 'local importance'. There are many countries in the world that allow states or provinces to levy income tax in addition to the levy by the Centre or the Federal Government. In all these countries, the central income tax is the dominant one. For example, both the US and Canada give powers to states to levy income tax. In fact, in the US, several states have zero or low tax rates. Competition among states helps to keep the rate low. It is also possible to limit it by law. This will help higher-income states relatively more and will help to calm down some of the states who complain about the low allocation of resources to them. One has to think through this idea and evolve a suitable scheme. The second suggestion is to let states tax additionally, certain goods in the GST scheme. Some revenue autonomy may be accessed by the state governments by being permitted an additional levy on the basic GST rate on selected goods. The concept of goods of local importance has been discussed in the GST Council earlier. I think this is permissible even under the present law. Of course, the GST regime needs several modifications and simplifications to make it more productive. The performance of GST in 2021–22 is encouraging.

Raising the share of states to 41 per cent of shareable taxes of the Centre should provide adequate revenue to the states. In this context, it is also important to point out that the Centre should desist from levying cesses that are 'permanent'. Either we should impose a limit on cesses as a percentage of a base or strictly limit the time period of a cess to one year. 'Cesses' should not provide a route to get around the higher tax devolution.

Fiscal transfers are necessary as long as there are differences between tax assignment and responsibilities of states and also as long as states differ in their fiscal capacities. I have made some suggestions for narrowing the gap between tax assignment and responsibilities. At the horizontal level, it is the accelerated growth of lower-income states that will require relatively less redistribution for achieving greater equalization.

15

Interacting with the Political System

Short Sojourn at the Rajya Sabha

In 2008, I was nominated to the Rajya Sabha. At that time I was chairman of the Economic Advisory Council to the prime minister. I had mentioned to Manmohan Singh at one time my desire to be in the Rajya Sabha. That was, in fact, many years earlier. He had remembered this and the timing was a surprise to me. After a brief discussion with the prime minister, I accepted the suggestion and it was duly announced.

Unlike my previous roles, this was entirely in a new area and I had to learn a lot in order to make myself useful. Since the Rajya Sabha was not in session at the time of the nomination, I was sworn in by the vice president (Ansari) in a special room and Manmohan Singh attended it.

My stay in the Rajya Sabha was short. This was because of two reasons. First, I was nominated to a vacancy that had only a short period left. Unless I was renominated, in any case, it would have been far less than a full term. Second, I reassessed my role at the end of one year and had serious doubts whether that was the position in which I would be most useful.

A nominated member has certain advantages. He or she is free from any political baggage. One can therefore look at the merits of the proposals that come up for discussion independently. But the support system for a nominated member is weak. One has to dig into the materials oneself. In fact there is a need to give to all members of Parliament adequate research support.

Many of the problems that I faced came perhaps from my lack of familiarity with the procedures of the house. But in general, I found that the opportunities given to nominated members for intervention were limited. The time allowed was too short. For example, even in the discussions on the Budget, nominated members used to get a chance to speak after all the political parties had made their observations and the time allowed was short. On occasion, one did not even know when a particular issue was to be discussed. During the period I was in the Rajya Sabha I did intervene and spoke on the Budget and the President's Address. But beyond that, the possibilities were limited. During the short period I was in the Rajya Sabha, I had not mastered the art of asking questions. The year at the Rajya Sabha was also a bit unusual. That was the year in which fresh elections for the Lok Sabha were announced. This resulted in most of the committees not functioning. I was not inducted in any of the important committees. I was waiting for it. Perhaps more time was needed to get acquainted with the procedures. But I was feeling restless. I then met the prime minister and discussed with him my dilemma, and wondered whether I could play a more effective role elsewhere. We allowed the matter to rest for some time. Finally, I submitted my resignation.

Very often, people complain about members of Parliament being paid excessively. This is not true. In fact, I personally felt that with the emoluments one got, it was difficult to maintain two households, one in Chennai and one in Delhi. Without another job, it is difficult to sustain the expenditure. What follows is, being a member of Parliament cannot be a full-time job.

During the time I was in the Rajya Sabha, it was my privilege to have had the company of three distinguished economist–administrators: Bimal Jalan, Arjun Sengupta and N.K. Singh. While Bimal was a nominated member, Arjun represented the Congress Party and N.K. the Janata Dal (United). It was a pleasure to listen to all of them. Each had a distinct style and approach.

In my intervention on the Budget of 2008–09, I pointed out that the high level of fiscal deficit projected was not appropriate. In fact, I felt while it might trigger some immediate growth, in the long run we might run into problems. This was what actually happened. I was quite sure that had I continued in the Rajya Sabha, I could have made some contribution to the analysis of issues that came up. What bothered me was whether that could be significant enough to influence policy.

During the time I was in the Rajya Sabha, I also thought about the usefulness and the role of a second chamber. Let me spell out my concerns.

Most large countries have bicameral legislatures. It is estimated that 41 per cent of the countries with parliaments are bicameral. In India too, as in many other countries, the adoption of a bicameral system was preceded by intense discussions on the usefulness of having two houses. Some members of the Constituent Assembly were highly critical of a second chamber and regarded it as redundant and a 'clog in the wheel of progress'. However, the majority felt the need for a second house and that was how the Rajya Sabha was created.

There are three major reasons advocated for the creation of a second chamber. The first reason is that it would introduce an element of sobriety in the legislative process and may act as a check on 'hasty and ill-conceived legislations'. Thus, the second chamber provides an opportunity for a 'second look' at the legislations and is therefore desirable. The oft-quoted observation in this context was the one made by George Washington who said, 'We pour legislation into the Senatorial Saucer to cool it.' Thus, much is expected from the second chamber—a cool and dispassionate study of legislations. Is this possible in a political system which is dominated by a party system and party whips?

Second, there is also an implicit assumption that the composition of members of the second chamber will be different from the other chamber. In fact, the vice president, Naidu, in an article described the second chamber as one 'whose members are expected to be sober, wise and well informed with domain knowledge'.[1] Because of the indirect election for members of the Rajya Sabha, this may be possible. But there is no guarantee. Very often it turns out to be the chamber of retired politicians or politicians who have failed to win in direct elections.

Third, it is claimed that the second chamber, because of the indirect election by members of the state legislatures, represents better the federal character of the country. It has to be remembered that the size of the state legislatures in India is also determined in proportion to the population. Unlike the Senate in the US, where every state irrespective of the size has two members in the Senate, the number of people elected to the Rajya Sabha from each state is determined by the size of the population in that state. In effect, it becomes a mini Lok Sabha.

The Rajya Sabha differs from the Lok Sabha in some important aspects. A no-confidence motion against the government can be moved only in the Lok Sabha. Again, a money bill can be introduced only in the Lok Sabha. While the Budget can be discussed in the Rajya Sabha, the final say is with the Lok Sabha. The Rajya Sabha has two exclusive powers. It can alone delete a subject under the exclusive state list and make it part of the concurrent list. It can alone create one or more new all-India services. There is also a provision for a joint meeting of the two houses when there are unreconcilable differences between the two. This provision has been rarely used. There have been only four instances of joint parliamentary sessions.

As pointed out earlier, members of the Rajya Sabha are elected by the state legislations. In the US, the Senate members are directly elected by the people. In the UK, the second chamber, which is the House of Lords, is an unelected body. It is clear from this why the Senate in the US is powerful.

One point that is made is that the second chamber is a continuous body and that it is not dissolved. Only a certain number of members get elected periodically. Hence, a legislation introduced in the Rajya Sabha never lapses. The Lok Sabha gets dissolved usually every five years and sometimes even earlier. It is therefore claimed that the two houses taken together represent 'continuity and change'. The Rajya Sabha has been dubbed as 'reactionary' or 'progressive' depending on the perceptions of the observers. It has been reported that during the bulk of the time, the ruling party was in a minority in the Rajya Sabha. The Rajya Sabha or the Council of States does not really represent states. The composition of the members elected represent only party strength in various legislatures. On many occasions, the members elected do not even speak the language of the state. Also, it is often a reflection of the legislatures not of the day but of some previous time when they were elected. The federal structure is not strengthened in any important way by the second house.

S. Radhakrishnan once mentioned that Parliament was not only a legislative body but also a deliberative one. He added, 'We should try to do everything in our power to justify to the public of this country that a second chamber is essential to prevent hasty legislation. We should discuss with dispassion and detachment proposals put before us.' As a deliberative body, has the Rajya Sabha performed better? It is difficult to give a categorical answer. 'Passion' and unruliness is seen as much in the Rajya Sabha as in the Lok Sabha. In this context, what does it mean to say, 'to discuss with dispassion and detachment'?

To call the houses of Parliament deliberative bodies must imply that members of Parliament are willing to change their stand on any issue as they listen to others. But that is not how the houses function. This is so elsewhere in the world too. As someone put it, the stand one takes depends on where he or she sits. This should change. There is scope in relation to a large number of legislations for members to speak and vote according to their best judgement. It is not a matter of voting according to conscience. It is voting according to one's own assessment after listening to all sides. In 1998, when I was governor of Andhra Pradesh and when I was addressing new members of Andhra Assembly, I said,

'The success of democracy depends to a great extent upon the efficiency and effective functioning of its legislative bodies. If the primary function of enacting of laws has to be effectively fulfilled by the parliamentary institutions, it is essential that the members of Parliament or the state legislature critically examine any legislation coming before it for consideration and assess the overall impact it will have on people and the country as a whole. In our parliamentary system, so far, voting on various legislations has been strictly on party lines. It is worth examining whether, except in the case of money bills or when the issue of leadership is involved, members can be given the freedom to vote according to their judgement. In fact, in some parliamentary democracies, such a move is clearly seen. In the US, because of the presidential form of government, voting in the

Congress or Senate has not necessarily been on party lines. The issue of whips on party lines could be limited to specific types of legislations, leaving the balance area in which members can be given freedom to express their views and vote according to their judgement. This is an aspect which deserves consideration, taking into account the basic principles of the parliamentary system of government and legislations such as anti-defection laws.'

In fact, I had found a member of Parliament giving expression to the same view. He writes: 'The aim is to ensure MPs make the most informed decision every time they are called upon to vote. But with the autonomy of voting long gone, debate has become meaningless. Armed with these, every MP should be an independent actor capable for consensus and dissent beyond narrow partisan lines. Party fiat and whips should be restricted only to no-confidence motion'.[2] Can we move in this direction at least in the Rajya Sabha which is often called the House of Elders?

16

Advice to Government

Days at Economic Advisory Council

It was sometime in May 2004 when I, along with other members of the Twelfth Finance Commission, were visiting one of the North-eastern States that I got a call from Manmohan Singh. He had just become prime minister. He wanted to know when the work of the Finance Commission would be completed. He said he was considering me for the position of deputy chairman of the Planning Commission. I told him that the work of the Finance Commission would take six months more to complete. Even though members of the Planning Commission had been members of the Finance Commission, there was no case of the deputy chairman being chairman of the Finance Commission. Obviously, there was some conflict of interest. The matter was dropped there. But I knew that Manmohan Singh wanted me to be involved in his government. After the Twelfth Commission Report was handed over, he was keen that I should stay in Delhi. But by that time, the new government was very much in the saddle, and I had packed my things and half of it had been sent to Chennai. In the course of a discussion, the idea came up that the Economic Advisory Council (EAC) could be revived in a new form and that I could chair it in a full-time capacity. At that time, I looked at the past history of EAC in India. It was first set up during the time when Indira Gandhi was prime minister. It was headed by Sukhamoy Chakravarty and there were four members, all of whom were on a part-time basis. Manmohan Singh, who was at that time governor of RBI, was a member of the council. However, within a year or two, he became deputy chairman of the Planning Commission and he resigned from EAC. The council was reconstituted and I was included as a member. At that time, I was deputy governor of RBI. The council did meet Rajiv Gandhi, who was then prime minister, on a few occasions. I distinctly remember talking to him about the need to control the fiscal deficit. While the council did prepare a few documents, which were also released to the public, there was no regular preparation of reports. When Rajiv Gandhi was succeeded by V.P. Singh, the council prepared a report that was somewhat critical of the Rajiv Gandhi years. I was somewhat unhappy about it because these criticisms were not put on paper earlier and given to Rajiv Gandhi. Later, Bimal Jalan became chairman for a short period. During the Vajpayee years, EAC became a large body comprising twenty or twenty-five economists as members. The prime minister himself chaired it. The members looked more like group of economists consulted to advise the finance minister before the presentation of the Budget. We decided to go back to the original model of EAC with a chairman and four or five members. This is somewhat similar to the Council of Economic Advisers in the US. It was also decided that the chairman would be full-time and the members would be part-time. It would have a separate Secretariat. The Secretary would be at the level of Additional Secretary or Secretary to the government. It was left flexible. The Planning Commission was the nodal ministry. One important change from the original council was that the chairman would have the rank of a cabinet minister and the members would have the status of ministers of state. This was something similar to the Planning Commission and Finance Commission. A lot of effort was needed to give shape to the new council. B.V.R. Subramanian, who was private secretary to the prime minister, did a lot of spadework to get the council going. He was always thorough in whatever he did. D. Subba Rao became the first Secretary of the council. Saumitra Chaudhuri, who was then a member of the Planning Commission, was also appointed as a member of EAC and he also put in a lot of effort in getting the council established. It was located in the Vigyan Bhavan Annexe. The first council had the following members: G.K. Chadha; Saumitra Chaudhuri; Satish C. Jha; M. Govinda Rao and Suresh Tendulkar.

When I was nominated to the Rajya Sabha, I left EAC but came back after a little over a year. Dr Tendulkar was chairman during the time I was in the Rajya Sabha. The reconstituted EAC in 2011 comprised the following members: Suman K. Bery; Saumitra Chaudhuri; M. Govinda Rao and V.S. Vyas.

The first secretary of EAC was Subba Rao, who had just returned from an assignment with World Bank. He was succeeded by Alok Sheel and later by K.P. Krishnan. The Secretariat was a compact one. It was good fortune that the council had a succession of eminent Secretaries, all of whom, besides being able administrators, were intellectually oriented.

EAC did multiple jobs. It answered references made to it by the Prime Minister's Office (PMO). It also sent notes to the prime minister on issues that it considered important. Besides, I was also involved in chairing a number of committees appointed by the government. In reviewing my involvement with EAC, these can be done on three broad categories: the annual publications of the council, references answered and important committee reports.

Economic Outlook

In 2005, the council decided to prepare a forecast for the economy in 2005–06 and send it to the prime minister. It was a fairly detailed report, making not only a forecast of growth but also providing a sector-wise analysis. There were comments on monetary policy, fiscal policy, BOP and reform agenda. After the presentation of the first report on the economy to the prime minister, I felt that such a report should be made public, to which the prime minister agreed. From 2006 onwards, EAC released sometime in August of each year a detailed report on the economy. The first such report, entitled 'Economic Outlook for 2006–07', was released in August 2006 and was put in the public domain. The chairman and members addressed a press conference and the main features of the report were highlighted. Subsequently, the council brought out a publication in January each year reviewing the developments during the year. The years between 2005 and 2014 covered a period that was characterized by sharp growth initially followed by a decline. This period also included the global crisis of 2008–09. Since

2010–11, the economy's growth rate started to decline largely because of domestic factors. Even to this day, the economy is somewhat staggering and has failed to pick up steam. The 'Economic Outlook' presented for the various years show that while the reports forecasted slightly lower growth in the high growth phase, they also underestimated the decline. These are according to 2004–05 base numbers. It is a different story with respect to 2011–12 base numbers. The latter set of data shows a lower growth in the high phase period. But the importance of the reports does not lie in the specific forecasts. They lie in the analysis of economic conditions that prevailed and, in particular, a critical analysis of agriculture, manufacturing, BOP, inflation and fiscal situations. More than once, reports dealt with decline in growth and the reasons behind it.

Issues raised in 'Economic Outlook'

As early as 2006–07, EAC raised the issue about whether the growth seen since 2002 was consumption=driven or investment-driven. It said:

'There has been some concern about the sustainability of our growth performance. It is argued that growth over the last three years has been driven largely by consumption demand, including demand for homes, financed by loans from the banking system. This consumption demand has been fuelled largely by monetary factors such as easy liquidity conditions and low interest rates, and benign inflation. The domestic comfortable monetary situation was further aided by easy liquidity and low interest rates at the global level which facilitated capital flows into India. This fortuitous combination of circumstances has now begun to reverse. Interest rates have increased and inflation is on the rise. Globally too, the era of cheap money has effectively ended with major central banks around the world all tightening monetary policy. The revised situation will dampen consumption demand and impede growth.

'In order to test this hypothesis, we analysed data on the sectoral deployment of bank credit during 2002–06. That led to two inferences: first, credit expanded rapidly in the period 2002–05, and second, during the first two years of this period, a larger share of incremental credit had gone to finance consumption, including home finance.

A plausible explanation of the economic dynamics underlying the above trends will be the following. The easy liquidity conditions in recent years encouraged a surge in demand for personal loans during 2002–03 and 2003–04. However, there was adequate capacity in the manufacturing sector, and the increased consumption demand could be met by stepping up production. This also facilitated the recovery of the manufacturing sector.

'The above analysis validates the hypothesis that growth over the recent period has been more consumption-driven than investment-driven. The credit market has since become tighter and this will restrain consumption demand to some extent. However, this need not necessarily result in a growth downturn. A consumption boom that lasts for a period has the potential to create an investment boom. In fact, the growth momentum can be accelerated if the government responds with a strong and credible policy to create a conducive climate for investment. Two specific responses are particularly important:

(i) First, government will have to supply more and better infrastructure. Investment in infrastructure can come by way of direct public investment or through public private partnership (PPP).

(ii) Second, investment capital needs to be made available at reasonable rates of interest. A critical requirement for this is for the government to reduce its fiscal deficit, particularly revenue deficit.'

On the policy framework for inflation management, the report said:

'Inflation management requires both sectoral responses as well as management of the macroeconomic situation at the aggregate level. The year on year growth in broad money (M_3) had accelerated to 19.5 per cent as on July 21, 2006, up from 14 per cent a year earlier. In view of the increase in prices across several sectors, containing money supply growth has to be an integral part of inflation management.'

In fact, the broad stability parameters had been met during the high growth phase. The BOP was strong. The current account deficit was low. In 2005–06 and 2006–07, there was a small surplus. The gross fiscal deficit of the Centre came down from 5.72 per cent of GDP in 2002–03 to 3.3 per cent in 2006–07. It must, however, be noted that the fiscal deficit remained above the mandated level of 3 per cent even in the high growth phase. The revenue deficit accounted for the major part of the fiscal deficit. The WPI inflation ranged between 3.4 per cent in 2002–03 and 6.6 per cent in 2006–07. The picture on the price front was mixed. What is interesting is that the period saw a significant rise in investment rates. This was relevant in terms of the discussion on consumption-driven and investment-driven growth. In a developing economy, for sustainable growth, investment is key. To a large extent, this was satisfied. Investment rates picked up strongly after 2003–04. The report for 2007–08 said:

'The strength of the investment boom may be seen from two inter-related facts. First is the big increase in the investment rate which is the proportion of total investment to GDP at current and market prices. For many years, the investment rate has stagnated in the low to mid-20s right from as far back as the mid-1970s. In the years immediately following the reforms of 1991, the investment rate rose to a peak value of 27 per cent in 1995–96, but fell off subsequently; the average value of the investment rate between 1996–97 and 2002–03 was 24.2 per cent, ranging between 22.9 per cent and 25.3 per cent of GDP. Starting from an investment rate of 28.0 per cent in 2003–04, the momentum of investment expansion gathered steam rising to 31.5 per cent and 33.8 per cent in 2004–05 and 2005–06. In 2006–07, the investment rate moved into the upper half of the 30s, with provisional estimates registering a figure of 35.1 per cent. In every sense, this change in the trajectory of investment is truly enormous.'

While welcoming the strong pickup in the investment rate, the report for 2007–08 also indicated the possibility of 'overheating'. It said:

'The term "overheating" has entered the lexicon of common usage in the discussion of our domestic policies over the past several months. "Overheating" refers to a situation where aggregate demand in the economy is significantly in excess of domestic productive capacity. In the short to medium term, if there is unutilized productive capacity in the economy, higher demand will lead to a rapid and above-trend expansion of GDP. But if the excess demand persists, it could lead to "overheating" and manifest itself in a rise in prices and/or a higher external trade deficit till such time that additional capacities are created to meet the rising demand. If fiscal expansion is a major cause of the surge in domestic demand, the fiscal balance will also begin to widen. Since domestic demand—whether public or private–for its materialization requires monetary accommodation by definition, there would be a rapid expansion of bank credit extended to public authorities and the private commercial sector.

'A sharp increase in economic growth could therefore be associated with a rise in inflation, a widening of the external (Current Account) and internal (fiscal) deficits, and a rapid expansion of bank credit and other forms of capital flows. Asset prices also tend to rise in response to increase in expected profits. During the last quarter of 2006 and the first few months of 2007 there were signs of overheating when the wholesale price index rose to over 6 per cent and the merchandise trade deficit also expanded to over 7 per cent of GDP indicating some pressure on the supply side. In such a situation, it would have been imprudent to let money supply accelerate. Since then, thanks to a series of monetary tightening measures undertaken by the RBI and fiscal measures initiated by the government, these signs have abated.'

The report for 2007–08 also dealt with the possible impact of the developments in the US, which burst out in the following year. In addition, the report wrote on the problem of accumulation of reserves. It said:

'There is an ongoing debate on the justification for central bank intervention in the foreign exchange market and its extent. In India the magnitude of the capital inflows and their potential to induce large changes in relative prices will have serious repercussions for domestic business in both the domestic and export markets. We do not therefore think that the solution is simply to stop intervention. The underlying imbalance between the CAD and capital inflows needs to be bridged.

'The argument has been made that if the excess of capital inflows is so much larger than the CAD, why not restrict such inflows? Any restriction—which by definition will be *ad hoc*—on equity investment, be it direct or portfolio investment, will be most unwise. Equity investment by its very nature is high-risk and policy continuity is an essential element to initiate and maintain such flows; they cannot be turned on and off at will. However, on the debt side there are some areas which can do with some scrutiny. Notably the best non-discretionary way of ensuring that such loans/bonds are used not to acquire rupee assets (where the by-pass becomes effective) is to limit the conversion of ECB proceeds into rupees. All in all, any such restriction that we may impose must be temporary.

'In substance, there are three instruments or channels through which policy makers can act in the face of strong capital flows. One is to let the rupee appreciate. However, there are limits up to which this can be done. Beyond a point it will hurt exports, as also the larger domestic economy. Besides we need to take into account the behaviour of the currencies of other developing countries, most notably China. Despite a strong trade surplus, China continues to permit its currency to appreciate only to a small extent. Appreciation finally works through widening the current account deficit and it is necessary to keep in mind the extent to which the country can comfortably allow the current account deficit to widen. Exchange rate appreciation will exact a fiscal cost if attempts are made to support exports through subsidies.

'The second channel is to absorb the capital flows into reserves and to sterilize the excess over what may be regarded as appropriate. The appropriate level would depend upon the desired expansion in money supply and the consequent level of reserve money expansion. It is currently estimated that expansion of reserve assets to the extent of $25 billion can be absorbed consistent with a money supply growth of 17.5 per cent. Intervention in excess of this has to be sterilized, which of course involves a cost. Sterilization through the issue of bonds will impose a fiscal cost which will be equal to the difference between the rate of interest paid on the domestic security and the return on reserves invested abroad. In this context it may be noted that with interest rates having risen in the developed world, the difference in yield has come down. Alternatively, sterilization can be done through raising the cash reserve ratio, in which case the burden will be borne by the banks. In either case, there will be some impact on the interest rate.

'A third channel is to liberalize outflows by removing administrative and procedural impediments, and to discourage inflows by putting restrictions in some capital items. Restricting capital inflow too has its limitations. It must not be seen as a signal that we are going back on liberalizing the capital account. However, as indicated earlier, there are some types of flows on which purely temporary restrictions can be imposed without it being seen as intrusive.

'Instead of arguing for the exclusive use of any one of the instruments, there must be a judicious mix of all of the three instruments. There are limits to which each instrument can be used by itself.'

The report for 2008–09 had a separate chapter on the impact of the global environment on India. The report also looked at factors that can act as barriers to further growth. It said:

'The economy continues to be supply constrained, most acutely in the areas of physical and social infrastructure, where the goods involved are to a greater or lesser extent public goods, and where Government is involved to a significant extent. These shortages require focused policy attention. Inadequacies in capacity creation in these infrastructural areas will determine the pace at which we will be able to benefit our citizens by sustaining a process of rapid economic growth in the medium and longer term. In the area of economic infrastructure the constraints are patent in electricity, irrigation and drinking water, road and rail transportation, urban and rural economic infrastructure, and in extending the benefits of technology to aid our farmers in raising productivity.'

The report for 2009–10 basically talked about the impact of the global crisis. In citing the reasons for the limited direct impact on the economy, the report said:

'The Indian economy escaped the global contagion primarily because the Indian banking sector was not exposed to the risky assets, similar to those financed in the advanced economies. The three important lessons to be drawn from this are, first, prudence is an essential virtue for financial and fiscal stability; second, deposit-based banking, as is practiced here, is perhaps the more solid foundation to bank lending than the one based on short-term borrowings from capital markets by banks; third, the financial regulators should be intimately conversant with the products and practices that they are enjoined to regulate.'

Talking of the international crisis and its impact on India, it said:

'The global economic crisis had two separate components. The first derived from a five year period of above-trend economic growth. In the developed economies the unemployment levels fell to historic lows and commodity and asset prices rose while the developing economies were impacted by the worldwide demand boom in the area of commodities and assets. Ordinarily the necessary adjustment should have been brought about by a tightened monetary policy but this did not happen leading to the second component of the crisis flowing entirely out of the financial systems in the developed economies. The easy money and fiscal policies adopted to leverage the US economy out of recession in 2001 resulted in a large liquidity overhang, blurring risk perceptions. This, in combination with the highly inadequate regulatory oversight and large-scale dilution of standards by financial market players resulted in the creation of bad assets leading to the financial crisis and recession in the advanced economies. The outcome was worsened by the global structural imbalances—a large current account deficit in the US and a matching current account surplus of oil exporting nations, China and Japan.

'The impact of the global economic and financial crisis on India operated through three channels—a) the financial channel which diminished the ability of Indian companies to mobilize equity and debt in foreign and domestic markets, b) the trade channel which operated by eroding the import demand in developed economies and c) the collapse of business and consumer confidence in the developed economies, which depressed sentiments worldwide, including in India. This was truer of the private corporate sector/consumers in the metropolitan centres than in semi-urban/ rural areas.'

On recovery, the report said:

'It is the Council's assessment that international economic conditions will strengthen further in the last quarter of 2009 and in 2010 and financial conditions, which have bounced back, will consolidate further. However, the low risk perception and ease in fund mobilization will not recur and the slow recovery of international trade will sharpen competitive conditions for exporters. The economic and financial conditions, while not being as supportive for rapid growth of the Indian economy, as in 2006 and 2007, will also not be adverse to growth as over the last year and a half.

'The principal risk that emanates from the global economy for India is inflation contagion, with crude oil prices once again in the lead. The other risk is the possibility of another setback to the world of finance, where even a small failure has an amplified capacity for destabilization.'

The report also cautioned as regards India:

'The highly accommodative and expansive monetary stance created due to exceptional circumstances, needs to be phased out. The timing and the pace of this will depend on the pace of expansion of the various sectors and the magnitude of inflationary pressures. Given the present inflationary pressures, we may have to act earlier than the US and European economies.'

In the Review of the Economy 2009–10, the council drew attention to the fiscal imbalance and wrote:

'Government cannot continue with the kind of large revenue and fiscal deficits recorded in the last two years and will have to initiate fiscal consolidation in the coming fiscal year (2010/11) itself. Although the large deficits this year and the last year did have a counter-cyclical impact, it is necessary to initiate measures towards fiscal consolidation in the forthcoming budget to ensure fiscal sustainability, enable greater flexibility in monetary policy calibration, contain interest payments and to avoid upward pressure on interest rates. The recommendations of the Thirteenth Finance Commission will spell out the magnitude of correction required, the strategy and roadmap to achieve the correction and the role of Centre and States in this task over the course of the next five years.'

In 2009–10, the council's projection of 6.5 per cent as growth rate fell well below the actual growth rate of 8.9 per cent as per the earlier base. The failure to anticipate such a high growth rate led to the continuance of easing measures beyond what might have been considered appropriate. Inflation touched the double digit level in February 2010.

The report for 2010–11 projected a growth rate of 8.5 per cent which was quite near the actual level. It wanted the easing measures to be withdrawn. It wrote:

'While the monetary easing and the fiscal measures during the crisis effectively limited the damage caused by the contagion, it was always clear that these would have to be rolled back as the economies gradually recovered.

'In those economies where the effects of the crisis have clearly worn off and the recovery is strong, an early exit from both the monetary and the fiscal stimulus is called for. Australia, India, China, Brazil and Singapore have been tightening their monetary policy by raising policy interest rates and/or rolling back specific liquidity measures that were adopted at the time of the crisis.'

And on policy actions, it mentioned:

'It is important to improve the revenue productivity of the tax system and phase out unproductive expenditures. The initiative to partially free prices of petroleum products is a significant measure but the government will also have to rationalise food and fertilizer subsidies. On the revenue side, two important initiatives relate to the passing of the Direct Taxes Code and replacement of domestic indirect taxes at the Central and State levels with the Goods and Services Tax (GST). GST is a major tax reform agenda in the country but a lot of work needs to be done to make it operational.'

The report for 2011–12 expected a decline in growth rate but not to the extent to which it actually fell. There was a precipitous decline from 8.9 per cent in the previous year to 6.7 per cent in 2011–12.

In July 2011, the council wrote:

'The gross domestic fixed capital formation has weakened significantly, with initial estimates for 2010/11 placing it at 29.5 per cent. High rates of domestic inflation, excessive government debt, political instability and the global situation have eroded business confidence impacting asset creation adversely. It is important to push through the reform agenda and generate conditions to increase the fixed investment rate to 33 per cent plus. This is imperative to achieve a stable 9 per cent rate of growth.'

The report went extensively into details on the factors for the decline in growth. It is worth reporting what the council said:

'However, the recovery in the fixed investment rate has not transpired and the pace of economic growth is also slower.[1] While quite clearly we were able to negotiate the global economic crisis quite well, we have been unable to find our way back to the path of rapid asset creation and growth. As a result, some of the momentum has gone out of the economy. Why that happened over the past two years is something that we need to reflect upon and understand if the situation is to be rectified. It is true that many economies, including the world's leading ones, are still embroiled in hard economic conditions and other developing countries like China are also facing difficulties. That, however, is not good enough reason to explain why we have not been able so far to do better than we have. The combined momentum of a stable government after the May 2009 general elections and the successful navigation through the crisis was a good opportunity to take those necessary steps to energetically get back to the imperatives: namely, of rolling out physical infrastructure, pushing through reforms and improving efficiency in public expenditure in the social sector. However, we have lost time. In part, the reasons were the apprehensions that the exceptional drought of 2009 created and the unfounded concerns about a double dip recession in the West. As a result, we found ourselves on the back-foot, as inflation began to spiral on account of international and domestic factors and new concerns began to emerge in the global economic canvas. There are several factors that clearly were important impediments in our effort to return to the path of high rate of asset creation and economic growth:

- First, there was clearly considerable over-confidence in both business and in the government as we came out of the crisis well. Compounding matters, the South-West monsoon was the weakest in 28 years and initial apprehensions of what that may imply for food availability were quite dire.
- Second, there was a disinclination to roll back fiscal and monetary stimulus quickly.
- Third, flaring up of inflation in food and thereafter in non-food items made it difficult to focus on broader policy initiatives.
- Fourth, the spate of corruption related controversies that has emerged over the past one year, has consumed the energies of Government and has led to an unintended slowing down of initiatives to restore investment and economic confidence.

'Asset creation in the private sector is always a matter of taking risk, since it expands the liabilities in the balance sheets and entails both greater market and financial risks into the enterprise. Therefore, for businesses to take these risks, the first precondition is the promise of stability—both financial and political. High rates of inflation are the antithesis of stability. Wild fluctuations in the price of assets—the exchange rate and, equity prices—are a symbol of lack of stability. Fear of crisis unleashed by the excessive debts of governments destabilizes the business environment. The last two years have seen all of this and also fears on account of political stability at home. The global canvas has been constantly jolted by the unhappy developments in the Euro-zone deriving from the sovereign debt crisis, as well as concerns about how the US is going to come out of its severe fiscal stress and halting pace of economic recovery.

'The Council had a structured consultation with business representatives, as also discussions with people from different fields. Certain key points that emerged that are relevant for the attention of policy, were:

- Bottlenecks in infrastructure, particularly power, as also roads and the port sector, are emerging as a major constraint in the manufacturing sector.

- In the case of power, inadequacy of fuel supply linkages, especially domestic coal, as well as restrictions on mining in previously allocated coal blocks, is posing a major constraint.
- Capital investment that is dependent on Government decisions, as also that on government funding, are experiencing difficulties on account of a slowing down in the approval process for projects.
- Within the manufacturing sector, some sectors are facing limited excess capacity and new investments are not coming up fast enough.
- Business sectors that are dependent on consumer expenditure are still doing reasonably well, but those which are dependent on capital expenditure are under pressure.
- Cost increases are eroding profitability and to that extent are adversely impacting new investment prospects.
- In the funding of infrastructure projects, commercial banks are reaching sectoral exposure caps and the limits for asset–liability mismatch. A corporate debt market for financing infrastructure has become vitally important.
- Delays in forest and environmental clearances are causing time and cost over-runs.
- A shortage of labour, especially skilled labour, is increasingly impacting negatively on the manufacturing sector.
- The uncertainty arising from political developments has had a very negative impact on business confidence and investment outlook.

'It was felt that Government could help in improving matters by a series of measures, which are purely within the policy domain. Key elements of these were:

- Pursuing fiscal consolidation, including rationalizing prices where there continues to be administrative control.
- Bring inflation under control as quickly as possible.
- Initiatives to improve the regulatory and governance framework and expediting the implementation of GST.
- Ensuring greater continuity and predictability of both policy and regulatory regimes.
- Providing clear evidence of taking the reform process forward, including modernization of the retail sector.
- Clearer emphasis on skill development, which is in any case a big social imperative, given the expected demographic dividend.

- Speeding up of clearances for projects that have got stuck.
- It will help if a clear announcement is made for projects which Government intends to take up in the balance of this financial year as well as in the next.

'There is scope on the domestic front for taking policy and administrative initiatives that will improve the investment context in 2011–12. What happens overseas is outside our control and we must take it as a given. However, over what happens at home, we have much more control. It is absolutely imperative that active measures to improve the investment climate be taken. This includes clarity on policy, removal of uncertainties on both policy and administrative fronts, pushing through the reform agenda and taking all other measures to strengthen the competitive character of the market and dealing with unresolved issues that are required to facilitate the expansion and acceleration of private investment over the medium-term. If we were to do this, we can reasonably expect to generate conditions that will result in the fixed investment rate moving upwards to over 33 per cent and enable a return to the trajectory of a stable 9 per cent rate of economic growth.'

The report also devoted a separate chapter, entitled 'Some Key Issues', to a wide variety of issues such as national food security, convergence of incomes of states, sustainable current account deficit and reforms in the power sector. On monetary policy, it recalled several steps undertaken by RBI to control inflation, such as a rise in CRR and a sharp increase in policy rates, and added: 'It is certain that the RBI will have to continue to maintain a tight monetary policy stance for quite some time, given the combination of domestic inflationary situation and the international backdrop.'

At the time of the Review of the Economy by February 2012, it became obvious that the decline in the growth rate during the year would be severe. Gross fixed capital formation as a proportion of GDP was estimated to have fallen from 32.9 per cent in 2007–08 to 29.3 per cent in 2011–12. While this may explain a fall in growth, it raises the other question of why the investment rate had fallen. The report in subsequent years went into this question.

The Economic Outlook Report for 2012–13 expressed serious concern for the fall in the investment rate, high level of inflation and continued imbalance in the government's fiscal. Looking at the industrial front, it reported:

> 'The inferences that unambiguously emerge—no matter what deficiencies of the Index of Industrial Production (IIP) data may suffer from—is that (a) investment demand has become a source of serious concern; (b) the textile industry where we should have a comparative advantage has industry-specific problems and (c) weak domestic demand and output seem to characterize even areas such as durable consumer goods and non-durables such as apparel. Clearly policy needs to take explicit cognizance of these elements in search of the solution for the restoration of the economy to a higher growth path.'

The report also elaborated on the steep rise in the current account deficit, which had reached a record level of 4.2 per cent of GDP, the largest ever. The report included 'Measures Suggested to Improve Economic Conditions' and prefaced the suggestions with the following observations:

> 'While we were able to negotiate the global economic crisis quite well, and saw an early recovery in domestic demand and in output, we have not been yet able to get investment back to the path of rapid asset creation and therefore sustainable higher growth. It is our assessment that if few immediate policy measures are taken, this will help in improving the domestic investment climate and help in raising the pace of asset creation and hence of economic growth.'

The list of measures touched on FDI in general and in multi-brand retail, reforms in the aviation sector, containing petroleum products subsidies, policy predictability, project clearance, encouragement to investment, containing inflation and improving the current account deficit.

In the Review of the Economy issued in April 2013, the council also brought attention to how the Incremental Capital Output Ratio (ICOR) had increased, which also dampened growth. The report said:

> 'Second, the extent to which delays in projects—mostly on account of delays in the issuance of clearances and lack of fuel for power

plants—were impacting the generation of incremental income in the current period was not fully appreciated. The ground situation was that projects with large sums of capital invested in them were not getting completed and therefore not yielding expected current output.

'The Incremental Capital Output Ratio (ICOR) has shot up from its historical level of around 4.0 in 2007–08 and earlier years, to much higher levels.'

The Economic Outlook for 2013–14 was the last of the reports submitted by the EAC chaired by me. The report projected a growth rate of 5.3 per cent in 2013–14. Since the low growth was causing concern, the report went over some of the issues already dealt with in earlier reports. It also pointed out:

'The second part, and possibly the larger part of the factors, that resulted in the abrupt decline in growth from 8.6 per cent in 2009–10 and 9.3 per cent in 2010–11 to 6.2 and 5 per cent in the two subsequent years, flowed from noneconomic factors. These created a climate of uncertainty resulting in hold-ups in projects awaiting clearances and a general deterioration in the investment climate.'

The report had a long section on 'Measures Suggested to Improve Economic Conditions'. Besides general measures, it also talked about sector-specific recommendations relating to the agricultural sector, public–private partnership in defence procurement and strategic interventions in the energy sector.

In light of the recent controversy over the farm legislations passed by the Parliament, which were subsequently withdrawn, it may be interesting to know what the council said in its report for 2013–14. The report said:

'The Council's recommendations on promoting High Value Agriculture are contained in Appendix I. Agricultural marketing policies also need to be streamlined to make the functioning of the market more efficient. State Agricultural Produce Marketing Committee (APMC) Acts have had the unintended effect of disincentivising private investment in market infrastructure and preventing development of competing markets and marketing channels. The process of ensuring greater efficiency in agricultural markets can be catalysed and facilitated through appropriate state reforms and central policies to aid development of competing, well-regulated private market operations.

'To this end, states may provide for state-wide licensing, setting up of private agriculture produce markets through a simple registration procedure, lower levies on agricultural commodities to encourage private buyers in commodities for which government procures, support farmer producer organisations through amendments to the state APMC Acts and in other ways, and provide for registered contract farming with safeguards to secure farmer interests.

'In addition, government may consider dispensing with movement and stock limit restrictions under the Essential Commodities Act for private buyers buying at the Minimum Support Price (MSP). To promote warehouse-based selling, strengthening of warehouse infrastructure for integrating with the agricultural marketing network, coupled with priority sector lending for accredited warehouses, is recommended. Agriculture trade policy must liberalise both export and import restrictions, do away with quantitative restrictions, and move towards a low, stable, tariff-based structure. However, trade policy in food grains may be dealt with in a more cautious manner.'

It is clear that the report recorded views on issues the new central legislations focus on. But there is one difference. The report wanted the changes to be made through amendments to APMC acts, which are state legislations.

In its various reports, the EAC drew the attention of the government to the various aspects of the economy that deserved consideration. It cautioned the government on 'overheating' when the economy was approaching 'full capacity', drew attention to the sharp increase in credit in its high growth phase, wanted the government to control the money supply even as inflation was about to explode and did not hesitate to highlight the factors contributing to the sliding down of the economy after 2011–12. At the point of slowdown, it drew attention to the non-economic factors as well.

Since the reports were widely circulated, the council's collective opinions were available not only to the government but to the public in general. On how the government took the advice and reacted is a different matter. I shall talk about it towards the end of the chapter when I discuss the council's role and effectiveness.

References Answered

EAC was in constant touch with the prime minister's office and several issues were sent to EAC seeking its views. This is in addition to what EAC wrote to the prime minister on issues that it felt necessary to draw his attention. The issues referred to EAC covered all key policy matters ranging from agriculture to external trade to taxation and to banking and finance. In that sense, EAC's advice was one of the inputs which the prime minister took into account when he made his final decision. Very often when there were differences between ministries, the matter was referred to EAC.

It is not proper to go into the actual advice offered by EAC on various issues. However, many of the issues were dealt with by it in its annual Economic Outlook and are therefore in the public domain. Some of the important issues were also the subject matter of the committees I chaired. I shall get into them in the next section.

To give a flavour of the issues that were referred, let me highlight certain questions that came up for advice. In agriculture, the questions revolved around the fixation of MSP, payment of bonus in addition to MSP, the issue of the ban on exports of agricultural commodities particularly cotton in times of shortage, deregulation of the sugar industry (which subsequently became the subject matter of a committee chaired by me), restructuring of fertilizer subsidy, role of commodity futures, rural employment guarantee and national food security (which again was the theme of a committee chaired by me).

On the general economy, there were frequent discussions with the prime minister in meetings that comprised, besides me, the governor of RBI, the deputy chairman of the Planning Commission and the finance minister. The notes sent by EAC dealt largely with the control of inflation, managing foreign exchange volatility, overheating of the economy and later measures to revive the economy. In the area of external trade, questions discussed related to the regional trade agreements, export duty on iron ore, import duty on rubber, revenue and taxation in Special Economic Zones (SEZ) and various export promotion schemes. Questions on banking centred on such issues as the impact of Basel III on the Indian banking system, the mandate for IIFCL and FDI in asset reconstruction companies. Again, there were specific requests from chief ministers of states that were also sent for examination. To conclude this section, there were issues that came up for advice such as the national pharmaceutical pricing policy, duty on export of iron ore, imposing mineral resources tax on iron ore, concessions for certain states like those in the North-east, funding constraints on the road sector and mode of delivery on national highways. The purpose of mentioning the list of issues is only to underline the fact that EAC during this period was seen by the prime minister as an important consulting board.

Committees Chaired

My tenure at EAC was also marked by my being asked to chair several committees that were set up whenever key issues came up for consideration. For some reason or the other, I have been privileged to chair a large number of committees from my days at IIMA. In the mid-1970s, I was asked to chair a committee by the Department of Posts to look at its future. That was the time I came into contact with Amaresh Bagchi, who was a member. Our friendship and association lasted till his death. In our report, we had recommended that the savings bank function be separated and set up as an independent organization within the Department of Posts. If that suggestion had been implemented then, the post office savings bank could have become a full-fledged bank later. In the 1980s when I was in RBI, I had the opportunity to chair several committees. I have in earlier chapters referred to these committees and their recommendations. I list below the committees I chaired between 2002 and 2013:

- Chairman, Committee on Pricing and Taxation of Petroleum Products (February 2006)
- Chairman, Independent Commission on AIDS in Asia and Pacific, UNAIDS (2006–2008)
- Chairman, Committee on Financial Inclusion (2006–08)

- Chairman, High Level Committee on Estimation of Saving and Investment (2007–09)
- Chairman, Report of the Expert Committee on National Food Security Bill, 2010
- Chairman, Expert Group to formulate a jobs plan for Jammu and Kashmir formed by the prime minister (2011)
- Chairman, High Level Expert Committee to suggest measures for effective management of public expenditure, Planning Commission (2011)
- Chairman, Committee to look into the Design of Future Production Sharing Contracts in Hydrocarbon Exploration (2012)
- Chairman, Committee on Deregulation of Sugar Sector (2012)
- Chairman, Expert Group to Review the Methodology for Measuring Poverty (2014)

Pricing and Taxation of Petroleum Products

In October 2005, the government appointed a committee under my chairmanship[2] to look into the issue of pricing and taxation of petroleum products. The committee submitted its report in February 2006. Even though the Government of India had announced the dismantling of the administered pricing mechanism effective from 1 April 2002, it was not implemented and the burden-sharing arrangement continued, which began to collapse after the sharp increase in international oil prices from late 2002. The committee took the view that petroleum products should, as far as possible, be aligned with international prices and that subsidies should be minimal, targeted and restrained by a monetary ceiling. These issues continue to remain relevant. Given below are the sets of recommendations made by the committee in its own words:

'The first set of recommendations relating to pricing of petrol and diesel are the following: (i) shift to a trade parity pricing formula for determining refinery gate as well as retail prices; (ii) Government to keep at arm's length from price determination and to allow flexibility to oil companies to fix the retail price under the proposed formula; and (iii) reduce effective protection by lowering the customs duty on petrol and diesel to 7.5 per cent.

'The second set of recommendations relates to pricing of domestic LPG and PDS kerosene, viz: (i) restrict subsidized kerosene to BPL families only; (ii) raise the price of domestic LPG by Rs 75/cylinder; (iii) discontinue the practice of asking ONGC/GAIL/OIL to provide upstream assistance, but instead collecting their contribution by raising the OIDB cess.

'The third set of recommendations relates to restructuring excise duties from the present mix of specific and ad-valorem to a pure specific levy and calibrating the levies at Rs 5.00/litre of diesel and Rs 14.75/ litre of petrol.'

Financial Inclusion

A committee was set up by the government in 2006 to look into what needed to be done to expand the availability of financial services to weaker sections. The term 'financial inclusion' gained currency after that since the committee came to be known as the Committee on Financial Inclusion. This term was used in the terms of reference. I chaired the committee and had members[3] drawn from various segments of rural credit and finance. The chairman of NABARD was Member Secretary. The committee submitted its report in 2008. As many actions have been taken since then in the area of financial inclusion, it may not be necessary to go into the details of the recommendations. However, the approach to financial inclusion recommended by the committee is worth recalling.

The committee said in its introduction:

'Deliberations on the subject of Financial Inclusion contributed to a consensus that merely having a bank account may not be a good indicator of financial inclusion. Further, indebtedness as quantified in the NSSO 59th round (2003) may not also be a reflective indicator. The ideal definition should look at people who want to access financial services but are denied the same. If genuine claimants for credit and financial services are denied the same, then that is a case of exclusion. As this aspect would raise the issue of credit worthiness or bankability, it is also necessary to dwell upon what could be done to make the claimants of institutional credit bankable or creditworthy. This would require re-engineering of existing financial products or delivery systems and making them more in tune with the expectations and absorptive capacity of the intended clientele. Based on the above consideration, a broad working definition of financial inclusion could be as under: "Financial inclusion may be defined as the process of ensuring access to financial services and timely and adequate credit where needed by vulnerable groups such as weaker sections and low income groups at an affordable cost."

'The essence of financial inclusion is in trying to ensure that a range of appropriate financial services is available to every individual and enabling them to understand and access those services. Apart from the regular form of financial intermediation, it may include a basic, no-frills banking account for making and receiving payments, a savings product suited to the pattern of cash flows of a poor household, money transfer facilities, small loans and overdrafts for productive, personal and other purposes, insurance (life and non-life), etc. While financial inclusion, in the narrow sense, may be achieved to some extent by offering any one of these services, the objective of "Comprehensive Financial Inclusion" would be to provide a holistic set of services encompassing all of the above.'

The committee also urged the use of technology to facilitate financial inclusion and recommended the setting up of a financial inclusion technology fund.

On the overall strategy, the committee said:

'Overall strategy for building an inclusive financial sector may be based on:

- Effecting improvements within the existing formal credit delivery mechanism;
- Suggesting measures for improving credit absorption capacity especially amongst marginal and sub marginal farmers and poor non-cultivator households;
- Evolving new models for effective outreach, and
- Leveraging on technology based solutions.'

The committee looked at every institutional agency operating in rural areas and made recommendations on how each agency could be strengthened to widen its scope and thus enable wider financial inclusion.

While dealing with regional rural banks (RRBs), the committee recommended that there should be no further mergers of RRBs and a merger of all RRBs at state level was not required. While discussing micro financial institutions (MFI), the committee recommended:

- Greater legitimacy, accountability and transparency will not only enable MFIs to source adequate debt and equity funds, but could eventually enable MFIs to take and use savings as a low cost source for on-lending.
- The committee examined the structure and nature of operations of MFIs and took into account the proposed provisions of the MFI legislation which is under consideration of the GoI. Keeping in view the above aspects, the committee makes the following recommendations:

  - There is a need to recognize a separate category of Microfinance–Non-Banking Finance Companies (MF–NBFCs), without any relaxation on start-up capital and subject to the regulatory prescriptions applicable for NBFCs. Such MF–NBFCs could be defined as companies that provide thrift, credit, micro-insurance, remittances and other financial services up to a specified amount to the poor in rural, semi-urban and urban areas.
  - To ensure that this provision is used by NBFCs which are focused on providing microfinance to the poor, it should be specified that at least 80% of the assets of MF–NBFCs should be in the form of microcredit of upto Rs 50,000 for agriculture, allied and non-farm activities and in case of housing, loans upto Rs 1,50,000, per individual borrower, whether given through a group mechanism or directly.
  - If this recommendation had been accepted and acted upon, the serious problems that arose later with respect to micro finance institutions in Andhra Pradesh could have been avoided. A later committee made the same recommendation, which was accepted by RBI.

Estimation of Savings and Investment

A high level committee[4] on estimation of savings and investment was set up in 2008. Though set up by the Ministry of Statistics and

Programme Implementation, the Secretariat was provided by RBI. The report was submitted in early 2009. The committee examined in detail the conceptual aspects of the estimates of savings and investment, and refined the procedure by eliminating data gaps. It suggested measures to strengthen the databases used then for the estimation of savings and investment. A 'worksheet' approach was adopted wherein each and every component of financial savings was examined with respect to database, data quality and methodology. A comprehensive review of the rates and ratios used in the estimation procedure was undertaken.

Estimation of savings and investment is important for any economy because ultimately, the growth of an economy depends on these two key factors. But this task becomes difficult in a developing economy with a large unorganized sector. The procedures to be adopted for estimation are thus different from developed economies. For example, the household sector is a conglomerate consisting of both consumer and producer households. A few major recommendations of the committee are highlighted here:

Household Savings

The committee recommended that NSSO should initiate at the earliest a comprehensive income-expenditure survey for the consumer household sector for the purpose of estimation of savings. This needed to be accompanied by an enterprise survey. However, the committee recommended the continuation of the procedures then in vogue with suggested modifications. As mentioned earlier, detailed recommendations were made for the improvement of every item in the category of financial savings of the household sector.

With respect to household savings in real assets, the prevailing procedure of residual estimation was to be continued.

Private Corporate Savings and Estimates

The committee recommended the use of MCA 21 (Ministry of Corporate Affairs) data for estimating savings and capital formation of non-government, non-functional companies. In this respect, the committee also mentioned the need to wait till 'data quality and reporting issues' were resolved. The committee felt that the then prevailing sampling method had many pitfalls.

Estimation of Capital Formation

The estimation of capital formation through different methods might have to continue. However, capital formation arrived from the savings side should be treated as firmer relative to estimates based on commodity flow. The committee recommended the regular updation of rates and ratios used in the commodity flow. The committee had made specific suggestions on the various ratios.

While many recommendations were put into immediate effect, some of the key recommendations, such as an income-expenditure survey for consumer households, are still in the experimental stage. The use of MCA 21 data has given rise to certain doubts in relation to national income estimation. While there is nothing wrong in the methodology for establishing the 'purity of data', a closer examination of the data is called for. This data also needs to be put in the public domain.

Efficient Management of Public Expenditures

Against the background of the observations made in the Eleventh Plan documents on the various anomalies and inconsistencies that arise out of the present classification of expenditures, the Planning Commission set up a committee in April 2011 to study these problems. I was requested to chair the committee.[5] The main recommendations were:

1. Plan and Non-Plan Distribution: Dealing with one of the terms of references, the committee said:

> 'The classification of expenditure into Plan and Non-Plan, although not rooted in the Constitution, has evolved with planning process. Over a period of time, several issues have cropped up from the distinction between plan and non-plan, making it dysfunctional and an obstacle in outcome based budgeting. Therefore, this distinction should go for both Union and State Budgets. On removal of Plan/Non-Plan distinction in the Budget, there should be a fundamental shift in the approach of public expenditure management—from a segmented view of Plan and Non-Plan to holistic view of expenditure; from a one year horizon to a multi-year horizon; and from input based budgeting to the budgeting linked to outputs and outcomes. This shift to holistic view of expenditure would require, inter alia changes in organizational structure, mandates and processes. In the envisaged

system, the MOF will prepare proposed allocations for ministries with broad scheme-wise allocations and committed items and send it to Planning Commission for their feedback and scrutiny. The Planning Commission will scrutinise these allocations based on the overall development priorities, outcome targets and sectoral requirements. On the receipt of the comments of Planning Commission, the budget allocations will be further reviewed and incorporated in the budget by the MOF.'

2. Mode of Transfer of Funds: The Committee recommended the treasury mode of transfer of Central Plan funds. This recommendation was made against the background of rising direct transfers society mode. On this it said:

'The Committee recommends the treasury mode of transfer of central plan funds. The switchover to complete treasury mode of transfer of funds may be made straightforward possibly beginning all new schemes from the 12th Five Year Plan. For existing schemes, a short transition period is required to allow for necessary adjustment. However, till complete switchover to treasury mode is done, accounting, and submission of Utilisation Certificates under society mode should be rationalized and auditing strengthened through several measures in the manner described in one of the chapters.'

3. Revenue–Capital Classification

'The committee is in favour of continuing the Revenue–Capital classification. Capital expenditure should relate to creation of assets and be determined by ownership criterion. While all transfers should be treated as revenue expenditure in accounts, an 'adjusted revenue deficit' (adjusting the revenue deficit to the extent of grants for creating assets) may be considered only for FRBM compliance.'

There were several other recommendations relating to the monitoring of the transfer of plan funds, and the scope of the public sector plan.

The recommendations relating to the abolition of the distinction between Plan and Non-Plan expenditures has lost its significance with the abolition of the Planning Commission. However, it must be added that even though the committee had the finance member of the Planning Commission as one of its members, the then Planning Commission was dragging its feet regarding the suggestion. There was some feeling that the recommendation could result in the weakening of the Planning Commission. But this is not so. Actually, the implementation of the recommendation would have enhanced the role of the Planning Commission as it would be looking at the total expenditures of a sector and making its recommendations regarding what should be done. It would have avoided the classic example of 'schools with buildings but not teachers'.

Our recommendation regarding 'adjusted revenue deficit' was accepted and there is an item even today in the Budget. But the fear is that it could lead to 'manipulation' of revenue expenditures leading ultimately to the creation of non-assets. The Fourteenth Finance Commission was not in favour of this idea. Though conceptually valid, the concept of adjusted revenue deficit can lead to controversies.

Committees on J & K

Prime Minister Manmohan Singh was deeply interested in finding solutions to the problems of Jammu and Kashmir. While undoubtedly the political solution was key, he also wanted answers to the economic problems. He felt that the solution to the economic problems might create the necessary environment for finding solutions to the political issues. Prime Minister Manmohan Singh set up two committees, one comprising political leaders and another comprising experts and industrialists. I chaired both the committees. Let me highlight some of the recommendations of the latter committee[6] which was set up in 2010 to formulate a job plan or programmes. The prime minister had already initiated a special infrastructure plan for J & K. It included construction of tunnels, roads and power plants. It is against this background the committee (expert group as it was called) made specific recommendations for expanding the job opportunities.

On the broad strategy of job development, the group said:

'Creating a large number of jobs will require a two pronged strategy. The first would be to identify sectors with large employment generation potential and suggest interventions to kick start the growth process and the second, a human resource development initiative focussed on improving skill sets through improving access to education and focussed placement oriented training. Learning from the experience of the rest of India, the Expert Group focussed a lot of its attention on the latter.'

With respect to skill development, the group recommended two initiatives: 'The first is Skill, Empowerment and Employment Scheme for J&K (SEE J&K) and the second is a Special Industry Initiative for J&K (SII J&K).'

The expert group, in consultation with the Ministry of Rural Development (MoRD), developed a special placement-linked, market-driven skill training programme for the J & K youth. The scheme proposed to provide placement-linked, market-driven skill training to 50,000 to 1,00,000 youth in three to five years.

On the Special Industry Initiative, the group said:

'J&K has a large talent pool of youth who are well educated but are unable to find employment due to lack of soft skills or lack of practical/ hands-on training. To engage the youth, one initiative could be to identify 10-20 companies across industry sectors to partner with an educational institution and run special training programs to enhance employability of 8000 youth per annum in J&K over a five year period. This would translate to 40,000 youth in J&K becoming employable in various sectors across India. This could be operationalized through a scheme to be executed in the PPP mode with 50:50 cost-sharing between the government and the private sector.'

Many companies, including leading IT companies such as TCS and Infosys, came forward to support the scheme. The group also recommended a special scholarship scheme for J & K.

The second set of recommendations related to sectoral initiatives, that is, promotion of such sectors that would lead to increased employment.

The sectors identified were agriculture, livestock, horticulture, tourism and handicraft. A detailed analysis was done to identify specific action programmes in each of the sectors.

The group's recommendations were taken up seriously by the home ministry and EAC and there was a highly welcome response to the Special Industry Initiative. Several companies came forward to participate in the training-cum-placement initiative. I inaugurated several such programmes. Also, the Ministry of Rural Development was active in making a success of the skill empowerment and employment scheme. It is unfortunate that these initiatives were later abandoned.

Deregulation of Sugar

In 2012, the Government of India appointed a committee[7] to take a 'comprehensive look' at the issues related to regulation of the sugar sector. These regulations in fact span the value chain ranging from sugarcane production to actual distribution of sugar in the domestic market and export of sugar. Sugar industry is one of the few industries that contribute to the development of the rural economy through utilization of a rural resource. The regulations covered cane reservation area (for every mill), minimum distance criterion, pricing of sugarcane, levy sugar obligation, regulated release of free sale sugar, trade policy for sugar and regulation relating to byproducts. This elaborate network of regulations arose because of the anxiety to please different stakeholders such as sugarcane producers, sugar mills and domestic consumers of sugar.

The committee felt that many of the regulations had outlived their usefulness, whatever might have been their original justification. The committee also indicated what the interim measures could be.

The most important recommendation was related to sugarcane pricing and the committee said:

> 'There is general agreement that there is a need to rationalize the pricing of sugarcane. It is also generally agreed that there should be a sharing of the revenues/value created in the sugarcane value chain between the farmers and the millers in a fair and equitable manner. The question that needs to be answered is the exact level and manner of arriving at the cane dues.
>
> It would be fair to share the revenue pot of value created in the sugarcane value chain between the farmers and millers in the ratio of their relative costs. An analysis of the costs incurred by sugarcane

farmers and those incurred by sugar mills suggests that this ratio between farmers and millers, taking a recovery rate of 10.31 per cent, works out as 69:31 which, rounded off, can be taken as 70:30. (If by-products are loaded on the value of sugar, the value-sharing ratio for farmers is estimated to amount to roughly 75 per cent of the ex-mill value of sugar alone). However, farmers will in all circumstances be paid the Fair and Remunerative Price (FRP) as the minimum, and this will be paid up-front.'

Thus, the farmers are assured of a price under any circumstances. But normally, they would get 75 per cent of the ex-mill value of sugar. The committee recommended suitable measures to ensure that the mills correctly report the ex-mill value.

The sugar industry has been passing through several business cycles. The recommendation of the committee could give stability to this sector. Tamil Nadu and Karnataka have passed regulations to implement the recommendation. But Uttar Pradesh has refused to implement this recommendation. This is unfortunate. In this state, the state aided prices have been fixed way above the FRP fixed by the Government of India. This has led to accumulations of arrears. The policy towards by-products and production of ethanol needs re-examination. A holistic view embracing all stakeholders is needed.

National Food Security Bill

The prime minister set up a committee in October 2010 under my chairmanship[8] to examine the implications of the National Food Security Bill (NFSB) prepared by the National Advisory Council (NAC). The time given to report back was one month.

The salient features of the National Food Security Bill were:
- Legal entitlement to subsidized food grains to be extended to at least 75 per cent of the country's population—90 per cent in rural areas and 50 per cent in urban areas.
- The priority households (46 per cent in rural areas and 28 per cent in urban areas) to have a monthly entitlement of 35 kgs (equivalent to 7 kgs per person) at a subsidized price of Re 1 per kg for millets, Rs 2 per kg for wheat and Rs 3 per kg for rice.

- The general households (39 per cent rural and 12 per cent urban in phase 1 and 44 per cent rural and 22 per cent urban in the final phase) to have a monthly entitlement of 20 kgs (equivalent to 4 kgs per person) at a price not exceeding 50 per cent of the current minimum support price for millets, wheat and rice.
- The minimum coverage, entitlement and price to remain unchanged until the end of the Twelfth Five-Year Plan.
- The Government of India to specify the criteria for categorization of population into priority and general households.

Though the coverage under the bill is claimed to be 'universal', there were still two categories to be identified. The committee examined the foodgrain requirement to fulfil the entitlements under NFSB at that point in time and in the future, the impact of such procurement on open market prices, which would also affect the priority and general categories who purchased almost 25–30 per cent of their consumption from the open market, and finally the subsidy implications for both phases.

The group came to the conclusion that the foodgrain required to be procured would be larger than what was estimated by NAC, and this would amount to almost 50 per cent of the marketable surplus.

Foodgrain to be procured would have to include what was required for other welfare schemes as well as buffer stock. Given the cycles in agricultural production, the procurement level would have to be around 30 per cent of production.

The expert committee was fully in agreement with the spirit of NAC's recommendations. However, it wanted to ensure that the mandated entitlements kept in mind the availability of grain. The report said,

'The Expert Committee accordingly recommends that the entitled population may be defined as the percentage of population below the official poverty line + 10 per cent of the BPL population. Using the Tendulkar poverty line, this works out to 46 per cent rural and 28 per cent urban population. These percentages are the same as those recommended by the NAC for categorization as the 'priority' households. This captures not only the poor but also some at the margin, which is desirable given the objectives of the NFSB.'

The entitled population would get 7 kg per person per month. The price initially would be as indicated by NAC. Thereafter, it would have to be inflation adjusted. The expert committee feels that these can be indexed to the Consumer Price Index. Since there are currently three indices being generated, we could use an average of the indices to adjust the issue price of the foodgrain suitably. The committee also estimated that after meeting the entitlement of the entitled category, other welfare schemes, which must also be treated as mandatory, and buffer stock, there would be around 5.4 million tonnes of foodgrains available in 2011 for distribution at an issue price equal to MSP. In 2013–14, according to the current projections on production and procurement, 5.68 million tonnes of grain can be distributed to the non-entitled population at an issue price equal to the MSP.

The committee had made other recommendations relating to the identification of beneficiaries and streamlining the public distribution system.

The government more or less decided to act according to the recommendations of the expert group. Even this will have a substantial burden in the form of subsidy.

Production Sharing Contracts Mechanism in the Petroleum Industry

The prime minister appointed in December 2012 a committee under my chairmanship[9] to examine some of the key issues faced by the petroleum industry. There is a twofold problem in the exploration of petroleum. First, operators invest huge amounts of money under conditions of uncertainty. They need to be adequately compensated so that they are encouraged to invest in exploration. At the same time, the government's interests as the owner need to be protected. The terms of reference to the committee included review of the existing production sharing contracts mechanism, mechanisms for managing the contract implementation, mechanisms to monitor and audit the Government of India's share of profit-petroleum and guidelines for determining the basis or formula for the price of domestically produced gas.

The committee comprised, among others, a retired judge of the Supreme Court, a member of the Planning Commission who had earlier dealt with the petroleum industry as Secretary, and a distinguished economist who had studied problems relating to natural resources.

The most important recommendation of the committee was related to the production sharing mechanism. What the committee recommended was truly production sharing. The earlier system was not in effect production sharing. The committee said:

'The committee recommends a new contractual system and fiscal regime based on a post-royalty-payment revenue-sharing to overcome the difficulties in managing the existing model based on the Pre-Tax Investment Multiple (PTIM) methodology and the cost-recovery mechanism. The extant fiscal model, with primary focus on upstream costs, has been found to be a major bottleneck in expeditious performance of exploratory work. The proposed model should overcome the constraints inherent to the cost-based monitoring mechanism of the existing PSC, and should meet the Government's objective of promoting rapid exploration and development in the oil and gas sector.

'The committee recommends that the proposed contractual model be based on a two-dimensional matrix. The proposed model envisages that the production or post-royalty value of the combined output of oil and gas be shared between the Government and the Contractor. Such a 'production sharing' will be linked to the average daily production and prevailing average of oil and gas prices in a well-defined period. The committee notes that in the proposed system, the Government will be able to capture economic rent in the form of royalty and revenue share of hydrocarbons, right from the onset of production. The committee further recognises that the Government will be able to secure a share in any windfall profits accruing on account of a price surge or a geological surprise by way of a huge hydrocarbon find.

'The production share for each cell of the matrix will be biddable, and the winning bid will be determined on the basis of competitive bidding. The bid has to be progressive and incremental with respect to the Government take, i.e., the Government take will be in an ascending order for increases in production and price. The NPV of Government's share in revenue, using the benchmarked production profile for the block, will be one of the deciding criteria for assessing a bid.'

The committee felt that the then existing model, which involved cost recovery before sharing with the government of profit-petroleum, led to many controversies, including complaints of inflating costs. As mentioned earlier, the new model recommended by the committee was sharing of the post royalty value of the combined output of oil and gas.

On the second important recommendation related to the pricing of domestic production of gas, the committee said:

'Since a competitive domestic price for gas does not currently exist and may not be expected to come about for several more years, the policy will have to be based on searching out from global trade transactions of gas the competitive price of gas at the global level. As the global market is not fully integrated in terms of physical flows and is also not everywhere liquid enough, it is proposed to combine two methods of search for such prices.

'First, the netback price of Indian LNG import at the wellhead of the exporting countries should be estimated. Since there may be several sources of gas imports, the average of such netback of import prices at the wellheads would represent the average global price for Indian imports. It may be assumed that each gas exporting country also faces competition and, therefore, there is no reason to suppose that India faces any bias of being over-charged or undercharged vis-à-vis other competing buyers in the global gas market constructed through such aggregation for averaging. Such a netback average price may be interpreted as the arm's length competitive price applicable for India, and such price may be estimated on the basis of recent historical transactions.

'A second method of searching for a competitive price for India is to take the average of pricing prevailing at trading points of transactions—i.e., the hubs or balancing points of the major markets of continents. For this, (a) the hub price (at the Henry Hub) in the US (for North America), (b) the price at the National Balancing Point of the UK (for Europe), and (c) the netback price at the sources of supply for Japan (a big buyer treated in the Asia–Pacific region as setting a benchmark for the region) may be taken as the prices most relevant for the purpose of approximating India's average price for producers at their supply points across continents. Such a global average price may also be interpreted as an arm's length competitive price for India.

'Finally, the average of the prices arrived at through the aforementioned two methods may be taken. Such an overall average of global prices, derived on the basis of netback and hub / balancing point pricing principles, can be taken as the economically appropriate estimates of the arm's length competitive prices applicable for India. While the formulae detailed in this section directly or indirectly take into account the data of a wide range of transactions including those with India, the methodology neutralizes any bias for India and ensures the arm's length aspect of pricing, as best as possible.'

In the case of oil, no complicated formula is necessary because there is a competitive market worldwide and the imported landed cost becomes the basis of price. But in the case of gas, there is no such competitive market even abroad.

There was much controversy over the recommendation of gas pricing because it was felt that it might be applied even to enterprises that were already in operation. That was a mistaken impression.

The committee was clear and it said: 'It is clarified that the proposed pricing formula would only apply prospectively and is not proposed for application to gas prices already approved.'

The committee's statement on the subject was categorical and yet the controversy continued.

Expert Group on the Measurement of Poverty

The Planning Commission appointed an expert group under my chairmanship[10] in June 2012 to go into the methodology for the measurement of poverty and drawing up an appropriate poverty line. The Planning Commission had constituted expert groups on poverty measurement usually after a gap of about twelve to fifteen years. However, this new group was appointed within less than three years after the submission of the recommendations of the Tendulkar expert group. The apparent urgency with which the new group was appointed reflected perhaps the changed aspirations regarding minimally acceptable standards of living in the country.

Our group continued with the practice of defining poverty in terms of income or, in the absence of such data, in terms of expenditure. Multidimensional indicators for defining poverty face several problems, which are indicated in the report. In defining the new consumption basket separating the poor from the rest, the group was of the view that 'it should contain a food component that addresses the capability to be adequately nourished as well as some normative level of consumption expenditure for essential non-food item groups (education, clothing, conveyance and house rent) besides a residual set of behaviourally determined non-food expenditure'. The introduction of essential non-food consumption expenditure in the basket is an innovation. The group also went in favour of separate consumption baskets for the rural and urban areas. The net result of the changes introduced by the new group was that the new poverty line was 19 per cent and 41 per cent higher in the rural and urban areas than the Tendulkar group estimates. According to our group, the poverty line translates into monthly per household expenditure of Rs 4880 in rural India and of Rs 7035 for urban India— assuming a family of five members in each case in 2011–12. While the Tendulkar group methodology gives a poverty ratio in 2011–12 of 21.9 per cent, our methodology shows the ratio at 29.5 per cent.

We can look at the proposed poverty line level in terms of PPP dollars per capita per day. As per the (World Bank, 2014) PPP values, the poverty line translates to $2.14 per capita per day for rural India, $3.10 per capita per day for urban India and $2.44 per capita per day for the country as a whole. (In PPP conversion, US$1= Rs 15.11.)

Two comments can be made on the poverty ratios as they emerge from our estimates. One, there was a sharp decline in the poverty ratio between 2009–10 and 2011–12 from 38.2 per cent to 29.5 per cent—a drop of 8.7 percentage points. The same conclusion follows from the estimates based on the Tendulkar methodology as well. In fact, during periods of high growth, poverty ratios tend to fall significantly. Second, in absolute numbers, the number of people below the poverty line came down from 454.6 million in 2009–10 to 263 million in 2011–12, a fall of 91.6 million. In fact, the Oxford Study that estimates poverty through a multidimensional poverty index said: 'India has made momentous progress in reducing multidimensional poverty. The incidence of multidimensional poverty was almost halved between 2005–06 and 2015–16 climbing down to 27.5 per cent. Thus, within ten years, the number of poor people in India fell by more than 271 million—a truly massive gain.' With the recent slowdown in growth, perhaps the reduction in the poverty ratio may have slowed down.

The use of National Sample Survey (NSS) data for computing the poverty ratio has been contested on the grounds that the total private consumption expenditure as per NSS is much lower than that in the National Accounts Statistics. In fact, the difference between the two estimates is widening over time. Since size-distribution of private consumption expenditure is available only under NSS, we are left with no choice but to use it. However, with the difference rising to 68 per cent, a relook at the problem has become necessary.

The report of our group was submitted to the new government in 2014, which did not take any view. It has been in limbo since then.

Commission on AIDS in Asia

One committee[11] which I chaired during this period had nothing to do directly with economics. That was the independent commission on AIDS in Asia appointed by UNAIDS. I was somewhat surprised when I was approached. But I was told that they wanted a development economist from Asia to head this committee so that a holistic view could be taken. The committee comprised eminent people from various countries in Asia and outside. They also came from different walks of life. The Member–Secretary of the committee was Prasada Rao, who was earlier Health Secretary, Government of India, and who had also headed the Aids control organization in India. His knowledge and experience were of immense help to the committee. For familiarizing myself with the situation, he and I met with the vulnerable groups in India, such as sex workers, male to male sex practitioners, etc. In Kolkata, I visited Sonagachi and had extensive discussions on how to prevent the spread. The commission appointed several study groups to understand the different aspects of the spread of the virus. The report clearly defined the epidemic characteristics in Asia as distinguished say from Africa and forecasted its progression with and without interventions. It also quantified the number of people who were vulnerable to the epidemic out of the large population of 3.1 billion in the region. Given the limitation of resources, the commission had to decide on the relative emphasis on prevention and treatment. We came to the conclusion that the most cost-effective approach would be to lay greater emphasis on prevention. However, the need for taking care of the treatment could not be overlooked. The commission also recommended the decriminalization of male to male sex. The commission's report turned out to be a comprehensive study on Aids. The 230-page report contained a technical annexe. I handed over the report to UN Secretary-General Ban Ki-moon in June 2008 at a special meeting convened in New York. The Secretary-General received the report with great enthusiasm. He also spoke to me about his India connection. I handed over the report to Manmohan Singh on 30 June 2008, once again at a special meeting. The prime minister's finding time to receive the report was an affirmation of the commitment of the government to tackle AIDS seriously. Oscar Fernandes, the minister in charge, was also present.

An important development during the commission's work from 2006 to 2008 was the rapidly changing political scenario in Thailand. On 19 September 2006, my wife and I had been invited by Prasada Rao for dinner. The Indian ambassador in Thailand was among the invitees. After the dinner, when we were ready to leave, the ambassador received a call on his mobile. He came back and announced that there was an army coup and the prime minister of Thailand was deposed. We somehow managed to return to the hotel. We had to delay our departure by one day. This was the most non-violent coup ever. Not even one gunshot was heard.

Utility of EAC

I have outlined the kind of work that EAC had done between 2005 and 2014. Prime Minister Manmohan Singh made frequent use of the council. One would have thought that an economist prime minister would have less need of such an organization. On the contrary, he felt the need more. As the prime minister, he had to deal with multitudes of issues well beyond purely economic issues. He felt sometimes that he could not pay adequate attention to economic issues. Once he told me, 'Think for me.' The structure that EAC had during this period is perhaps the appropriate one. Too large a body without a secretariat or leader can serve only a limited purpose. In the final analysis, the question we have to ask is, 'Do we need such a body?' Each ministry has an economic adviser. The finance ministry has a chief economic adviser who plays a critical role. Prime ministers do not normally have full-fledged economic advisers. However, what the prime minister needs is someone or a small group above the bureaucratic level. One can ask the question whether the prime minister needs an additional structure besides the Planning Commission or now, Niti Aayog. The Planning Commission had grown in size. It was not just a think tank. It had become a quasi-administrative body. A small compact body like EAC that Manmohan Singh had can play a useful role and that depends on how the prime minister uses it. I met the prime minister regularly. It is important that the chairman of EAC must have the rank of a cabinet minister like the deputy chairman of the Planning Commission. That status is important to make his or her impact felt. Manmohan Singh recognized that. However, we have a brief history of EAC. Dismantling EAC in 2014 was a wrong step. I am glad it has been revived now. To make the organization more effective, we need to develop certain conventions and procedures. In fact, I was made a member of several groups comprising purely cabinet ministers. I felt I was useful during my tenure as chairman of EAC. Of course, towards the end of UPA II when the government was caught in several controversies, I could not play much of a role. The usefulness of EAC also depends on how other cabinet ministers, particularly the finance minister, react to EAC. Sometimes, this is a problem. Manmohan Singh had trust in me and in the EAC and that gave us the satisfaction. However, there is one problem with purely advisory bodies. Sometimes, they may not know whether the advice given was accepted or not. Since I met the prime minister regularly, I would get to know his reactions most of the time. But there were occasions when one was not sure of how the advice was taken.

One issue on which I was not consulted was the decision in the Budget of 2012–13 on an amendment to the Income Tax Act, 1961, seeking to tax with retrospective effect from 1962, mergers or acquisitions transactions involving foreign companies, which enabled them to control assets in India. This move was aimed at negating the

Supreme Court judgment that went in favour of Vodafone. I met the prime minister after it was announced. I also met the finance minister (Pranab Mukherjee) and expressed my disagreement. But the finance minister mentioned how there were so many legislations in the past from the Nehru era onwards that were made applicable with retrospective effect. I tried to point out to him that there was a difference between social legislations and tax legislations. I also mentioned that had such a legislation been introduced immediately after the Bombay High Court decision, which went in favour of the government, there would have less grounds for concern. But bringing in such a legislation after the Supreme Court had overruled the Bombay High Court was not in good taste. I was not arguing about the merit of the proposed change. What was disquieting was to modify a tax legislation with retrospective effect. In fact, this particular decision of the government had a dampening effect on the investment climate and was one of the factors responsible for the decline in the investment rate.

Finally, to end on a half-serious note, I must refer to one 'rumour' that was floating during the period that I was being considered for the position of finance minister. This is not without foundation. However, the idea of bringing a technical person as finance minister did not go far and it faded away!

17

Some Ruminations

The preceding chapters have dealt with what I did in various capacities since 1982. In 2014, I left Delhi and came to Chennai. In fact, I have not lived for any continuous period in Chennai after the 1950s. Of course, my official work took me to Chennai often. But these were all brief visits. Since 2014, I have been involved with the academic world. The four institutions with which I am associated are the Madras School of Economics; C.R. Rao Advanced Institute of Mathematics, Statistics and Computer Science; the ICFAI University and Ahmedabad University. I was for a time chancellor of the Central University of Hyderabad. I started my professional life in academia and am ending it there. A full circle!

In this chapter, I look back over the last seven decades and reflect on some of the key developments in the economy. When India gained Independence, I was in the first year of college. Thus, my entire adult life was spent in Independent India and I was a witness to many developments. Many people do not realize that India's economic progress in the first half of the twentieth century under British rule was dismal. During the five decades, India's annual growth rate was just 0.9 per cent. With population growing at 0.83 per cent, per capita income remained almost flat.[1] Immediately after Independence, growth became the most urgent concern for policymakers.

The dominant view in the literature on development economics in the 1950s and 1960s was that the government had an important role to play and that it should undertake activities that would compensate for 'market failure'. Market failure was perceived particularly in its inability to allocate resources over time, that is, for investment because of the 'myopic' nature of market participants. The literature also emphasized the benefit of a coordinated and consistent set of investment decisions. It is this line of reasoning that led most developing countries, including India, to formulate economy-wide plans. Though India adopted a mixed economy, the mix was tilted heavily towards the state, at least incrementally.

Policymakers in India in the 1950s and 1960s cannot be blamed for the decisions they took. At that time, there was no clear model available for accelerating growth in developing countries. State intervention on an extensive scale seemed to be appropriate, even though there were some critics even at that time. However, by the 1970s, it was becoming clear that the model we had chosen was not delivering and that it needed to change.[2] By that time, there were many more critics of the Indian strategy. But our policymakers refused to recognize this. It was around that time that China made a big change.[3]

It was the crisis of 1990–91 that compelled the policymakers to turn to an 'idea whose time had come'. The break with the past came in three important directions. The first was to dismantle the complex regime of licences, permits and controls that dictated almost every facet of production and distribution. Barriers to entry and growth were dismantled. The second change in direction was to reverse the strong bias towards state ownership of means of production and the proliferation of public sector enterprises in almost every sphere of economic activity. Areas once reserved exclusively for the state were thrown open to private enterprise. The third change in direction was to abandon the inward-looking trade policy. By embracing international trade, India signalled that it was boldly abandoning its export pessimism and was accepting the challenge and opportunity of integrating into the world economy. This approach is very different from what we used to do when faced with BOP problems earlier.

There is a common thread running through the various measures introduced since July 1991. The objective is simple: to improve the efficiency of the system. The regulatory mechanism involving multitudes of controls had fragmented capacity and reduced competition even in the private sector. The thrust of the new economic policy was towards creating a more competitive environment in the economy as a means to improving the productivity and efficiency of the system. This was to be achieved by removing the barriers to entry as well as the restrictions on the growth of firms. While the new industrial policy which dismantled licences and controls seeks to bring about a greater competitive environment domestically, the trade policy seeks to improve international competitiveness, subject to the protection offered by tariffs which are themselves coming down. The private sector is being given a larger space to operate in, as some areas earlier reserved exclusively for the public sector are now also allowed to the private sector. In these areas, the public sector will have to compete with the private sector, even though the public sector may continue to play the dominant role. What is sought to be achieved is an improvement in the functioning of the various entities, whether in the private sector or the public sector, by injecting an element of competition in them. There is, however, nothing in the new economic policy that takes away the role of the state or the public sector in the system. The New Economic Policy of India has not necessarily diminished the role of state; it has only redefined it, expanding it in some areas and reducing it in others. As has been said, somewhat paradoxically, more market does not mean 'less government' but only 'different government'.

What has been the impact on the economy because of the reforms? Did India's growth rate pick up? Did the BOP situation improve? What happened to inequality in income and poverty?

India's average growth till the end of the 1970s remained modest with the average growth rate being 3.5 per cent. With population growing at 2.2 per cent, the per capita income growth rate was extremely modest at 1.3 per cent. However, on certain parameters, there have been noticeable improvements, such as the literacy rate and life expectancy (Table 17.1). The Indian economy did grow at 5.6 per cent in the 1980s. But it was accompanied by sharp deterioration in the fiscal and current account deficits and the economy faced the worst crisis in 1991–92 when the growth rate fell to 1 per cent. It is extremely doubtful if, without a change in the strategy of development, growth

Table 17.1 Literacy Rate and Life Expectancy

Parameter	1951	1981	1991	2001	2011	Current Value
Literacy Rate	30.7	43.1	51.6	64.8	73.0	
Crude Birth Rate (per 1000 population	39.9	37.2	32.5	24.8	21.8	20.0
Crude Death Rate (per 1000 population)	27.4	15.0	11.4	8.9	7.1	6.2
Infant Mortality Rate	146	110	80	66	44	32
Total Fertility Rate	6.0	4.5	3.6	3.1	2.4	2.2
Expectation of life at birth (in years)						
Male	37.1	54.1	60.6	61.8	66.9	68.2
Female	36.1	54.7	61.7	63.5	70	70.7

Source: Handbook of Statistics on Indian States, RBI.

would have picked up.[4] However, it must be admitted that the 1980s did see the beginnings of reforms. But the conviction to break totally with the past was not there.

Trends in Growth Post Liberalization

Between 1992–93 and 2000–01, GDP at factor cost grew annually by 6.20 per cent (Table 17.3). Between 2001–02 and 2012–13, it grew by 7.4 per cent and the growth rate between 2013–14 and 2019–20 was 6.7 per cent. The best performance was between 2005–06 and 2010–11 when GDP grew by 8.8 per cent, showing clearly what the potential growth rate of India was. This is the highest growth experienced by India over a sustained period of five to six years. This is despite the fact that this period included the global crisis year of 2008–09. During this period, the investment rate reached the peak of 39.1 per cent in 2007–08. There was a corresponding increase in the savings rate, touching the high of 36.8 per cent in 2007–08. The current account deficit in the BOP remained low at an average of 1.9 per cent. However, the growth story suffered a setback after 2011–12. The growth rate fell to 4.5 per cent in 2012–13 according to the 2004–05 series. According to 2011–12 base series, the corresponding figure is 5.5 per cent.

Table 17.2 Per Capita Income at Current US$

Country	Bangladesh	Indonesia	India	South Korea	Sri Lanka	Malaysia	Pakistan	China
1960	89.04		82.19	158.25	142.78	234.94	83.34	89.52
1970	140.00	79.71	112.43	279.30	183.93	357.66	172.47	113.16
1980	227.75	491.58	266.58	1715.43	267.67	1774.74	303.05	194.80
1990	306.27	585.08	367.56	6610.04	463.62	2441.74	371.68	317.88
2000	418.07	780.19	443.31	12256.99	869.70	4043.66	576.20	959.37
2010	781.15	3122.36	1357.56	23087.23	2799.65	9040.57	987.41	4550.45
2020	1961.61	3869.59	1927.71	31631.47	3680.67	10412.35	1188.86	10434.78

Source: World Development Indicators.

Table 17.3 Key Economic Indicators since the 1991 Economic Reforms

Year	GDP Growth Rate	Per Capita Income Growth Rate	GFD as a Percentage of GDP	Bank Credit Growth Rate	WPI Inflation	CPI Inflation	GFCF	GCF	GDS
1992–93	5.4	3.4	6.8	21.0			25.1	24.9	21.3
1993–94	5.7	3.7	8.0	8.2			23.7	24.0	21.7
1994–95	6.4	4.3	6.9	28.7	12.6		23.4	26.8	23.6
1995–96	7.3	5.3	6.3	20.1	8.0		25.1	27.3	23.6
1996–97	8.0	6.2	6.1	9.6	4.6		24.5	25.6	22.4
1997–98	4.3	2.2	7.0	16.4	4.4		25.4	27.7	24.2
1998–99	6.7	4.6	8.7	13.8	5.9		25.5	26.2	23.2
1999–00	8.0	6.0	9.1	18.2	3.3		27.5	28.8	25.5
2000–01	4.1	1.7	9.2	17.3	7.2		26.0	26.2	23.7
2001–02	5.4	3.3	9.6	15.3	3.6		29.9	26.2	24.8
2002–03	3.9	2.3	9.3	23.7	3.4		28.3	26.8	25.9
2003–04	8.0	6.5	8.3	15.3	5.5		28.3	29.0	29.0
2004–05	7.1	5.0	7.2	30.9	6.5		30.7	35.2	32.4
2005–06	9.5	7.8	6.5	37.0	4.5		32.8	36.4	33.4
2006–07	9.6	7.9	5.1	28.1	6.6		33.6	36.0	34.6
2007–08	9.3	8.1	4.0	22.3	4.7		35.8	39.1	36.8
2008–09	6.7	4.7	8.3	17.5	8.1		34.7	38.4	32.0
2009–10	8.6	6.8	9.3	16.9	3.8		34.0	38.9	33.7
2010–11	8.9	6.8	7.8	21.5	9.6		33.2	39.8	33.7
2011–12	6.7	5.1	6.9	17.0	8.9		34.3	39.0	34.6
2012–13	5.5	4.2	6.7	14.1	7.4		33.4	38.7	33.9
2013–14	6.4	5.0	6.7	13.9	5.2	9.3	31.3	33.8	32.1
2014–15	7.4	6.1	6.9	9.0	1.3	6.0	30.1	33.5	32.2
2015–16	8.0	6.6	6.9	10.9	-3.7	4.9	28.7	32.1	31.1
2016–17	8.3	6.9	5.8	8.2	1.7	4.5	28.2	32.0	31.3
2017–18	6.8	5.6	5.8	10.0	2.9	3.6	28.2	33.9	32.1

Table 17.3 Continued

Year	GDP Growth Rate	Per Capita Income Growth Rate	GFD as a Percentage of GDP	Bank Credit Growth Rate	WPI Inflation	CPI Inflation	GFCF	GCF	GDS
2018–19	6.5	5.4	6.9	13.3	4.3	3.4	29.2	32.7	30.6
2019–20	3.7	2.7	6.3	6.1	1.7	4.8	28.8	32.2	

Source: MOSPI, RBI. Economic Survey 2021–22.
Note:
- Till 2011–12, GDP at factor cost (at constant prices) is estimated with 2004–05 base. From 2012–13, GDP at market price (at constant prices) with 2011–12 base.
- Till 2011-12, per capita income growth is calculated on GDP (at constant prices) with 2004–05 base. From 2012–13, per capita income growth rate is based on GDP (at constant prices) with 2011–12 base.
- GFD is the gross fiscal deficit of both state and Central governments combined.
- Base year of the WPI inflation till 1993–94 is 1981–82. From 1994–95 to 2004–05, the base year is 1993–94, after that the base year is 2004–05.
- Base year for CPI combined inflation is 2012.
- GFCF and GCF as a percentage of GDP at current prices.
- Gross Domestic Savings (GDS) as a percentage of GDP at current prices.

The downturn after 2011–12 was the result of many causes. It was partly cyclical. The economy, after having reached its full potential, had begun to decline. Capacity utilization had reached its peak of 83.2 per cent in the fourth quarter of 2011. And the decline was accentuated by the rise in non-performing assets of banks. The extraordinary increase in bank credit between 2005 and 2011—the annual growth rate was as high as 23.9 per cent—is one of the causes for the rise in non-performing assets. Once growth rate started falling, projects that were viable turned unviable. In the context of the international financial crisis of 2008, the government decided to push the economy forward by a highly expansionary fiscal policy. The fiscal deficit of the Centre in 2008–09 and 2009–10 was 6 per cent and 6.5 per cent of GDP respectively. While there was the immediate benefit of a sharp rise in growth rate in 2009–10 and 2010–11, it also led to an inflationary spike. WPI inflation reached a peak of 10.9 per cent in April 2010 and continued to remain at a high level for the next two years. The sharp rise in price level also had a dampening effect on growth post 2010–11. Besides, there were other factors that had a dampening effect on the investment climate. The introduction of a tax law with retrospective effect in 2012–13 shook the business community. Even though that particular legislation affected only a few, the possibility of a tax law with retrospective effect sent shivers down the spine of entrepreneurs. Another factor of concern was the delay in getting environmental clearances on projects. This essentially led to a rise in ICOR. In fact, the downturn in general was not well managed. The government was also caught up with resolving many controversies.

The decline in growth rate that started well before the advent of Covid-19 should make the policymakers reflect and introspect. The growth performance since 2012–13 is a bit difficult to interpret. The introduction of a new series on national income with the base 2011–12 has raised many controversies. The methodological changes that were introduced—particularly the use of MCA 21 data for calculating manufacturing growth—have not found general acceptance. In any case, we have no other data to go by. As per the new data, 2015–16 and 2016–17 were good years with the growth rate around 8 per cent. The high growth rate of 2016–17 came as a surprise to all those who were witnessing the harsh situation following demonetization. Thereafter, it started declining and touched the level of 3.7 per cent in 2019–20. In fact, this period is marked by a sharp decline in gross fixed capital formation rate from 33.4 per cent of GDP in 2012–13 to 28.8 per cent in 2019–20. The private sector investment during this period fell from 26.4 per cent of GDP in 2012–13 to 21.8 per cent in 2019–2020 (Table 17.4). The shocking management failure with respect to demonetization announced in 2016 and the continuing teething problems of GST had their adverse impact on the economy. Certainly it appears from the data that the investment climate deteriorated.

The growth story cannot be complete without reference to the two recent events —one, Covid-19 and the other, the Russia–Ukraine War. The economic impact of Covid-19 is largely because of the actions taken to contain the spread of Covid-19, such as the lockdown. The net result has been a decline in growth rate by 6.6 per cent in 2021 and a rise in growth rate by 8.7 per cent in 2021–22. The economy is virtually

Table 17.4 Sector-wise Gross Fixed Capital Formation as Per Cent of GDP at Current Market Prices

Year	Public Sector	Private Sector	Total
2004–05 Series			
2000–01	6.7	16.0	22.7
2001–02	6.8	18.3	25.1
2002–03	6.6	17.1	23.7
2003–04	6.7	17.8	24.5
2004–05	6.9	21.8	28.7
2005–06	7.3	23.0	30.3
2006–07	7.9	23.4	31.3
2007–08	8.0	24.9	32.9
2008–09	8.5	23.8	32.3
2009–10	8.4	23.3	31.7
2010–11	7.8	23.1	30.9
2011–12	7.1	24.7	31.8
2012–13	7.8	22.6	30.4
2011–12 Series			
2000–01	6.9	19.1	26.0
2001–02	7.1	22.9	29.9
2002–03	6.9	21.4	28.3
2003–04	7.0	21.3	28.3
2004–05	7.2	23.6	30.7
2005–06	7.5	25.2	32.8
2006–07	8.1	25.5	33.6
2007–08	8.3	27.5	35.8
2008–09	8.8	25.9	34.7
2009–10	8.6	25.3	34.0
2010–11	8.0	25.2	33.2
2011–12	7.3	27.0	34.3
2012–13	7.0	26.4	33.4
2013–14	7.1	24.2	31.3
2014–15	7.0	23.1	30.1

Table 17.4 Continued

Year	Public Sector	Private Sector	Total
2015–16	7.5	21.3	28.7
2016–17	6.9	21.3	28.2
2017–18	6.7	21.5	28.2
2018–19	7.1	22.1	29.2
2019–20	6.9	21.8	28.8

Source: Economic Survey 2013–14 and 2021–22.

where it was in April 2020. We have lost two years. The decline in output is even greater when looked at from the trend rate of growth.

2022–23 could have been the first normal year after Covid-19. Even that assumption has been shattered by the Russian invasion of Ukraine. The economic impact of this war can be severe, if it continues for long. The sudden surge in crude oil prices can severely affect our BOP and the current account deficit can rise to 3 per cent of GDP. The impact of the rise in crude prices as well as other imported commodities on the general price level can be severe and overall inflation may well exceed 6 per cent, given the trends in liquidity. The expectation that the growth rate in 2022–23 could be around 8 per cent was optimistic even before the Russia–Ukraine War. Perhaps, we should settle for a growth rate of 7 per cent.

Balance of Payments

In the post-liberalization period, the BOP situation had remained comfortable (Table 17.5).[5] It is, in fact, a success story of liberalization. There were three years in which the current account showed a small surplus. Most of the years showed a small deficit. The exceptions were 2011–12 and 2012–13 when the current account deficit exceeded 4 per cent of GDP. This was taken care of quickly. Foreign exchange reserves showed a substantial increase and reached a peak of $635 billion in early 2022. Of course, the reserve accumulation is because of the excess of capital inflows over current account deficits. The opening up of the external sector, which included a liberal trade policy, market-determined exchange rate and liberal flow of

Table 17.5 Balance of Payment Indicators

Year	Export Growth Rate	Import Growth Rate	Import Cover of Reserves	Current Account Balance
1992–93	3.8	12.7	4.9	-1.4
1993–94	20.0	6.5	8.6	-0.4
1994–95	18.4	22.9	8.4	-1.0
1995–96	20.8	28.0	6.0	-1.6
1996–97	5.3	6.7	6.5	-1.2
1997–98	4.6	6.0	6.9	-1.3
1998–99	-5.1	2.2	8.2	-1.0
1999–00	10.8	17.2	8.2	-1.0
2000–01	21.0	1.7	8.8	-0.6
2001–02	-1.6	1.7	11.5	0.7
2002–03	20.3	19.4	14.2	1.2
2003–04	21.1	27.3	16.9	2.3
2004–05	30.8	42.7	14.3	-0.3
2005–06	23.4	33.8	11.6	-1.2
2006–07	22.6	24.5	12.5	-1.0
2007–08	28.9	35.4	14.4	-1.3
2008–09	13.7	20.8	9.8	-2.3
2009–10	-3.5	-5.0	11.1	-2.8
2010–11	40.5	28.2	9.5	-2.9
2011–12	21.8	32.3	7.1	-4.3
2012–13	-1.8	0.3	7.0	-4.8
2013–14	4.7	-8.3	7.8	-1.7
2014–15	-1.3	-0.5	8.9	-1.3
2015–16	-15.5	-15.0	10.9	-1.1
2016–17	5.2	0.9	11.3	-0.6
2017–18	10.0	21.1	10.9	-1.8
2018–19	8.7	10.4	9.6	-2.1
2019–20	-5.1	-7.7	12.0	-0.9

Source: RBI DBIE.

external resources, has greatly strengthened the external sector. However, we still run a high merchandise trade deficit, which is offset to a large extent by the surplus in services. The merchandise export growth during 2005–11 was high at 20.9 per cent. Of course, there were periods from time to time when the currency came under pressure because of the sudden outflows of capital largely triggered by external factors. In the final analysis, the exchange rate of the rupee cannot be stable, if there are significant inflation differentials. The management of the rupee in such times of stress needs special attention. The accumulation of reserves is a facilitating factor in this context. What the global environment for trade will be in future is a major question mark.

Poverty Ratio

Besides growth, the other major objective of economic policy is to reduce the number of people living below the poverty line.[6] There are many problems associated with the definition of poverty and the kind of data required to measure it. Going by the procedure adopted by the erstwhile Planning Commission using the Tendulkar expert group methodology, the overall poverty ratio came down from 45.3 per cent in 1993–94 to 37.2 per cent in 2004–05 and further down to 21.9 per cent in 2011–12 (Table 17.6). The per year reduction in percentage points in the poverty ratio between 1993–94 and 2004–05 was 0.7 and between 2004–05 and 2011–12 it was 2.18. The annual per capita income growth in the first period was 4.3 per cent and in the second period it was 6.7 per cent (Table 17.3). The post-reform period up to 2011–12 saw a significant reduction in the poverty ratio because of faster growth supplemented by appropriate poverty reduction programmes such as the Rural Employment Guarantee Scheme and Extended Food Security Scheme. This decline in poverty is also corroborated by the multiple indicator index computed by the Oxford Study.[7] With the decline in growth rate since 2011–12 and with a negative growth in 2020–21, the decline in poverty reduction may have slowed down. The key lesson to be learnt is that for poverty reduction, high growth is needed. We also need appropriate safety net measures. Together, the two can speed up the reduction in the poverty ratio.

Table 17.6 Percentage and Number of Poor Estimated from Expert Group (Tendulkar) Methodology

Year	Poverty Ratio (per cent)			Number of Poor (Million)		
	Rural	Urban	Total	Rural	Urban	Total
1993–94	50.1	31.8	45.3	328.6	74.5	403.7
2004–05	41.8	25.7	37.2	326.3	80.8	407.1
2009–10	33.8	20.9	29.8	278.2	76.5	354.7
2011–12	25.7	13.7	21.9	216.7	53.1	269.8

Decline in Poverty Ratio Estimated from Expert Group (Tendulkar) Methodology			
			(Percentage points per year)
Period	Rural	Urban	Total
1993–94 to 2004–05	0.75	0.55	0.74
2004–05 to 2011–12	2.32	1.69	2.18
1993–94 to 2011–12	1.36	1.01	1.3

Source: Rangarajan, C. and S. Mahendra Dev (2017), 'Counting the Poor in India: Where Do We Stand', Academic Foundation.

Lessons from the Reform Experience

Had the growth trend seen up to 2011–12 continued, we would have an unqualified answer to the impact of reforms on growth. Growth requires more than reforms. Reforms do not automatically translate into growth. Reforms are, in the words of economists, only a necessary condition— they are not sufficient. In a developing economy, in the final analysis, growth is driven by investment. It is the decline in the investment rate by 6.8 percentage points since 2011–12 that has led to the progressive decline of the growth rate. Reforms normally create a natural climate for investment. But 'animal spirits' are also influenced by non-economic factors, such as social cohesion. Reforms supplemented by a careful nurturing of the investment climate are needed to spur growth again. Growth should also become the sole concern of policymakers.

The reform agenda must continue as it has been under various regimes. There has been a flurry of reform measures in the recent period. Many of them were initiated earlier but they took a concrete shape in the last few years. Good examples are the introduction of

GST, real estate regulation and development, and the bankruptcy and insolvency code. The reform regime will be incremental in character. It has to be. The paradigm shift occurred in 1991. Policymakers should be clear about the direction in which they should move. We need to move in the same direction in which we have been moving in the past three decades. Policymakers should identify the sectors that need reforms in terms of creating a competitive environment and improving the performance efficiency. The Centre and states must be joint partners in this effort.

Reforms do attract criticism. The 1991 reforms were dubbed by some as dictated by IMF and World Bank. Some criticized some of the reforms as a sell-out to capitalists. Under the shadow of a crisis, some of the reforms in 1991 could have been pushed. But today, this is no longer possible. The power sector, the financial system, governance and even agricultural marketing need reforms. But we need more discussion and consensus-building. Timing and sequencing are also critically important. For example, labour reforms are best introduced when the economy is on the upswing. Looking at the recent controversies over agricultural marketing reforms, the best course of action may have been to leave these measures to each state to decide whether they wanted these changes or not. That will set the stage for experimental economics and farmers themselves will be able to see the best possible solution in terms of marketing for different agricultural crops and conditions.

Some years ago, there was talk about India becoming a $5 trillion economy. As of 2020, we were a $2.7 trillion economy. To reach the goal of $5 trillion, on some assumptions relating to price and exchange rate stability, India needs to grow at 9 per cent per annum for at least five consecutive years. That is the challenge before us, as growth is the answer to many of our socio-economic problems. It was only during the high-growth period that the poverty ratio came down fast. High growth enabled the government to introduce several social safety nets.

To be credible and acceptable, reforms must not only result in higher growth but also benefit all sections of society. In that sense, reforms are not ends in themselves. At the same time, equity will remain a dream, if it is not supported by growth spurred by reforms. Reforms, growth and equity must form the triad of economic policy. All three are mutually reinforcing.

Challenges and Opportunities

After Covid-19 and after the Russia–Ukraine war, there is need to lay down a clear roadmap for India's future development. Initially, we need to raise the growth rate to 7 per cent and then follow it up with a growth rate of 8 to 9 per cent. Is this possible? We have shown that in the past we can have a growth rate of 8 to 9 per cent over a sustained period of six to seven years. That is the potential rate of growth of India. What is needed is to raise the investment rate steadily back to around 33 per cent of GDP. This will require a big effort. While public sector investment particularly in infrastructure may 'crowd-in' rather than 'crowd-out' private sector investment in crisis years, this cannot be the permanent solution. Private investment—corporate as well as non-corporate—must pick up. Obviously, technological change will have an important impact on investment decisions. Absorption of new technology will require skill development of various types. New technologies can have serious employment implications both for the immediate and the long run. For example, the conversion of the current motor vehicles into electric vehicles will have many repercussions. At the macro-level, there will be saving of foreign exchange because of the reduction in the import of petroleum products. However, electric vehicles may need other kinds of imports for their manufacture. The concomitant need of manufacturing new imports like chips will require attention. The employment implications are more widespread. On the whole, the future development of industry, agriculture and other services sectors will require considerable amount of planning and thinking. Bearing in mind the need for faster growth and containing the current account deficit, we should enhance the investment rate. While FDI is welcome and desirable, its share in the total investment will always be small. Net inflow of resources into the country is equal to the country's current account deficit. That has to be kept at a low level.

On the strategy of development, there are many models. In the 1950s, the focus was on investment to spur growth. This is valid even now. But strategy goes beyond that. The critical issue was whether the focus should be on import substitution or export promotion. Good examples of countries that made rapid progress adopting export-led growth were the East Asian countries like South Korea and Taiwan.

Their economic growth had been truly impressive. However, there are relatively smaller economies. Then came China, a large country with a huge population, which moved strongly on exploring export opportunities. China's share in world merchandise exports moved from 1 per cent in 1973 to 15.2 per cent in 2021. India relied more on import substitution until 1980 and thereafter shifted gears more particularly after the reforms of 1991. India's share in world exports moved from 0.5 per cent in 1973 to 1.6 per cent in 2021. Obviously, a strong export sector also requires a strong domestic economy. China's exports primarily comprised manufactured goods and quite clearly this required in turn an efficient domestic manufacturing sector. Sri Lanka depends on export of services for its growth. India has a mix. But India's growth is not mainly driven by export. In fact, India's future growth path cannot be unidimensional. We need a strong export sector, both of goods and services. We also need a strong manufacturing sector domestically, both with a view to meet the domestic demand as well as provide employment to a wide cross section of talent. The growth of the high-tech service sector will provide employment to a small segment of highly skilled persons. Our own 'sunrise industries' will be different from those of other countries. In this category, the food processing industry must get a high importance in our country so that our agriculturists earn more. India's population will stabilize only after three decades and that too at a high level of 1.6 billion. The manufacturing and the services sectors of the future will need different training and skills, and our education system needs restructuring. The rapid pace of globalization that we saw since the beginning of the 1990s will slow down for a variety of reasons. Some countries that were champions of globalization are making a retreat on the grounds that the rules of the game are not being followed by all countries. Some countries feel that dependence on other countries for certain key inputs like crude oil or chips may land them in difficulties at times. The recent Russia–Ukraine war has exposed this problem starkly. Free (and fair) trade presupposes a global environment of peace and harmony. If that is broken, the whole argument for free trade and the dictum that each country should produce that commodity or service for which it is best suited falls apart. The state of war cannot also be a permanent situation. *Atmanirbhar* should not result in pure import substitution. That is neither economically sound nor is it desirable. An open economy with some limitations is still the best route to follow.

Just as peace and harmony are needed globally for promoting international trade, it is equally true that, domestically, 'animal spirits' favouring investment thrive only when there is social cohesion and calm. This is a non-economic factor that we should not ignore.

India's ability to grow between 7 and 8 per cent is a proven fact. As already emphasized, we need to raise the savings and investment rates rapidly. We need to keep the ICOR around 4, which is a reflection of the efficiency with which we use capital and labour. Growth is the answer to many of our socio-economic problems. In a fast-growing economy, we can take care of the community's social problems more easily.

Dilemmas of Monetary Policy

The flexible inflation targeting model adopted by the government and RBI fits well with the needs of our country. It is a proper blend of the objectives of price stability and economic growth. However, there are several aspects of the mandate that remain fuzzy and can be subject to multiple interpretations. For example, how long can RBI stay beyond the comfort zone without undercutting the spirit of the mandate? How much value should RBI attach to the mid value of 4 per cent? Which is more relevant and central—stability at 4 per cent or being in the comfort zone? Interpretations may vary according to circumstances. But the spirit of the arrangement is that over a period of time, the system needs to be close to 4 per cent. We must recognize that 4 per cent inflation itself is well above what developed economies consider appropriate. This has implications for the exchange rate.

Consumer inflation did remain at a modest level after the adoption of the flexible inflation targeting programme. Analysts attribute several factors, such as soft crude oil prices, as favouring a low inflation climate. But it is also a fact that money supply growth slowed during the period. But the advent of Covid-19 changed the picture. Inflation in 2020–21 was 6.2 per cent. During 2021–22, the monthly average stood at 5.5 per cent.

The Covid-19 period combined with the Russia–Ukraine war has thrown up some interesting problems with respect to inflation. In fact, inflation has become a worldwide phenomenon. In March 2022, the consumer price inflation in the US had touched 8.56 per cent, a level not reached for four decades. India's CPI inflation had remained at a high level of over 6 per cent since April 2020. It hit a peak of 7.61 per cent in October 2020. Thereafter, it came down and started rising significantly only after January 2022. It touched a peak of 7.8 per cent in April 2022. At that same time, the WPI inflation had remained in double digits since April 2021. The GDP implicit price deflator-based inflation rate for 2021–22 was 9.6 per cent. Even though RBI's mandate is with respect to CPI inflation, can the policy-makers ignore the behaviour of other price indices? In the 2008–09 crisis, central banks of developed countries, particularly the Fed, had been blamed for overlooking the sharp rise in asset prices, even though CPI inflation was modest.

After the advent of Covid-19, the major concern of policymakers all over the world was to revive demand. This was sought to be achieved by raising government expenditure at a time when revenues were falling. This is the standard Keynesian prescription. The severe lockdowns imposed to prevent the spread of Covid-19 restricted the mobility of people, goods and services. Thus, the expansion in government expenditure did not immediately result in increased production in countries where the lockdown was taken seriously. India belonged to this category. As V.K.R.V. Rao pointed out in the 1950s, the Keynesian multiplier did not work when there were supply constraints as in developing countries. That was why he argued that the multiplier operated in nominal terms rather than in real terms in such countries. Something similar has happened in the present case where the supply constraint came from non-mobility of factors of production. Nevertheless, the prescription of enhanced government expenditure was still valid under the circumstances that prevailed. Perhaps the increase in output could happen with a lag and also with the relaxation of restrictions. Initially, the focus of monetary policy in India had been to keep the interest rate low and increase the availability of liquidity through various channels, some of which were newly introduced. However, the growth rate of money was below the growth rate in reserve money (see Table 17.7). This is because of lower credit growth, which also depended upon business sentiment and investment climate. Thus, the money multiplier was lower than usual. Nevertheless, the money supply increased over a time when real growth, taken two years together,

Rs crore

Table 17.7 Growth in Reserve Money and Broad Money

Month	Reserve Money		Broad Money		Non-Food Credit	
	Stock at the end of the period	Y-o-Y Growth Rate	Stock at the end of the period	Y-o-Y Growth Rate	Absolute Amount	Y-o-Y Growth Rate
Apr–21	3585499.95	18.74	18980415.30	11.43	10802151.38	5.69
May–21	3705431.46	18.32	19012125.69	10.34	10740559.48	5.89
Jun–21	3698987.35	16.92	19168204.11	10.70	10754940.00	5.89
Jul–21	3715957.38	16.80	19372714.42	9.91	10833089.78	6.18
Aug–21	3679192.14	15.22	19330427.06	9.53	10828801.02	6.69
Sep–21	3659381.97	14.74	19397300.04	9.34	10894475.88	6.75
Oct–21	3703450.87	14.15	19524125.56	9.66	10980922.14	6.90
Nov–21	3736106.80	12.76	19646645.57	9.53	11079778.48	7.09
Dec–21	3802775.14	14.74	20114036.38	11.40	11591625.86	10.88
Jan–22	3814348.18	13.46	19946628.19	8.37	11500052.30	8.32
Feb–22	3847490.56	13.88	20183528.17	8.73	11643716.86	8.19
Mar–22	3920298.48	8.90	20489597.28	8.73	11891314.34	8.71
Apr–22	4059240.76	13.21	20712062.92	9.12	11956344.02	10.29

Source: RBI

was almost negligible. The government's borrowing programme, which was large, went through smoothly, thanks to abundant liquidity.

Even as the economy picked up steam in 2021–22, inflation also became an issue. As mentioned earlier, this was a worldwide phenomenon. In the US, the explanation had been quite simple. There was a balance sheet explosion of the Fed. On 1 January 2020, the total assets (less some items) of the Fed stood at $4.17 trillion and in April 2022, they stood at $8.96 trillion. This massive expansion in assets is the result of quantitative easing, which essentially meant liquidity support provided by the Fed. The Fed chairman made strong statements expressing the need to reduce the size of the assets. The Fed was planning to shrink its balance sheet by $95 billion a month. In India, too, there was a shift in monetary policy. The May monetary policy reiterated the stance as one of 'to remain accommodative while focusing on withdrawal of accommodation to ensure that inflation remains within the target going forward, while supporting growth'. Without efforts to curtail liquidity, inflation cannot come down.

In the context of analysing inflation, I wish to make one point. While discussing inflation, analysts including policymakers focus almost exclusively on the increases in the prices of individual commodities like crude oil as the primary cause of inflation. The Russia–Ukraine war was cited as the primary cause of inflation in 2022. True, in many situations these may be the triggers. Supply disruptions due to domestic or external factors may explain the behaviour of individual prices but not the general price level, which is what inflation is about. Given a budget constraint, there will only be an adjustment in relative prices. Besides the fact that any cost-push increase in the price of one commodity may get generalized, it is the adjustment that happens at the macro level that becomes critical. A long time ago, Friedman said, 'It is true that the upward push in wages produced inflation, not because it was necessarily inflationary but because it happened to be the mechanism which forced an increase in the stock of money.' Thus, it is the adjustment in the macro level of liquidity that sustains inflation. There was thus the famous statement of Friedman which went, 'Inflation is always and everywhere a monetary phenomenon.'

The possible trade-off between inflation and growth has a long history in economic literature. The Phillips curve has been analysed theoretically and empirically. Tobin called the Phillips curve a 'cruel dilemma' because it suggested that full employment was not compatible with price stability. The critical question flowing from these discussions on trade-off is whether cost-push factors can generate inflation by themselves. Tobin said at one place that inflation 'is neither demand-pull nor cost-push or rather it is both', even though he did not agree with Friedman's extreme position that there would be no pure cost-push inflation.[8] Sometimes it is argued that inflation will come down, if some part of the increase, say, in crude prices, which may be a trigger, is absorbed by the government. There may be a case for reducing the duties on petroleum products for the simple reason that one segment of the population should not bear an excessive burden. The same consideration applies to an increase in food prices. But to think that it is a magic wand through which inflation can be avoided is wrong. If the additional burden borne by the government (through loss of revenue) is not offset by expenditures, the overall deficit will widen. The borrowing programme will increase and additional liquidity support may be required, which will have an effect on price levels.

Inflation in India in 2022 cannot be described just as 'cost-push'. Abundance of liquidity was an important factor. The April 2022 monetary policy statement talked of a liquidity overhang of the order of Rs 8.5 lakh crore. Beyond a point, inflation itself can hinder growth. Negative real rates of interest on savings are not conducive to growth. If we want to control inflation, action on liquidity is always needed with a concomitant rise in interest rates. In the final analysis, quantitative contraction, which obviously implies a rise in the policy rate, is the answer to control inflation whatever may be the trigger.

Fiscal Management

While growth is the primary aim of policymakers, it must meet certain stability conditions to be sustained. Stability, in short, has three dimensions—one, a low current account deficit; second, a reasonable price stability; and third, a modest fiscal deficit. We looked at the first two dimensions earlier. We now consider the third dimension of fiscal deficit. It needs to be pointed out that the prescription of any level of fiscal deficit by itself is not adequate. The same level of deficit can occur at a higher or lower level of tax/GDP ratio. The literature on the sustainable level of deficit or debt is extensive. The issue can be examined from various angles. One of the elements in the reform agenda initiated in 1991 was the containment of fiscal deficit. This took a more definitive shape after the passing of the Fiscal Responsibility and Budget Management Act of 2003. It prescribed that the fiscal deficit of the Government of India should not exceed 3 per cent of the GDP. After the report of the Twelfth Finance Commission, which offered certain incentives for states to adopt similar legislations, all the state governments passed legislations over a period of time prescribing 3 per cent of the state domestic product as the limit. The actual experience is not that encouraging. Except in one year (2007–08), the deficits of the Centre have remained above the prescribed level and on several occasions, well above the level. The performances of the state governments have been mixed. The FRBM Review Committee prescribed a target debt–GDP ratio of 60 per cent to be achieved by 2023, 40 per cent by the Centre and 20 per cent by states. To achieve a desired level of debt–GDP ratio, the governments have to act only on the fiscal deficit. Therefore, the prescription of a mandated level of fiscal deficit appears more reasonable. There is a strong argument in favour of a prescription of 6 per cent for both the Centre and states taken together. In India, the household sector is the only surplus sector that saves more than it invests and the excess becomes available in the form of financial savings to be utilized by the private corporate sector, the public sector enterprises and the government. Therefore, the financial savings of the household sector sets the limit on what the other sectors can borrow. The financial savings of the household sector have ranged between 7 and 7.5 per cent of GDP for several years (Table 17.8). Against this background, 6 per cent of GDP limit appears not only appropriate but also tilted towards the government even after taking into account the inflow of resources from abroad. Of course, if the financial savings of the household sector as a proportion of GDP increases, the fiscal rule can be modified. But that is very much in the future.

It is sometimes pointed out that the debt–GDP ratio of India is not that high as compared to other countries, particularly Japan. But that is not an appropriate comparison. Since tax revenue to GDP is high and the interest rate is low in Japan, interest payment on debt constitutes only 4.7 per cent of revenue receipts (Table 17.9).

Table 17.8 Financial Saving of the Household Sector

(per cent of GNDI)

Item	2011–12	2012–13	2013–14	2014–15	2015–16	2016–17	2017–18	2018–19	2019–20
1	2	3	4	5	6	7	8	9	10
A. Gross Financial Saving	10.4	10.5	10.4	9.9	10.7	10.4	11.9	11.1	11.0
of which:									
1. Currency	1.2	1.1	0.9	1.0	1.4	-2.1	2.8	1.4	1.4
2. Deposits	6.0	6.0	5.8	4.8	4.6	6.3	3.0	4.2	4.2
3. Shares and Debentures	0.2	0.2	0.2	0.2	0.2	1.1	1.0	0.4	0.4
4. Claims on Government	-0.2	-0.1	0.2	0.0	0.5	0.7	0.9	1.1	1.3
5. Insurance Funds	2.2	1.8	1.8	2.4	1.9	2.3	2.0	1.9	1.5
6. Provident and Pension Funds	1.1	1.5	1.5	1.5	2.1	2.1	2.1	2.1	2.2
B. Financial Liabilities	3.2	3.2	3.1	3.0	2.7	3.0	4.3	4.1	3.2
C. Net Financial Saving (A-B)	7.2	7.2	7.2	6.9	7.9	7.3	7.5	7.1	7.8

GNDI: Gross National Disposable Income.

Note: Figures may not add up to the total due to rounding off.

Source: NSO.

Table 17.9 Fiscal Parameters for General Government (per cent)

Countries	Revenue receipts/GDP	Interest payments/ Revenue receipts	Debt/GDP
India	18.1	25.8	72.4
US	29.5	13.8	108.7
UK	36.6	5.6	85.4
Japan	35.0	4.7	238.0

Data pertains to 2019–20 for India. For the UK, the US and Japan, data for revenue receipts pertain to 2018 and for interest payments and debt to 2019.

The corresponding figure for India, taking the Centre and states together, was 25.8 per cent in 2019–20. In the case of the Centre alone, interest payments will equal 42.7 per cent of revenue receipts in 2022–23. This is a large pre-emption leaving less for other productive expenditures. This is not a tenable situation.

It is also argued sometimes, since the stability of the debt–GDP ratio can be achieved if the growth rate is equal to or higher than the interest rate, stability can be achieved by manipulating the interest rate, i.e., by keeping the interest rate low. But by artificially keeping the interest rate low, we will usher in a regime of financial repression. If real rates of interest are negative for long, it can only lead to diversion of savings into speculative investment. Gold hoarding and rise in land values will be the consequence.

We cannot make the level of public borrowing loose and elastic. As stressed earlier, the demands on public expenditure will be strong. Reforms have not reduced the role of states. In some areas, it has expanded and in some areas, it has shrunk. Therefore, while keeping the fiscal deficit within the permitted range, the effort must be to raise revenue to GDP ratio. After the tax–GDP ratio of the Centre rising steadily to touch 11.86 per cent in 2007–08, it has fallen since then. All effort must be directed towards raising this ratio.

There have been many suggestions on improving the fiscal deficit rule. Should we insist that the rule of, say, 3 per cent of GDP for the Centre be achieved every year? Can it be made a cyclical average? There is some logic to this. But our own experience has been that even in good years, that is, years of high growth, the deficit rule has not been met.

In fact, this rule has been honoured more often in the breach than the observance.

In fact, Covid-19 posed a major problem to the adherence of this rule. Since the near unanimous recommendation was to raise government expenditure, the deficit has touched extraordinarily high levels. The Centre's fiscal deficit in 2020–21 was 9.2 per cent of GDP. Part of it was, of course, due to some cleaning up operations, which are desirable. Even then, it is extremely high. In 2021–22, it was 6.9 per cent of GDP and is expected to be 6.4 per cent in 2022–23. The norm that we had set was 3 per cent of GDP. As a consequence, the Centre's debt–GDP ratio is expected to be at 60.2 per cent of GDP in 2022–23 as against the desired level of 40 per cent of GDP. For the Centre and states taken together, it would touch 90 per cent of GDP. One can understand the compulsions; the economic impact of Covid-19 had brought the economy to a grinding halt at one stage. GDP fell in 2020–21. In 2021–22, it has grown to go a little beyond the level of where we were in 2020. Extraordinary measures had to be taken to kick-start the economy. Government expenditures had to rise. All economists and analysts were agreed on it. But we should not belittle the situation that we are facing.

In 2022–23, the Centre and the states taken as a whole will borrow an amount equivalent to 10.4 per cent of GDP. As already mentioned, the savings of the household sector in financial assets do not exceed 7.5 per cent of GDP. Thus, the borrowing programme can be completed only with the support (though indirectly) of RBI. This is what we used to do in the 1980s. Such support from RBI will have its impact on inflation, if not immediately, at least with a lag. Of course, one has to take into account its favourable impact on output. At present, the target appears to be to take the Centre's deficit to 4.5 per cent by 2025–26. Even this may or may not be achieved. But will this be adequate? A medium-term plan of fiscal consolidation is urgently needed, showing the period over which a sustainable level of fiscal deficit will be reached. Crowding out of private investment may not happen now. But eventually, it will become a problem, if we have prolonged high fiscal deficit.

In this context, one other issue relates to borrowing by state governments and the Centre's role in it. The Government of India agreed to raise the limit of states to borrow from 3 per cent to 4 per cent of State Domestic Product (SDP) for 2022–23. But it imposed the condition that 0.5 per cent of this will be contingent on the states meeting power sector reforms. This condition is unnecessary. Power sector reforms are needed and the inducement for this can be provided through other means. The limit for 2022–23 should have been raised without imposing any condition. Article 293 of the Constitution stipulates that states need permission from the Centre to borrow as long as the states are indebted to the Centre. Prior to the Twelfth Finance Commission, the Government of India used to borrow for the purpose of lending to states. The Twelfth Finance Commission recommended that this system might be stopped and that at least all major states should be allowed to borrow directly from the market. In fact, it was our hope that as this new system took root, a stage would be reached when states would not be indebted to the Centre and that states would then borrow based on their own assessment. It is also appropriate here to recall one recommendation of the Twelfth Finance Commission, which was to set up a loan council comprising the Union Government, states, the Planning Commission and RBI that could take the decision on how much states should be allowed to borrow. This recommendation was not acted upon earlier. This needs a relook.

To Conclude

It is customary for policymakers to say that the fundamentals of the Indian economy are strong when faced with a critical situation. Certainly, we could not say this in 1991. We had to admit that things had gone wrong and that we had to move on a new track. While for a time, we maintained reasonably high growth after reforms, it has not continued. The pandemic has queered the pitch further.

The immediate focus of policymakers must be to raise the growth rate of the economy. We have earlier indicated some of the actions that need to be taken to achieve this. Achievement of a $5 trillion economy is a good short-term aspirational goal. As already mentioned, this will take a minimum five years of sustained growth of 9 per cent. Even then, at the end of it, India's per capita income will be only $3472 and we will still be classified as a lower middle income country. To be classified as a developed country, the per capita income will have to be at a much higher level and that will take more than two decades of strong growth to achieve it. This is the true challenge we face. Growth must also be accompanied by a more equitable distribution. We cannot sequence it, growth first and equity later. They need to go together. Growth and equity should not be posed as opposing considerations. They must be woven together to give an acceptable pattern of development. Therein lies economic wisdom and economic statesmanship.

Acknowledgements

This is a book that should have been written many years ago. Anyway, here it is at last.

Let me at the outset most sincerely thank Dr Manmohan Singh for allowing me to dedicate this book to him. Our friendship dates back to the late 1960s. In the early 1990s, I was fortunate to be part of the team led by him which gave a new direction to India.

In the writing of the book, there are many who have to be acknowledged. First and foremost, there are three who prodded me constantly to write and finish the book quickly. They are T.C.A Srinivasa Raghavan, Y.V. Reddy and Shaji Vikraman. I am truly grateful to all of them.

My sincere thanks to Y.V. Reddy, Usha Thorat and B. Sambamurthy who read some parts of the book and offered their comments. Their comments not only made the book better but also encouraged me to go ahead with the writing of the book. I am, however, responsible for any errors that may remain.

I must thank my many friends at RBI for their assistance and help. In any case, this book has grown out of my association with the institution for fifteen years, and I fondly recall this association. I have drawn heavily on the publications of RBI in the writing.

There are three institutions which provided the environment and facilities to write the book. My thanks to Pankaj Chandra, vice chancellor of Ahmedabad University, J. Mahender Reddy, former vice chancellor of ICFAI Foundation for Higher Education and K.R. Shanmugam, director, Madras School of Economics (MSE). At MSE, I must thank V. Sudha who bore the major responsibility of transcribing and putting in an appropriate form my handwritten notes. She went beyond that and also checked references and helped me in a number of ways to complete the book. At MSE, I must also thank K. Baskar for obtaining the various books I needed from different libraries. At Ahmedabad University, B.G. Varghese provided the secretarial support whenever I was there and my thanks are due to him.

I would like to thank my family members for their affection and help. I must thank my son-in-law Santanu Paul for suggesting the title of the book and my grandson Ishan Rangarajan for carrying out the library work on the role of a state governor and the function of an upper chamber in a parliamentary form of government. My late wife Haripriya always thanked me in all the books she had written. Today I would like to thank her as my way of remembering her for all that we shared in our decades together.

                                                    C. Rangarajan

Notes

Introduction
1. Martin Bronfenbrenner, 'A "Middlebrow" Introduction to Economic Methodology', in Sherman Roy Krupp (ed.), *The Structure of Economic Science: Essays on Methodology* (Englewood Cliffs, New Jersey: Prentice-Hall, 1966), p. 6-24.

Chapter 1: Tryst with IMF: 1981
1. *History* hereinafter refers to the *History of RBI Volume 4.*

Chapter 2: BOP in the 1980s: A Crisis in the Making
1. Economic Survey 1988–89, p. 128.

Chapter 3: Monetary Policy in the 1980s
1. First Five Year Plan, Government of India
2. In fact, much of the discussion between RBI and the government happened at the time of determining the borrowing programme before the Budget was presented. Generally speaking, the government used to insist on a larger borrowing programme than what RBI had in mind. In addition, the government wanted, despite an increase in borrowing, no increase in interest rate. Interestingly, after Manmohan Singh took over as the chairman of Planning Commission, he was also under pressure to have a larger borrowing programme. Once he told me not to quote what he had said as governor. Smilingly, he added that his 'dharma' had changed.

3. How comprehensive the influence of the government was can be seen by one episode, which is detailed in *History* (p. 172). In October 1987, two days before the credit policy meeting, a text message came from the finance secretary to put the proposed increase in CRR on hold. The government, it said, had a different perception. In fact, the proposed increase had earlier been agreed to by the finance minister. The meeting had to be postponed. Even though the government finally agreed, the postponement itself was an embarrassment. This was just one instance.

Chapter 5: At the Planning Commission
1. Budget Speech, July 24, 1991.
2. https://www.southcentre.int/wp-content/uploads/2013/02/The-Challenge-to-the-South_HRes_EN.pdf
3. Eighth Five Year Plan (1992–97), Vol. I

Chapter 15: Interacting with the Political System
1. Venkaiah Naidu, 'The Need for a Second Chamber,' *The Hindu*, 12 May 2020.
2. Chidambaram, Karti, 'Restrict Whips to No-Confidence Motions, Please', *Deccan Chronicle*, 6 October 2020.

Chapter 16: Advice to Government
1. Part of the reason for expecting the fixed investment rate to pick up soon was that the fixed investment rate was initially reported at 32.4 per cent in the revised estimate of 2009–10 but revised sharply down to 30.8 per cent in the quick estimate, in part due to the revision of the entire data series following the new price index with 2004–05 as the base year.
2. The committee comprised Kirit S. Parikh, member, Planning Commission; Saumitra Chaudhuri, prime minister's Economic Advisory Council and chief economist, ICRA, New Delhi; Ashok Lahiri, chief economic adviser, Ministry of Finance; Prof. Bakul H. Dholakia, director, IIM Ahmedabad; M.S. Srinivasan, Secretary, Ministry of Petroleum and Natural Gas; and S.C. Tripathi, former Secretary, Ministry of Petroleum and Natural Gas, as members.

3. The committee comprised Vinod Rai, Secretary (Financial Sector), Ministry of Finance, Government of India; R. Bandyopadhyay, Additional Secretary, Ministry of Telecommunications, Government of India; M.B.N. Rao, chairman and managing director, Canara Bank; Yogesh Agarwal, chairman and managing director, IDBI; Prof. Mahendra Dev, director, Centre for Economic and Social Studies (CESS), Hyderabad; Vijay Mahajan, chairman, BASIX, Hyderabad; R. Gopalakrishnan, executive director, TATA Sons, Mumbai; A.P. Fernandez, executive director, MYRADA, Bangalore; Member Secretary Y.S.P. Thorat, chairman, National Bank for Agriculture and Rural Development (NABARD) and permanent invitee Usha Thorat, deputy governor, RBI, as members.

4. The committee comprised Kirit Parikh, member-in-charge of Perspective Planning Division, Planning Commission, Government of India, New Delhi; Prof. Ravindra Dholakia, Indian Institute of Management Ahmedabad; S.L. Shetty, EPW Research Foundation, Mumbai; Saumitra Chaudhuri, member of the Economic Advisory Council to the prime minister, Government of India, New Delhi; Ramesh Kolli, additional director general, National Accounts Division, Central Statistical Organization, Government of India, New Delhi; Member Secretary R.B. Barman, former executive director, Reserve Bank of India, Mumbai (till 31 July 2008) and Member Secretary K.U.B. Rao, adviser, Department of Economic Analysis and Policy, Reserve Bank of India, Mumbai, as members.

5. The committee comprised Prof. Abhijit Sen, member (FR), Planning Commission; Sudha Pillai, Secretary, Planning Commission; Subir Gokarn, deputy governor, Reserve Bank of India; Sushama Nath succeeded by Sumit Bose, Secretary, Department of Expenditure, Ministry of Finance; Kaushik Basu, chief economic adviser, Department of Economic Affairs, Ministry of Finance; C.R. Sundaramurti, controller general of accounts, Ministry of Finance; Rekha Gupta, Deputy Comptroller and Auditor General of India,; M.G. Rao, director, National Institute of Public Finance and Policy, New Delhi; Nitin Desai, honorary professor, ICRIER, New Delhi; Prof. D.K. Srivastava, director, Madras School of Economics; Prof. Ravindra Dholakia, professor,

IIM Ahmedabad; C.M. Bachhawat, Principal Finance Secretary, Government of West Bengal; K. Shanmugan, Principal Finance Secretary, Government of Tamil Nadu; G.P. Singhal, Principal Finance Secretary, Government of Madhya Pradesh; Himanshu Shekhar Das, Principal Finance Secretary, Government of Assam; Principal Finance Secretary, Government of Maharashtra; and Member Secretary Tuhin. K. Pandey, adviser (FR), Planning Commission, as members.

6. The committee comprised N.R. Narayana Murthy; Tarun Das; T. Nanda Kumar, member; Shakeel Qalander; Y.V. Sharma; Bharat Vyas, Member Secretary; Sanjay Mitra, special invitee and K. Skandan, special invitee.

7. The committee comprised T. Nandakumar, member, NDMA; initially Kaushik Basu followed by Raghuram Rajan, chief economic adviser; Ashok Gulati, chairman, Commission for Agricultural Costs and Prices; Secretary, Department of Food and Public Distribution; Secretary, Department of Agriculture and Cooperation and K.P. Krishnan, Secretary, EAC to the prime minister–Convener.

8. The committee comprised Member Secretary, Planning Commission, Chief Economic Adviser, and the Secretaries of Departments of Agriculture and Cooperation, Expenditure and Food and Public Distribution.

9. The committee comprised Justice Jagannadha Rao, former judge of the Supreme Court; B. K. Chaturvedi, member, Planning Commission; Prof. Ramprasad Sengupta, distinguished fellow, India Development Foundation, former professor of economics, JNU; J.M. Mauskar, retired Special Secretary to the Government of India; Joeman Thomas, former MD, ONGC Videsh Ltd; K.P. Krishnan, initially Secretary, Economic Advisory Council to the prime minister and currently Principal Secretary (Coordination); Giridhar Aramane, Joint Secretary (Exploration), Ministry of Petroleum and Natural Gas, Secretary, Government of Karnataka—Convenor, as members.

10. The committee comprised S. Mahendra Dev; K. Sundaram; Mahesh Vyas and K.L. Datta—Convener.

11. The committee comprised Nerissa Corazon Soon Ruiz, Congresswoman from Cebu, the Philippines; Rajat Kumar Gupta, senior partner worldwide, McKinsey and Co., United States; Mahmuda Islam, professor of sociology, Dhaka University, Bangladesh; Tadashi Yamamoto, president for Japan Centre for International Exchange (JCIE), Japan; J.V.R. Prasada Rao, former health secretary, Government of India as Member-Secretary; Frika Chia Iskandar, coordinator of the women's working group in APN+, Indonesia; Tim Brown, epidemiologist and senior research fellow in East West Centre, Hawaii, United States; Wu Zunyou, director of National Centre for AIDS and STD Control and Prevention in Chinese Centre for Disease Control and Prevention, China.

Chapter 17: Some Ruminations

1. Sivasubramanian, S. (1997), 'Revised Estimates of the National Income of India, 1900–1902 to 1946–17', *The Indian Economic Social History Review*, No. 34, Issue 2, pp. 113–68.

2. In the early period, India's strategy of development, besides emphasizing the need for economic planning and dominance of state intervention, also rested on import substitution and domestic manufacture of capital goods. The intellectual support for an emphasis on 'heavy industry'-led growth came from the Mahalanobis model, which was strictly valid only in a closed economy. The 'export pessimism' that prevailed at that time went in support of the approach of import substitution. One consequence of this approach was that India became a high-cost economy. The net result was that India's share in world exports, which stood at 2 per cent of world trade, fell to less than half of 1 per cent by 1973.

3. The famous Deng's speech was delivered on 13 December 1978. He called to 'explore new ways and generate new ideas'. It is interesting to note that in 1980, in current dollars, India's per capita income was 266 while that of China was 194. In 2020, India's was 1900 while that of China was 10,500. Of course, one cannot attribute the big difference to only a change in policy.

4. While India's post-Independence economic performance was reassuring compared to the pre-Independence period, it is not

that impressive when compared with several developing countries outside South Asia (Table 17.2).

5. For an extended treatment of the subject, see my article 'Some Issues in External Sector Management', *Economic & Political Weekly*, 26 May 2018, Vol. LIII, No. 21, pp. 34–42.

6. In the context of the developing countries, it is best to see the behaviour of the poverty ratio rather than look at inequality coefficients. Of course, inequality by itself has its own relevance. But it is bound to remain high in the early stages of development. Eliminating poverty must be the initial goal.

7. The report on the global multidimensional poverty index (MPI) 2018 released by UNDP and Oxford University says, 'India has made momentous progress in reducing multidimensional poverty. The incidence of multidimensional poverty was almost halved between 2005/6 and 2015/16, climbing down to 27.5%. The global Multidimensional Poverty Index (MPI) was cut by half due to deeper progress among the poorest. Thus within ten years, the number of poor people in India fell by more than 271 million—a truly massive gain.' This is indeed high praise.

8. In his presidential address to the American Association in 1971, Tobin elaborated this idea further and said, 'Postwar experience destroyed the identification of full employment with the economy's inflation threshold. The profession, the press, and the public discovered the "new inflation" of the 1950's (inflation without the benefit of gap), labelled but scarcely illuminated by the term "cost-push". Subsequently, the view of the world suggested by the Phillips curve merged demand-pull and cost-push inflation and blurred the distinction between them.'

References

(For Chapter 11)

Bernanke, B.S., and F.S. Mishkin. 1997. Inflation Targeting: A New Framework for Monetary Policy?, *The Journal of Economic Perspectives*, Vol. 11, No. 2, American Economic Association.

Clarida, R.H. 2019. The Federal Reserve's Review of its Monetary Policy Strategy, Tools, and Communication Practices. *The Bank of Finland Conference on Monetary Policy and Future of EMU (Economic and Monetary Union)*. Helsinki.

European Central Bank. 2013. *European Sources Online*. Retrieved from European Central Bank: http://aei.pitt.edu/74892/1/European_Central_Bank.pdf

Federal Reserve System. 2016. *The Federal Reserve System: Purposes and Functions*. Federal Reserve System Publication.

Fischer, S. 1996. Why Are Central Banks Pursuing Long run Price Stability. *Proceedings – Economic Policy Symposium* (pp. 7–34). Jackson Hole: Federal Reserve Bank of Kansas City.

Friedman M.. 1975. Unemployment versus Inflation: An Evaluation of the Phillips Curve. London: *IEA Lecture No. 2*, Institute of Economic Affairs.

George, E. 1996. *Economic Policy Approaches, Some Reflections*. Bank of England Quarterly Bulletin Q4.

Goodfriend, M. 2007. How the World Achieved Consensus on Monetary Policy. *The Journal of Economic Perspectives*, Volume 21, Number 4—Fall 2007—Pages 47–68.

Kydland, F.E., and E.C. Prescott. 1977. Rules Rather than Discretion: The Inconsistency of Optimal Plans. *The Journal of Political Economy*, Vol. 85, No. 3, pp. 473–92.

Pierce, D.G., and P.J. Tysome. 1985. *Monetary Economics: Theories, Evidence and Policy*. London: Butterworth-Heinemann.

Planning Commission. 1952. *Report of the First Five-Year Plan*. Government of India.

Rangarajan, C. 1998a. Dimensions of Monetary Policy. In C. Rangarajan, *Indian Economy: Essays on Money and Finance*. New Delhi: UBSPD.

Rangarajan, C. 1998b. Development, Inflation and Monetary Policy. In I. Ahluwalia, and I. I.M.D. Little, *India's Economic Reforms and Development: Essays for Manmohan Singh*. New Delhi: OUP.

Rangarajan, C., and A. Samantaraya. 2017. RBI's Interest Rate Policy and Durable Liquidity Question. *Economic and Political Weekly*, Vol. 52, No. 22.

RBI. 1934. *The Reserve Bank of India Act*. Government of India.

RBI. 1998. *History of Reserve Bank of India 1951-67*, Vol. 2. Mumbai.

RBI. 1985. *Report of the Committee to Review the Working of the Monetary System*. Mumbai.

RBI. 2016. *Amendment Act of 2016*. Government of India.

RBI. 2002. *Report on Currency and Finance, 2001–02*. Mumbai.

Sarel, M. 1996. Nonlinear Effects of Inflation on Economic Growth. *IMF Staff Papers*, Vol. 43, No. 1, pp. 199–215.

Simons, Henry C. 1936, 'Rules Versus Authorities in Monetary Policy', *Journal of Political Economy*, Vol. 44, No. 1, (Feb.) pp. 1–30, University of Chicago Press.

Tarshis, L., and E.S. Furniss. 1947. *The Elements of Economics: An Introduction to the Theory of Price and Employment*. Houghton Mifflin Company.

Taylor, J. 1995. The Monetary Transmission Mechanism: An Empirical Framework. *Journal of Monetary Economics*.

Taylor, J.B. (1993). Discretion versus Policy Rules in Practices. *Carnegie-Rochester Conference Series on Public Policy*, (pp. 195–214). North Holland.